Urban planning and the development process

DAVID ADAMS

Department of Land Economy
University of Aberdeen

UCL
PRESS

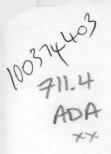
© C. David Adams 1994

First published in 1994 by UCL Press.
Second impression 1995.

UCL Press Limited
University College London
Gower Street
London WC1E 6BT

The name of University College London is a registered
trade mark used by UCL Press with the consent of the owner.

ISBN:
1-85728-021-0 HB
1-85728-022-9 PB

British Library Cataloguing-in-Publication Data
A catalogue record for this book
is available from the British Library

Printed and bound by
Biddles Ltd
Guildford and King's Lynn, England.

Contents

CONTENTS

CONTENTS

Preface

This book is based on the conviction that urban planning is fundamentally concerned with the process of development, and that to separate one from the other weakens the potential of both. Indeed, such artificial separation in the past helps explain why many people, when they first encounter urban planning, often believe that it can change everything, but subsequently conclude that it can change nothing. People who share this experience are quite diverse and include local councillors, those active in environmental organizations, those working in the various professions and industries that create the built environment, and those still in higher education who meet the planning process in land management, geography, politics, architecture or urban studies courses, as well as in urban planning education itself. Whatever your experience of planning, this book is written to help you explore how far development activity can be influenced by the work of urban planners.

The book is intended as an applied rather than an introductory text and assumes that its readers already appreciate basic economic concepts such as supply and demand, understand the relevance of welfare economics to urban areas, and have gained an initial knowledge of the British planning system. Readers who require specific explanation of these matters may find it helpful to refer to such texts as Begg et al. (1994) on economics, Walker (1982) on welfare economics and urban problems, and Rydin (1993) or Cullingworth & Nadin (1994) on the planning system. Although I have sought to draw the reader's attention to any significant differences in planning law and procedure between Scotland and England & Wales, I have otherwise tried to provide a contemporary account of practice throughout the United Kingdom.

Finally, I wish to acknowledge what I have received throughout this book from the source of inspiration for all intellectual endeavour: "To him who by means of his power working in us is able to do so much more than we can ever ask for or, even think of: to God be the glory in the church and in Christ Jesus for all time, for ever and ever! Amen." (*Good News Bible*, Ephesians 3: 20–1).

David Adams   January 1994
Aberdeen

Acknowledgements

This book derives from almost eleven years research and teaching at the Universities of Reading, Manchester and Aberdeen. I am grateful to all those who during that period helped and encouraged me to explore the relationship of urban planning to the development process, especially the many students and staff with whom I shared ideas during nine challenging years at the Department of Planning and Landscape, University of Manchester. In this respect, particular thanks are due to Mike Yates, who set me thinking, Roger Bristow, Gwyn Williams, Christopher Wood, Stephen Young and my fellow researchers, Richard Kent, Helen May, Gillian Pawson, Timothy Pope, Lynne Russell and Clare Taylor-Russell. The Economic and Social Research Council provided funds for part of the work on which this book is based. The University of Manchester generously granted me two terms sabbatical leave in 1991/2, during which the foundations were laid, and on my arrival north of the border, the University of Aberdeen allowed me time to complete the task. Such forms of support were very much appreciated.

I am grateful for permission from the following sources to reproduce copyright material: Investment Property Databank (Figs 2.1, 2.2), HMSO (Figs 3.3, 6.6, 8.1, 8.2), Dartmouth Publishing Co. Ltd (Fig. 3.4), Peter Ambrose (Fig. 3.5), Routledge (Fig. 5.1), Elsevier Science Publishers and Paul McNamara (Table 6.1), Kipper Williams (Fig. 6.2), MEPC (Fig 6.3, 6.4, 6.5), and the American Planning Association (Fig. 9.1).

I have greatly appreciated the time and trouble taken by many people to comment on the initial concept for the book and on subsequent parts of the draft text, especially Roger Bristow, Alan Disberry, Ken Gillespie, Alan Hooper, Greg Lloyd, Bryan MacGregor, Paul McNamara, Nanda Nanthakumaran, David Robinson, Jeremy Rowan-Robinson, William Walton and Stephen Young. Roger Jones at UCL Press has taken particular care to guide me through my first publishing venture. I have found all their contributions enormously helpful, but they are, of course, absolved from any responsibility for what has now emerged.

> ## To Judith
> whose love, support and encouragement
> helped create this book

Tables

PART 1

THE DEVELOPMENT FRAMEWORK

CHAPTER ONE

Introduction

This book is about the very essence of urban planning in a market economy. It is concerned with people – among them landowners, developers, investors, politicians and ordinary members of the public – who shape the built environment as they relate to each other and react to development pressure. Whether urban planning exists or not, people such as these ensure that most towns and cities gradually evolve through a continuous process of change and development. Urban planning neither overrides nor fully controls this process, but aims instead to influence it. Indeed, as an explicit programme for the management of land-use and environmental change (Healey et al. 1988), urban planning is best defined as a form of state intervention in a development process dominated by the private sector.

Any justification for urban planning thus demands evidence that such intervention produces a better urban environment than that which could be generated by the market alone. Nevertheless, urban planning does not replace the market but works through it, affecting the value of land as it is bought and sold and creating potentially lucrative development opportunities for others to implement. In a market economy, no theory of urban planning which assumes that the planning authority controls the urban environment is therefore valid. Rather, the extent to which any such authority can successfully influence the development process is dependent on the resources it can attract, the powers with which it is entrusted, and particularly on the depth of its relationships with landowners, developers, investors and other significant actors. Such relationships do not flow merely in one direction, for these very people whom urban planning tries to influence may themselves wish to see urban plans modified to their own advantage.

Urban planning in practice therefore has little to do with scientifically discovering the best technical solution to be implemented by the planning authority in the public interest. Rather, it is about the processes of bargaining, negotiation and compromise over the distribution of scarce environmental resources, in which the planning authority, in attempting to mediate between conflicting claims on land, may promote particular interests above others. This approach does not devalue the vision of a well designed and attractive urban environment, nor deny the significance of fundamental urban linkages, such as those between the housing and employment markets. Rather, it seeks to put them in proper perspective by relating them to how planners operate in practice. Moreover, since urban planning has the potential to alter the resource distribution that market forces produce, causing some people to gain and others to lose, it is an inherently political activity in which controversy is never far from the surface. For this reason, authorities often reach urban planning decisions that may appear technically defective.

Earlier conceptions of urban planning

Urban planning was not always seen in this light. For example, it has been variously regarded as an exercise in civic design, a style of corporate management, and as a form of systems analysis. A brief historical excursion is helpful to explain the legacy of these approaches. The early pioneers of town planning believed passionately that the comprehensive design of new settlements and the reconstruction of existing ones could best achieve amenity, convenience, safety and public health in urban form, and reinforce the onward march of social progress. In this vision, the planner was considered the master-designer of the built environment, arranging land-uses to produce balance and order throughout the city. This required aesthetic appreciation and technical skills, natural qualities for a planning profession that had originated in architecture, engineering and surveying.

For the first five decades of the 20th century, urban planning was thus commonly equated with civic design in a tradition that remained for many years thereafter, a powerful influence on both planning education and the self-image of planners in practice. However, this consensus was shattered in the 1960s by new approaches to urban planning in three related areas of controversy, termed respectively by Yiftachel (1989) the analytical, urban form and procedural debates. Each of these debates can be traced back to the early days of urban planning at the turn of the 20th century. All three debates have since taken place in parallel and continue to do so today.

In the analytical debate, the fundamental question is "What is urban planning?" After the 1960s, urban planning was considered less a matter of civic design and more a function of state policy. Marxists saw urban planning as aiding and abetting the capitalist system, facilitating capital accumulation by paying for infrastructure, providing welfare and other services and ensuring social harmony (Blowers 1986). In contrast, pluralists, who believed in a neutral state capable of serving a variety of interests, resisted the Marxist challenge to the public interest as a basis for planning action. Those who took a managerial view of the state stressed the ability of a rational, independent and increasingly powerful bureaucracy, nominally subservient to politicians, to define the public interest. This coincided with the growing

3

popularity of corporate management in public service both centrally and locally, evident in the introduction of corporate plans that aimed to allocate resources according to the overall objectives of the service rather than by traditional departmental boundaries.

Corporate management was thus intended to prevent unco-ordinated action by the bureaucracy caused by the inherent tendency of its different sections to pursue mutually conflicting objectives. Local authorities who searched for expertise capable of preparing corporate plans often turned to those on their own staff originally trained as town planners. For a time, urban planning became caught up with the management and delivery of public services as a whole, including education, housing and social services in a working environment far removed from any notion of civic design. The planner was seen as "the master-allocator of the scarcest resources: land, and capital and current expenditure on the built environment and the services which are offered to the community" (Eversley 1973: 342). In the 1980s, as Yiftachel (1989) notes, the analytical debate continued to be divided along ideological lines, with the main strands then evident best described as managerialism, neopluralism and reformist Marxism.

Yiftachel (1989) identifies the fundamental question in the urban form debate as "What is a good urban plan?" Until late in the 1960s, it was widely believed that older industrial cities should be redesigned and re-developed at much lower densities, with the overflow of population dispersed to newly built settlements at some distance. This type of urban plan was physically led, reflecting the ascendancy of design thinking, often to the neglect of social and economic considerations. However, comprehensive redevelopment within cities came to be regarded as destructive of social and economic life and as poor value financially. Since the 1960s, the urban form debate has emphasized urban containment rather than urban dispersal, and has preferred conservation and rehabilitation to clearance and redevelopment. More recent attention has been given to the sustainability of alternative urban forms and to the relative merits of high- and low-density development.

The fundamental question in the procedural debate is "What is a good planning process?" Yiftachel (1989: 34) further contends that: "the first five decades of the century were dominated in what is termed here the 'design method', whereby substantial knowledge about a given object was translated into a plan via the intuition or inspiration of the planner." In the early days of urban planning, Patrick Geddes, one of the pioneers of the civic design tradition coined the phrase "survey before plan" to encapsulate this method, but to later generations of planners it became better known as "survey–analysis–plan". The narrowness of this consensual approach was again challenged in the 1960s by new approaches that defined the planning process as the application of reason to collective decision-making.

Rational comprehensive planning, as it became known, sought to employ scientific methods to social organization and control. This approach had originated in the USA in the 1940s and 1950s, and drew heavily on cybernetics, systems analysis and operational research. The planner's task became to identify all possible alternatives or courses of action, to evaluate the consequences of each against pre-stated ends, and as a result to select the most appropriate. Whether the planner in question sought to rebuild a city or put a man on the Moon mattered little, for planning was seen as a generic activity applicable in principle to any task. The planning graduate, educated to take an overall view in co-ordinating the work of others and to appreciate the longer-term perspective, was considered qualified not only for the town planning profession but for a management career in any part of the public or private sectors. During the early 1970s, such procedural planning theory came to dominate planning thought as a whole, with urban planning almost caricatured as a set of techniques for rational decision-making. The most influential application of the rational comprehensive approach in British planning practice proved to be systems analysis, and its employment particularly in the initial wave of structure plans in the 1970s.

The systems approach regarded the city not as a place of chaos but of order, functioning as a richly integrated urban system with complex inter-connections between its component parts (McLoughlin 1969, Chadwick 1970). Since certain land-uses were considered to generate particular traffic requirements, movement around the system could be predicted, once it was known how land at each node of activity was used. Advanced mathematical models could therefore be employed to simulate the urban system. This approach was thus linked to the quantitative revolution in the social sciences more generally. The planner was seen as a helmsman, controlling and directing the process of change throughout the urban system, at the same time continuously monitoring the impact of such action through the model. Plan-making therefore became not a single event but a continuous process.

Although rational comprehensive planning was highly influential on urban planning practice research and education in the 1970s, Yiftachel (1989) comments that it was never supported by a similar consensus to that achieved by the design method during the early decades of the century. Competing concepts of the planning process included disjointed incrementalism (Lindblom 1959), mixed scanning (Etzioni 1967) and advocacy planning (Davidoff 1965). In later years, McLoughlin (1985) himself bravely acknowledged criticism that the systems approach reinforced the existing social order by accepting it as given, depended too much on the availability of information that was often difficult or expensive to collect, and ignored political and bureaucratic realities. By the 1980s, rational comprehensive planning had given way in the procedural debate to two competing strands which Yiftachel (1989) identifies as positive discrimination and rational pragmatism.

Neither civic design, corporate management or systems analysis, powerful as they have each been at times within these debates, adequately explain the nature of urban planning in a market economy. Although civic design sought to improve the built environment directly, it often neglected social and economic factors responsible for poor physical conditions. At its most naïve, the pretension that better living conditions would inevitably create social harmony and a sense of belonging represented no more than a highly simplistic form of environmental determinism (Allison 1986). Indeed, civic design primarily reflected the values and attitudes of the middle class, and tended to be regressively redistributive in practice, since it concentrated on creating or preserving environments unaffordable by the urban poor. In contrast, within corporate management, urban planners have been required to act as educationalists, housing specialists and welfare officers, for which many have neither the training nor the expertise. Systems analysis certainly brought a new logic and rigour to planning thought, as a result of which most planners today automatically set out the aims and objectives of any policy recommendations. However, it is highly questionable whether urban systems bear any real resemblance to the systems evident, for example, in biological phenomena. Indeed, to many people, urban areas appear chaotic and unpredictable places, with any sense of order far removed.

Much as civic design and systems analysis seem distinctly different, they both regard urban planning as a politically neutral activity in which rational choices technically identified by experts readily gain popular consent. Such a philosophy fails to acknowledge that every piece of land affected by a plan has not only a use but a value and an owner. It is therefore helpful to consider alternative approaches that examine how various types of interest relate to the planning system (Healey et al. 1988). For example, plans that suggest new uses for land affect monetary value and cause owners pleasure or displeasure. Landowners are certainly not the only people who stand to gain or lose through urban planning. Community groups, for example, may value their local environment in a quite different sense for the amenity it bestows. If urban plans threaten that local amenity, whether justified or not on wider grounds, controversy can normally be expected. Indeed, urban planning produces winners and losers of all kinds, who in a mature democracy know how to bring pressure on politicians to overturn the supposedly neutral recommendations of planning experts.

The implementation of urban plans in a market economy

A market economy is conceived differently in neoclassical, welfare and Marxist economics. Markets, in neoclassical economics, are structured principally by the behaviour of buyers and sellers. Since no single buyer or seller can affect market price, perfect competition exists. The price mechanism ensures that supply and demand are balanced unproblematically. In welfare economics, the propensity of markets to fail is emphasized. Competition is seen not as perfect but often as highly imperfect. Market efficiency then depends on the success of political and institutional measures taken to correct market failure. Marxist economists dismiss the notion of markets in the conventional sense. Although particular Marxist interpretations differ from one another, they share the view that resources are distributed by the outcome of the continuous struggle between the forces of capital and labour.

This book seeks to examine urban planning and the development process from an approach grounded within a welfare economics perspective. It contends that, since the development process is dominated by the private sector, the implementation of urban plans is highly dependent on the extent to which the planner can successfully influence landowners, developers, investors and other significant actors. Earlier conceptions of urban planning that fail to understand the critical relationship between plan-making and implementation are seriously flawed. For example, both civic design and systems analysis start from the mistaken belief that the planner is in control of the urban environment and that the implementation of plans is an unproblematic administrative process that follows on naturally from the setting of policy. This "top-down" view of the world assumes that plans, formulated at the top of a hierarchy, are passed down to compliant agents who are responsible to the plan-makers for implementation (Bruton & Nicholson 1987). If such unrealistic thinking were applied in the real world, where planners are in constant negotiation with landowners, developers, infrastructure companies and other agencies, each of whose powers and resources may be greater than those of the planning authority, it would merely produce paper plans with little prospect of implementation.

A more helpful explanation of real life provided by Barrett & Fudge (1981) rejects such sequential and hierarchical assumptions, instead seeing policy formulation as an interactive process of negotiation and bargaining between policy-makers and implementing agencies. The power, resources and influence of relevant agencies and their ability to bargain thus determine not only what is and what can be implemented but also what is feasible in the first place, in policy terms. In this perspective, urban plans result from a dynamic relationship between policy and action in which those responsible for implementation negotiate to maximize their own interests during policy formulation and in which urban plans are open to constant modification as bargaining takes place.

By the beginning of the 1980s, urban planning practice had thus left behind earlier notions of civic design, corporate management and systems analysis. However, by failing to develop a new basis in theory and instead concentrating on the job in hand (reflected by the catchphrases of the time

such as "getting things done" and "making things happen"), urban planning proved easy prey to the New Right thinking of the Thatcher Government. For until 1979, postwar urban planning had sought to promote economic efficiency, protect the environment and fulfil community needs, but
under Thatcherism "the first of these has become paramount, the second
important only in specified geographical areas and the third is no longer
seen as the remit of planning" (Thornley 1991: 219). This ideological shift
was facilitated by British planning legislation which defines procedures but
not policy content, enabling politicians, officials and pressure groups to fill
the system with whatever content is considered most important at the time
(Healey 1992b).

   Although planning returned decisively to the political agenda in the early
1990s, within the heightened concern for environmental quality and sustainability, Healey contends that the relationship between the state and the
market had by then been fundamentally reorganized. She suggests (1992b:
412) that: "The challenge for planning in the 1990s is to 'adapt' not only to
new substantive agendas about the environment and how to manage it, but
to address new ways of thinking about the relation of state and market, and
state and citizen, in the field of land-use and environmental change."
Subsequent chapters consider the importance of this challenge. For, in a
market economy, the state acts primarily as a regulator and enabler, rather
than as a controller and provider. Urban planners thus work in partnership
with such people as landowners, developers, investors, community groups
and ordinary members of the public to improve the urban environment
through specific acts of intervention in the development process. Such
intervention can and should be fully justified by evidence of market failure
and government success. Urban planning, at its best, therefore aims to challenge and transform market thinking, practices and products in order, not
that urban plans should be market-led, but that markets should be plan
influenced. However, in reality, British urban planning has been poorly
equipped for this purpose, in theory and in practice.

Urban planning as intervention in the development process

Urban planning can intervene in the development process through three
main instruments: plans, control and promotion. At certain times, such
intervention has been closely tied to its impact on the value of land by
broader land policy measures, including land taxation. Attempts to achieve
this generated considerable controversy and never gained political consensus. Yet, as subsequent chapters show, when matters of land use are artificially separated from those of ownership and value, urban planning is
inevitably weakened.

   Development plans provide a context for control decisions by stating the strategies and principles that the planning authority will adopt in seeking to manage land-use and environmental change. A development plan indicates where an authority wishes to encourage development (by allocating land for specific uses) prevent it (e.g. by designating land as green belt) and direct it (through a combination of the previous two, e.g. by allocating land for a new shopping centre within a city while preventing its development on the fringe). Such guidance provides a framework for the land market, by helping landowners, developers and investors to know in advance what is likely to be acceptable on their own land as well as on neighbouring land.

Development control provides an administrative mechanism for the planning authority to exercise discretion on specific development proposals, by deciding in each case whether to uphold the development plan or depart from it. Development control thus enables landowners, developers and investors to challenge the development plan, after its adoption. The planning authority may try to control the form of a development as well as its location, specifying requirements for matters such as access, scale, design and external appearance. Although development control is a passive process, responding to proposals submitted for the approval of the planning authority, it is far from negative, since many authorities aim by negotiation to transform proposals that conflict with the development plan into ones that contribute to its implementation. Refusal is usually a last resort, except in green belts and other areas of particular restraint.

Development promotion is the most active way in which urban planning interacts with the development process. Authorities seek to stimulate development and investment within their areas by promoting and marketing locations, making land available to developers and providing grants and subsidies. Such important activities are often neglected in academic accounts of urban planning, since they are not statutory duties under town and country planning legislation and are often undertaken in specialist units or departments which have no responsibility for development planning and control. However, as a form of intervention in the development process, development promotion is conceptually no different from plans or control and, in many parts of the country, may be far more effective.

This book concentrates on development promotion and especially on statutory development planning at the local level, making only limited reference to development control. There are three reasons for this. First, the relationship of development plans, promotion *and* control to the development process is too much to examine in detail in a book of this length. Indeed, the extent to which development as a whole is influenced by the statutory control framework of applications, appeals and enforcement is worth a book in its own right. Secondly, an intensive new wave of development plan preparation was initiated at the local level in England and Wales by the Planning and Compensation Act 1991, which sought also to enhance the status of statutory development plans in individual planning decisions.

Much debate, of course, already surrounds the interpretation of this Act (Gatenby & Williams 1992). Thirdly, conflict over land-use and environmental change between, for example, landowners, developers and local residents, is most fully displayed during local plan preparation. This creates a rich investigative environment for the type of research that informs this text.

What this book contains

This book is in four parts. Part 1 sets out the development framework. Chapters 2 and 3 therefore respectively explain how land & property markets and land & property development processes function in practice. Market imperfections and failure are identified, and development activity is shown to be both volatile and uneven. The extent to which such weaknesses justify planning is discussed in Chapter 4, which explores the nature and purpose of urban planning in a market economy. The chapter contends that, for such planning to be effective, it must be regarded as a form of state intervention in the development process. The chapter therefore gives particular attention to the importance of equity, efficiency and sustainability in the built environment. It also examines the relationship between land-use planning and wider land policy, and concludes by investigating the growth of planning gain.

Part 2 concentrates on the strategies, interests and actions of particular actors who play a critical rôle in shaping the built environment. Chapter 5 investigates how landowners formulate their land management and development strategies, and distinguishes between active and passive behaviour by owners in planning and development. Chapter 6 looks at developers, investors and professional advisers, and explores both the risks and returns that development can generate. The chapter shows how different types of developer, at varying stages of maturity, pursue different strategies. Chapter 7 examines the variety of agencies in the public sector which promote development or affect its viability. The chapter gives particular attention to entrepreneurial planning or development promotion, and concludes by investigating various types of public–private development partnership.

Part 3 looks in detail at statutory local development planning. Chapter 8 explains current practice and procedure, and investigates the impact of local planning on development by reference to case studies in Cambridge, Greenwich and Surrey Heath. An outline of development planning practice elsewhere in the European Union is also given. Since urban planning is an inherently political activity, Chapter 9 explores the politics of local development planning through an investigation of the political controversy that surrounded the preparation of the Cambridge Green Belt Local Plan. Chapter 10 seeks to identify which groups and organizations are best placed to influence the content of local development plans. Chapter 11 evaluates the effectiveness of local development planning with particular reference to its distributional impact and its relationship to land & property markets and development processes. The chapter concludes that statutory local plans have been marginalized as an active form of intervention in such markets and processes.

Part 4 sets out an agenda for planning practice, education and research in Chapter 12. This is not intended to be comprehensive in coverage but rather to stimulate debate by identifying ways in which urban planning might be enabled to intervene more effectively in the development process. Throughout the book, case studies and examples from recent research and practice are used to illustrate points of particular interest or importance.

CHAPTER TWO

Land & property markets

Since activities undertaken on one plot of land may constrain what is possible on neighbouring plots, land is intrinsically a social rather than a private commodity. However, private property rights control access to land and enable it to be traded in private markets that pay only scant attention to its social characteristics. Indeed, market processes ensure that: ". . . land tends to be put to its most profitable use, depending on the local circumstances, for the underlying criterion of commercial development is profitability, not the usefulness of particular buildings nor local people's need for them" (Kirk 1980: 32). Unless urban planners understand and relate explicitly to these processes, plans will tend not to shape market behaviour, but be shaped by it.

This chapter explains how land & property markets arise and function. By reference to English land law (but not Scottish), it shows how a whole variety of rights and entitlements can be created in the same land, each of which may be traded separately. Attention is given to the ways in which land & property markets are subdivided, and in particular, to the important distinction between the user, investment and development markets. The chapter suggests that certain subsectors are so riddled by imperfections and failure that they cannot really be described as markets at all, in the strict economic sense. However, as the chapter concludes, urban planning may produce unexpected market outcomes, which need to be identified and debated well in advance, if such intervention is to be effective.

The nature of land ownership

The ownership of land has been a source of power throughout history. The defence of private property is deeply entrenched in English law and culture. From this perspective, urban planning represents a recent statutory interference in property rights. The nature of land ownership in English law is determined by two fundamental doctrines: the doctrine of tenures and the doctrine of estates.

The doctrine of tenures

Since the Norman Conquest, the basis of English land law has been that the absolute ownership of all land is vested in the Crown. The Crown itself occupies only a very small proportion of the nation's land. According to the doctrine of tenures, all other land is held under the Crown. Tenure refers to the terms and conditions under which the right to possession of the land was originally granted by the Crown. In feudal times, there were many different forms of tenure, such as Knight service (providing a fixed number of fully armed horsemen for 40 days a year) or petty sergeanty (providing the King with, for instance, straw for his bed). Under the tenants-in-chief, who held land directly from the King in the feudal system, existed a whole pyramid of mesne (or intermediate) tenants, all the way down to those who actually occupied the land, known as tenants in demesne.

All the terms and conditions under which land was held, came in time to conform to the tenure known as socage or freehold, in which payment was made in money rather than by services in kind. Indeed, all the various forms of tenure were eventually converted directly into freehold by statute and, with few exceptions, all conditions of such tenure were abolished. As a result, feudal laws of tenure are no longer relevant to disputes over land. The absolute ownership of land continues to be vested in the Crown, but this has no practical significance, since the freeholder's right to possession is not restricted by any feudal burdens. Indeed, as Harwood (1975) comments, the right to possession, rather than some abstract concept of ownership, is central to English land law. Although the freehold is the highest form of property right in English law, lesser rights to the benefit of other persons, may also exist in freehold land. If so, such rights must be respected by the freeholder. Today, the word tenure is applied in a different sense to the relationship between landlord and tenant. However, this particular relationship, which is not feudal in origin, is governed by the doctrine of estates.

The doctrine of estates

While the doctrine of tenures refers to the manner in which land is held, the doctrine of estates refers to the duration or period of time over which land is held. The Law of Property Act 1925 reduced the number of legal estates to two. These are the fee simple absolute in possession, commonly called the **freehold estate** and the term of years absolute, commonly called the **leasehold estate**. These will each be explained further.

The freehold estate All land, apart from the Crown Estate, is held by someone somewhere in freehold ownership under the Crown. A freehold estate is known technically as a fee simple absolute in possession. It is absolute because no time limit is placed on its existence. It is in possession because, unlike a fee simple in remainder or in reversion, possession is not dependent upon the expiry of lesser interests, but rather exists at the present time. A fee simple in reversion may arise, for example, when a man leaves property to his widow for the remainder of her natural life and thereafter to his children. In this case, the widow has a life interest, while the freehold is held by trustees until her death, and only then passed to the children.

The freeholder has both natural and proprietary rights existing in perpetuity and is entitled to use the land without restriction, unless so prevented by either statute or other estates and interests in the same land. The right to the light and air vertically over the land is an important natural right. The most valuable proprietary rights are those that allow the freeholder to develop, sell, transfer or create lesser interests in the land, without needing to obtain the consent of anyone else. The Town and Country Planning Act 1947, which nationalized the right to develop, was one of the most far-reaching statutory restrictions placed upon the rights of freeholders. Although the freeholder retains the right to use agricultural land for the grazing of cattle or the right to use retail premises for the sale of goods, the traditional right to build shops on grazing land and sell goods can now be exercised only if planning permission is given.

The leasehold estate A leasehold estate or a term of years absolute is defined as any period of time which, at its minimum, is of fixed and certain duration. It can include a monthly or weekly tenancy, since in each case, there is a fixed and minimum duration of a month and week respectively over which the tenancy can exist. The landlord in a leasehold estate lets the tenant into exclusive possession of the land or property for a specified period, usually in return for either an initial payment (known as a premium) or periodic rent, or a combination of both.

The terms and conditions, including the exact description of the land or property, the duration of the estate, the premium or rent payable and the covenants or obligations entered into by both landlord and tenant, are set out in the lease or tenancy agreement. Responsibility for repairs and insurance, for example, is normally defined in the covenants. A **lease** is a document correctly signed, sealed and delivered in law, which thus testifies by deed that both landlord and tenant have agreed terms. A **tenancy** is merely an agreement in writing. Normally, a legal estate can be created only by deed. However, tenancies for three years or less, at the best rent reasonably obtainable without taking a premium, can be created as legal estates, either orally or in writing, provided they take effect in possession.

The landlord and tenant enjoy separate rights in the same land or property. At any time, the landlord is entitled to sell the freehold estate, irrespective of the existence of any leasehold estate. The stream of income due to be received over the years in the form of rent, provides the basis on which the landlord's freehold can be valued. The sale of the freehold does not affect the existence of the leasehold. One landlord or property investor

14

simply replaces another. In the meantime, tenants are entitled to sublet for any period shorter than their own lease or tenancy, unless expressly forbidden by the covenants. If a sublease (or underlease) is created, the original freeholder becomes the head landlord, the original tenant becomes the head lessee or sublessor, while the tenant under the sublease becomes the sublessee. A whole chain of subleases can be created. More than one leasehold estate may therefore exist in the same land or property. Each estate may be valuable.

For example, a tenant may occupy premises on a 25-year lease, entered into 20 years ago. If the lease contained no provision for periodic rent reviews, the rent payable under the terms and conditions of the lease (known as the passing rent) would be substantially less than the current full letting value (known as the rack rent). The tenant could therefore sublet the premises at the rack rent, while continuing to pay only the passing rent to the head landlord, thus making a profit on the difference between the rack and passing rents. Alternatively, unless prohibited by the covenants, the tenant could transfer (or assign) the remaining five years of the lease and receive a capital sum to take account of the difference between the rack and rents. This explains the paradox "lease for sale".

Building land may be sold freehold or let on a ground lease. Ground leases may be for any duration but in commercial development, terms of 99, 125 and 999 years are common. The freeholder, as ground lessor, receives either a premium or a periodic ground rent, or a combination of both, from the developer who becomes the ground lessee. A ground lease enables a freeholder to exercise control over the type and quality of development constructed. Once finished, the developer will let the property to tenants on rack rents, for periods normally up to 25 years. Any developer who chooses not to remain as sublessor will sell the leasehold estate to a property investor. In due course, tenants who wish to move, will either assign their leases or create subleases. At the end of the specified period of 99, 125 or 999 years (or whatever alternative term is agreed), any buildings that remain revert with the land to the freeholder. No compensation needs to be paid for such buildings, unless agreed in the original ground lease.

Interests in land

Apart from the two types of legal estate, all other rights and entitlements in land and property take effect as **interests in land**.[1] Whereas the word estates refers to rights over one's own land, interests normally refers to rights over the land of another. There are five specified categories of legal interest, each of which is usually granted on a commercial basis for money or other valuable consideration. All other estates, interests and charges in or over land now take effect as equitable interests, most of which are created within families on a non-commercial basis. Discussion will therefore concentrate on legal interests.

Examples of important legal interests include restrictive covenants, mortgages, easements and options. A restrictive covenant, for instance may arise when part of a large garden is sold for residential development. The original owner may wish to prevent the use of the dwellings for non-residential purposes, and will therefore impose a restrictive covenant to this effect, at the time of sale. This enables the vendor's use and enjoyment of the original house to continue, without the fear of commercial or industrial activity taking place on the land that has been sold. The rights of those buying new dwellings are thus limited by the restrictive covenant imposed for the benefit of the original freeholder.

A developer may to wish to secure the right to purchase land, while trying to obtain planning permission. This can be achieved by means of either an option, granted by a freeholder to the developer normally in return for payment, or a contract for sale conditional on planning permission. As Goodchild & Munton (1985: 70) explain, "An option is an agreement that allows a developer to buy land at an agreed, fixed price by serving notice on the owner at any time within a specified period, normally two years. A conditional contract is one that does not take effect until a specific event occurs, usually the granting of planning permission. A time limit is imposed by which date the event making the contract unconditional must have taken place. The difference between the two is this. A developer who holds an option *can* buy the land at any time during the duration of the agreement. A developer who holds a conditional contract *must* buy the land if the event on which the contract is conditional occurs. Thus, if planning consent is granted, the developer must purchase the land." Options and conditional contracts thus allow developers to seek planning permission, safe in the knowledge that if it is granted, the land can be acquired.

Licences

A licence is not a property right, but merely a personal permission given by an estate owner to allow the licensee to do what would otherwise be a trespass. For example, permission may be given to allow someone to exercise dogs on private land. Where a development site is due to be made available on a ground lease, the developer may initially enter the site under a building licence or contract. The ground lease itself will commence only when construction is complete.

Who is the landowner?

It is apparent that, in any one parcel of land, there may be several estates and interests. For example, a farm may be held freehold by an investor but let to a tenant. The tenant may have sublet one of the fields for show-jumping to the local pony club. The investor may have mortgaged the land to a bank who took out a legal charge. A developer may have obtained an option on part of the farm. Who owns the farm? None of the parties can

16

claim exclusive ownership of the land, but each enjoys particular rights or entitlements in the land. Each of these rights is capable of being traded as a commodity. None of the parties is entitled to violate the rights or entitlements of the others. If, for example, the developer obtains planning permission and acquires the freehold, the tenant and the subtenant are entitled to remain for the duration of their leasehold estates. Development cannot proceed immediately unless the developer is able to buy out such existing rights and entitlements and clean up ownership of the land. We can therefore think of rights in land as existing in "bundles" (Denman & Prodano 1972). The greater part of the bundle held by one individual or organization, then the better placed is that individual or organization to control the present use and future development of the land. However, unless otherwise stated, the word "landowner" is used in the remainder of this book to refer to the owner of the freehold estate, which is regarded as the highest form of property right in English law.

The nature of markets in land and property

Transactions

A market exists when buyers and sellers involved in the production and consumption of a single commodity come together to undertake transactions. Some markets, such as those for fruit and vegetables have a clearly identifiable location. In contrast, rights in land and property are exchanged through informal and decentralized networks. Most communication between buyers and sellers (or normally between their respective agents) takes place by telephone or letter, rather than face to face. However, the absence of a specific location or of face to face communication, does not prevent the existence of a market.

Transactions in land and property occur through private treaty, formal tender or public auction. Under private treaty, land or property is advertised for sale normally at a specified price. If offers are received below the asking price, negotiations may take place with prospective purchasers. The vendor may wait until the asking price is offered or alternatively may withdraw the land or property from the market, if no such offer is received. Under formal tender, the vendor invites bids in sealed envelopes by a specified date. On that date, the vendor opens the envelopes, having usually reserved the right not always to accept the highest bid. In normal circumstances, a purchaser must proceed, if a bid is accepted. Public auction provides the one example where land & property markets adopt a specified but temporary location. Often, auctioneers book a function room in a hotel for this purpose. Land and property are offered by open competition to the highest bidder. However, vendors are free to set reserve prices, below which even the highest bid will not be acceptable.

Prices and values

Prices for land and property refer either to the amount sought (asking prices) or the sum received (prices paid). In contrast, values of land and property are price estimates that reflect subjective expectations and perceptions of worth. The more efficient the market, the more likely is value to correspond to price. Three types of value can be recognized. **Use value** represents the utility or profitability that the land or property affords to a particular user in a particular use. **Exchange value** represents the expectation of what the particular land or property would fetch, if it were to be offered for sale. Although home-owners may well spend money improving the use value of their properties, for example by knocking walls down between rooms, this may not necessarily enhance the exchange value. **Open market value** reflects the exchange value rather than the use value since it is an estimate of the best price at which the land or property might reasonably be expected to be sold, given certain assumptions. Of course, in order to estimate open market value, professional valuers need to take full account of prices actually paid in recent open market transactions.

Supply and demand

According to neoclassical theory, market prices are determined by the forces of supply and demand. By exploring such theory, its limitations can be identified. Demand is the quantity of land and property that buyers wish to purchase at each conceivable price. The demand for land and property is derived from the utility or profitability of the proposed use. Supply is the quantity of land and property that vendors wish to sell at each conceivable price. Many argue that the supply of land is fixed. In fact, where land is in extremely scarce supply, expensive reclamation from the sea may be profitable. Much of the Central Business District of Hong Kong is built on land reclaimed from the harbour. More crucially, the flow of land offered for sale each year may vary enormously in response to market forces. In any event, the supply of property rights is not fixed, as they can be readily subdivided.

Markets and land-use patterns

According to neoclassical marginalist models (Hurd 1903, Alonso 1964, Muth 1969), competitive bidding for land determines the pattern of urban land-use. As Rhind & Hudson (1980: 191) explain: "For each type of activity, a location has utility which is measured by willingness to pay rent for use of that location. Activities bid competitively in a land market for use of different locations. In the long run, this competitive allocation process results in a tendency for the overall land-use pattern to adjust so that each location is occupied by the activity which can pay the highest rent. This yields an ordered pattern of land-use in which all activities are optimally located, in the sense that utilities are maximized." Relative profitability and utility in neoclassical marginalist theory are thus determined by accessibility. This confers the comparative advantage of lower cost and enables higher rents to be paid.

Neoclassical marginalist theory assumes that land is readily supplied to meet demand by the highest bidder. However, in practice, the supply of land may be restricted by planning, physical, valuation or ownership constraints (Adams et al. 1988). Although owners may prefer to receive rent, if only on a short-term basis, rather than leave land and property vacant, Goodchild & Munton (1985), for example, argue that the decision to sell is complex and reflects each owner's personal, financial and taxation circumstances (see Ch. 5). If the maximum price that developers are able to afford is below that which owners will accept, no sale will take place.

Discussion has therefore centred on the extent to which the individual preferences of particular landowners can be accommodated in models of land supply (Evans 1983, Wiltshaw 1985, Evans 1986a, Wiltshaw 1988). Evans, for example, acknowledges that the reluctance of elderly couples to sell up and move at any price, or the high regard in which wealthy landowners may hold the amenity of their estates above any tempting offers received from developers, may be the kinds of exceptional cases, where individual preferences are more important than monetary considerations. Wiltshaw (1985) discusses the extent to which land affords an owner satisfaction in such non-market uses as a garden, and subsequently (1988) explains the extent to which non-land income is likely to affect supply prices. Such personal preferences can be considered part of what Baum & Crosby (1988) call the "psychic income" or positive feeling that land or property ownership may create.

Once theory begins to take account of the individual behaviour of landowners, it becomes much more difficult to explain land-use patterns by demand-side analysis alone, irrespective of whether planning controls exist or not. Competitive bidding is certainly an important determinant of urban land-use, but in practice, the application of neoclassical marginalist models needs to be tempered by an understanding of both the behaviour of landowners and of imperfections and failure in land & property markets, which are subsequently discussed in detail. Indeed, no two parcels of land or no two properties are exactly the same, although many parcels and properties are close substitutes for one another. As a result, a series of recognizable submarkets in land and property arise in three main ways: by the motive for acquisition, geographically and sectorally. Each of these ways will now be considered.

Submarkets by motive for acquisition

Users, investors and developers acquire land and property for different motives. The user rents or buys space in the **user market**. The user is interested in use value, and especially in matters affecting business productivity and operating costs, such as appearance, comfort, convenience and efficiency. The investor buys and sells existing or recently completed property in the **investment market**. The investor is interested in the income flow from user rents, capitalized into the exchange or investment value of the property. The developer aims to exploit development value created by opportunities such as building sites or redundant premises suitable for renovation, available in the **development market**. The developer seeks to minimize development costs and maximize development revenues in order to maximize development returns or profits.

An individual or organization may adopt more than one of these rôles. A user, for example, may undertake development for owner-occupation. A mature developer may diversify into investment and an adventurous investor may initiate development. However, development and investment need to be appraised and justified on their individual merits, even when undertaken by the same organization or individual. The important distinction between the user, investment and development markets will now be explored further.

The user market

Users evaluate the accessibility, specification and tenure of available accommodation against their own particular needs. Accessibility and location are critical to users. Richardson (1971) distinguishes between general accessibility, or nearness in travel costs to all other urban uses and facilities, and special accessibility, or nearness to particular types of complementary facilities. Office users evaluate proximity to clients and related companies, while retailers consider location in relation to nearby pedestrian flows. Rapid motorway connections are essential for many industrial and warehouse users. As far as specification is concerned, users such as industrialists concentrate on physical characteristics, since a well designed factory on a flat site with enough room for circulation, servicing and car parking, is likely to make production more efficient. Others, such as professional firms seeking prestige offices, may pay more attention to the image that the accommodation is likely to display to clients.

Users can rent or buy property. Most rented premises are constructed to a standard specification in order to appeal to a wide variety of potential tenants. By renting, a company does not tie up resources in property when they could produce higher returns from business expansion. Indeed, many small companies may be unable to afford freehold premises. Users retain greater flexibility to move by choosing to rent, subject to the terms of the lease. Although investors prefer to let premises on a standard 20–25 year lease, more flexible terms may offered to attract tenants in a downturn, when the supply of property exceeds demand. However, once an upturn causes demand to exceed supply, tenants may face substantial rent increases at the next review. In contrast, owner-occupiers are protected from such shocks. If rents rise rapidly, developers may be prompted into new construction and some users who rent may decide to buy.

Since each user has particular requirements for accessibility, specification and tenure, user demand is highly diverse. Some users, such as small manufacturing companies, may be unable to find affordable accommodation to meet their needs, since supply never matches the diversity of demand (Adams 1990). Although small workshops and nursery units have often been built by the public sector, the quantity, quality and location of most commercial construction have traditionally been determined by developers and investors in the private sector. However, rented property built only 20–25 years ago can now be hard for investors to let, if it no longer satisfies modern user demand. Small commercial and industrial users appear increasingly interested in owner-occupation. Investors have therefore become more responsive to user preferences in order to retain their long-term loyalty. Yet, users who purchase land and construct their own accommodation are best placed to satisfy any special requirements. Nevertheless, if such development is funded externally, a bank will need to be convinced that the resale value of the property for more general use covers the loan.

Many users take only enough space to cope with existing or projected output, despite the desirability of some room for subsequent expansion. If business subsequently increases, such users may try first to adapt their existing accommodation. Manufacturing companies are notoriously reluctant to relocate, owing to the cost and disruption involved. Indeed, relocation is usually postponed until there is enough evidence that the new business is sustained. Such reluctance to move means that the user market, particularly in industrial property, lags behind national changes in output and employment.

The investment market

Property is a cost to the user but an investment to the owner (Ketelby 1983). A property investor seeks a return from owning existing buildings or completed developments over a period of time. Investment return is a function that combines income flow from user rents, capital growth and that intangible factor, psychic income (Baum & Crosby 1988). Standing property investments are traded in the investment market. These are buildings already occupied by tenants, which offer the investor a known present income in the form of rent, with the prospect of future capital appreciation. Investors may also acquire freeholds from owner-occupiers, such as retail chains who wish to raise capital for business expansion, on the basis that such properties are immediately rented back to the occupier on a long lease. A single investor may hold a collection of standing investments, known as a property portfolio. Investors who wish to extend their portfolio will normally acquire further standing investments. However, some may choose to participate in development, particularly if no suitable standing investments are available to purchase. This is discussed in Chapter 3.

An ideal investment combines three essential qualities: **security, liquidity** and **profitability**. The more secure an investment, then the lower the risk that the capital invested will be lost or the expected income will not be paid. A secure investment protects the investor from inflation. The capital value of the investment must therefore be maintained, at least in real terms. To achieve this, the nominal value must rise by at least the rate of inflation. The more liquid an investment, then the easier it is to sell, either in whole or in part. Liquidity depends on the existence of potential purchasers, on the costs of transfer, on the overall size of the investment, and on the extent to which it is capable of subdivision for the purposes of sale. Profitability may refer to either income or capital growth, or to both combined in the form of overall returns. In the long run, capital growth and high overall returns will depend upon the prospects for income growth.

No investment offers complete security, perfect liquidity and guaranteed profitability. Indeed, the balance between security, liquidity and profitability varies from one investment to another. Each investment represents a different combination of these attributes, with investors able to play security, for instance, off against profitability. Higher expected returns would therefore be required from higher-risk investments. This is expressed by the concept of yield. Initial yield is defined as the annual income at the date of purchase as a percentage of the capital value. Other things being equal, investors expect a higher initial yield from riskier investments on the same basis that dangerous employment commands higher pay (Millington 1988). The higher the initial yield, the more an investor sacrifices security in pursuit of profitability.

Property investment has traditionally been considered to provide a real asset which, at its best, offers an attractive combination of security, liquidity and profitability. Over time, property returns more than keep up with inflation. Nevertheless, property investment involves considerable risks. A building may remain unlet for a considerable period, with no income received. In the long term, expensive maintenance or refurbishment may be necessary. Management expenses may be high, particularly when a single building is let to many tenants. Liquidity may be poor, especially in the case of very large buildings which become unfashionable. Property returns are also more frequently affected by changes in legislation than are returns from the other forms of investment.

The most significant property investors in the UK are the insurance companies and pension funds. These financial institutions grew rapidly in the postwar period, especially from the late 1950s (Cadman 1984). About a hundred such institutions each with property assets in excess of £100 million existed in the late 1980s (Nabarro 1990). Among those with the most substantial property holdings are two insurance companies, Prudential and Legal & General, and two pension funds, Postel and Coal Industry Nominees. As the most important recipient for personal savings, apart from house purchase, financial institutions recorded a net inflow of funds of over £5 billion per quarter in 1987. Each institution constantly seeks the best way to invest such funds in order to offer existing savers the highest possible pension or life assurance payment and consequently, to attract new savers. Property provides one possible investment outlet. By the early 1990s, it was estimated that institutional investors owned approximately £55 billion of commercial and industrial property in the UK, or one fifth of all such property in private hands (Investment Property Databank 1991).

However, financial institutions have no sentimental commitment to property. They deposit funds in banks and invest in government securities (called gilts, because they were originally issued on gilt-edged certificates) company stocks and shares (called equities) and even works of art or antiques. Funds may be invested at home or abroad. Overseas equities, for instance, are an increasingly important vehicle for institutional investment. Baum & Crosby (1988) neatly summarize the respective merits of the most important types of investment, while Fraser (1993) explains their qualities in some detail.

Although institutions prefer to maintain a varied investment portfolio of gilts, equities and property, all investments are increasingly appraised in the same way. The investment property market is therefore more closely tied to other investment markets than to the user or development markets in property. If property performs badly, funds will be gradually switched into alternative investments. To capture the attention of investors, property must offer returns which, taking account of good investment practice, compare favourably with gilts and equities. Figure 2.1 shows the comparative overall returns from these three main types of investment between 1981 and 1992. Although property returns outpaced inflation for most of this period, it is apparent that except in 1981, 1987 and 1988, it took either second or third place behind gilts and equities. Significantly, the latter two years coincided with the Stock Market Crash of 1987 and with the onset of the development boom.

The relatively poor performance of property in the 1980s, particularly in relation to equities, reduced its attractiveness to institutional investors (Nabarro 1990). By 1993, property accounted for only 5 per cent of overall pension fund assets and only 9 per cent of those held by insurance companies. This was almost two-thirds below the levels prevailing at the start of the 1980s. Moreover, the share of new institutional investment claimed by property had fallen from about 15 per cent of overall flow around 1980 to only 5 per cent by 1993 (Debenham Thorpe 1993). This limited new money is directed primarily at the acquisition of standing investments rather than at new development. Indeed, as Chapter 3 explains, the development boom of the late 1980s was fuelled primarily by bank lending rather than institutional investment.

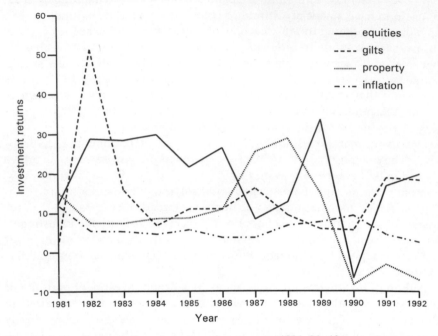

Figure 2.1 Comparative investment returns, 1981–92 (*Source:* Investment Property Databank).

In contrast, institutions have traditionally adopted a cautious approach to property investment, concentrating funds on what appear to be the most secure, liquid and profitable types of property. Such investments are termed "prime property". Prime property occupies the best possible location, such as the City of London or the West End for offices, or close to a motorway junction in the South East for business parks. In 1987, for example, the City of London and the West End accounted for 64 per cent of all institutional investment in offices (Nabarro 1990). Prime property is owned by the institution freehold or on a long leasehold of at least 99 years. The property is built to latest specification and design. The premises are leased for at least 21 years to tenants of unquestionable covenant, meaning that they will not disappear overnight without paying the rent. Only the very best property can therefore be considered prime.

Shops and offices meet such narrow criteria more readily than factories. In 1988, offices accounted for 53 per cent of institutional property holdings, shops for 36 per cent and industrials for less than 10 per cent (Nabarro 1990). Figure 2.2 shows the comparative overall returns from these three sectors between 1981 and 1992. This suggests that a successful property investor, having benefited from higher returns in retail property in the early and mid-1980s, would have moved funds into offices in 1987 and then to industrials in the late 1980s. However, the sheer scale of institutional property holdings deters such rapid switching. Moreover, expertise in property forecasting was rare until the late 1980s, so for most of the decade, the best returns were evident only in hindsight.

Although prime property has traditionally been considered to provide investors with the best possible returns, many prime investments of the 1960s and 1970s have now so deteriorated that they look extremely shabby. Such depreciation can be reversed only by expensive refurbishment, which may not be justified unless it regains or retains tenants prepared to pay higher rents. Buildings once considered prime have therefore been demolished. This has tarnished the image of prime property and further undermined the confidence of property investors.

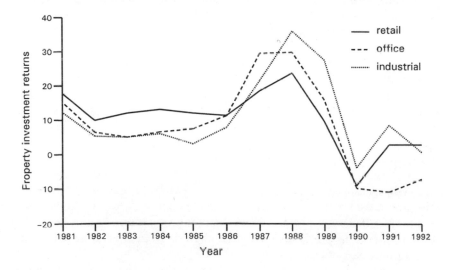

Figure 2.2 Property investment returns, 1981–92 (*Source:* Investment Property Databank).

Indeed, as Oakeshott (1985) argues, there is no guarantee that what is now considered prime property will maintain its appeal. The prime market is highly fickle. Investors who acquire prime property at expensive prices may well discover that, in due course, such property is considered too big, too old or badly located for the prime market and can be sold only in the secondary market. Oakeshott suggests that institutional investors need to take a more flexible approach and recognize that, in the long run, well located secondary property available at much lower prices can produce overall returns which outpace prime property.

McNamara (1993) contends that institutions could buy more commercial properties in inner cities, provided that the prospects of poor rental growth in such locations were reflected in lower purchase costs and particularly, that the substantial risks involved in such investment were reduced, for example, by the provision of more local information on actual returns. However, although institutions tend no longer to assess property on a building-by-building basis, but have moved towards overall portfolio management (Morrell 1991), there is yet little evidence of any widespread acceptance of the more flexible strategies advocated by both Oakeshott and McNamara.

The development market

Developers seek to enhance the value of land or property through capital expenditure or a change of use. The Town and Country Planning Act defines development as the carrying out of building, engineering, mining or other operations in, on, over or under land, or the making of any material change in the use of any buildings or other land. Users may undertake development, primarily to improve the use value of land or property, for example, by extending a house or a factory. Unsatisfied user demand provides developers and investors with an opportunity to profit from the development process.

Development opportunities that appear to offer the minimum acceptable profit are bought and sold in the development market. However, some transactions are so surrounded by secrecy that, although the purchaser may have every intention to develop, this is not revealed to the vendor. Developers, for example, may acquire sites suitable for commercial redevelopment but in multiple ownership, gradually and through third parties. Some users who sell at an early stage may believe that the transaction is taking place in the user market, and that the purchaser intends to use the property for a similar business. Secrecy enables the developer to pay only the value of the property in its existing use rather than the higher value which it may command as part of a redevelopment site.

Development land is normally valued by what is known as the residual method of valuation. This is illustrated in Table 2.1 by examining, for the sake of simplicity, a 4 ha residential site in a Surrey town, sold in the late 1980s. The residual method requires that the market value of the finished product should be estimated first. In this case, the developer proposes 100 dwellings, with a selling price at the time of the valuation of £150,000 each. The full costs of the development are then deducted, with allowance made not only for construction costs but also for professional fees and interest charges. For valuation purposes, it is assumed that working capital of £5,625,000 is borrowed evenly over the two-year construction period at

£234,375 per month. The average loan outstanding over the whole of the two-year construction period is therefore £2,812,500, or half the total cost of construction and professional fees. Interest is charged at 16 per cent per annum over the two years on this average sum. The developer's required profit at 20 per cent on gross development value is then deducted, leaving the balance or residual of £5,475,000, which when discounted at 16 per cent per annum over the two years, leaves £4,069,020 to purchase the four hectares.

In normal circumstances, the developer should therefore not bid above £1,017,255 per hectare. If the developer is able to acquire the site for less, profits will be boosted. However, in the late 1980s, fierce competition for building sites in the South East encouraged some residential developers to bid above their own residual valuations, in the belief that by the time the houses were finished, selling prices would have further increased (DOE 1992a). Yet subsequently, when mortgage rates rose steeply, housing demand receded and several prominent residential developers ran into financial difficulty (see Ch. 6).

Table 2.1 Residual valuation of residential development site.

Gross development value	£	£
100 units at £150,000		15,000,000
Expenditure:		
Construction: 10,000 m² at £50 per sq. m	5,000,000	
Professional fees, including architect, solicitor and quantity surveyor at 12.5% in total	625,000	
Interest charges at 16% per annum	900,000	
Developers profit at 20% of GDV	3,000,000	
Total costs		9,275,000
Residual site valuation		5,475,000
Discounted for 2 years at 16% per annum (5,475,000 × 0.7432)		4,069,020
Per hectare		1,017,255

Geographical submarkets

The characteristics of land & property markets vary geographically, on both an urban and a regional basis. Within cities, submarkets are often highly differentiated according to location. Models of urban use which derive from the work of Burgess (1925), Hoyt (1939) and Harris & Ullman (1945) subdivide urban areas into zones. Four zones recognized by many such models are the central business district, the inner city or zone of transition, the suburbs and the rural–urban fringe. In 1993, for example, a modernized inter-war semi-detached house cost between £61,000 and £67,000 in Newham in inner London, but between £85,000 and £110,000 in Barnet in outer London (Valuation Office 1993).

However, land & property markets are subdivided more locally within cities. For example, the central business district will contain both prime and secondary areas. In 1991, the best-quality newly built office accommodation in the centre of Manchester cost £22 per sq. ft per annum to rent in Mosley Street, the prime location, but only £18 per sq. ft in established secondary locations only ten minutes walk away, such as Quay Street and Peter Street. Land and property prices in the inner city and suburbs can also vary markedly within half a mile. Regional variations on land & property markets reflect the relative strength of regional economies. This is best illustrated by the cost of residential building land. For example, in 1993, a two-hectare residential building site with planning permission, would have cost £250,000 freehold in Blackburn, Lancashire, but four times that amount in Guildford, Surrey (Valuation Office 1993).

Sectoral submarkets

Land & property markets are divided sectorally according to the use or proposed development. The five traditional sectors of the market – agricultural land, residential, retail, office and industrial – were supplemented in the 1980s by two new sectors: business space and leisure. Capital available for investment and development will be switched between these sectors, in accordance with comparative returns. Each sector will now be examined further.

The agricultural land market

Agricultural land is divided between owner occupied and tenanted. Land sold with vacant possession is usually much more valuable than tenanted land. For example, dairy land in the South West fetched £2,200 per ha tenanted in 1993, but £5,900 if sold with vacant possession (Valuation Office 1993). However, as fully explained in subsequent chapters, owners able to obtain planning permission for urban use can reap very substantial development gains.

Residential market

More than two-thirds of dwellings in the UK are owner-occupied. This sector is highly specialized, with flats, terraced housing, semi-detached and detached houses each forming a particular submarket. New development is often targeted at particular niches of the market, such as starter units, executive housing and sheltered accommodation. In the rented sector, a substantial proportion of the local authority stock was sold off during the 1980s. Housing associations were able to expand their activity with extra funds from central government. Some recovery also took place in the private rented market as a direct result of special taxation incentives like the Business Expansion Scheme. Residential building land is subdivided into urban sites for flats or maisonettes, small sites of less than two hectares and bulk land, on which mass production can be organized. Bulk land is generally cheaper on a per hectare basis.

Retail market

Until the late 1960s, the retail market was concentrated in city centres and district or suburban centres. Many of these traditional locations remain vibrant, with substantial development having taken place in the 1980s. However, three waves of retail decentralization have occurred in the past 25 years. These trends reflect fundamental changes in the structure and organization of retailing, and in the behaviour and priorities of consumers. Superstores and hypermarkets, which formed the first wave, were developed from the late 1960s. Retail warehouses, developed from the mid-1970s, were proved the second wave. Regional shopping centres, which first caught public attention in the mid-1980s became the third wave. Following the opening of the first phase of the Metro Centre in Gateshead in 1986, development of other regional shopping centres followed at Dudley, Sheffield and at Thurrock on the eastern edge of London. These centres offer the complete range of convenience and comparison shopping in purpose-built undercover accommodation of at least 50,000 m²

Office market

The office market is heavily concentrated in the South East, with 40 per cent of floor-space located in Greater London. The City and the West End are the traditional market leaders. Decentralized locations include Croydon, developed as an office centre from the 1950s, and London Docklands, in which substantial office space was constructed in the 1980s. Decentralized locations have also been promoted in provincial centres, such as Salford Quays in Greater Manchester. Regional decentralization of certain central government administrative functions has also taken place to locations such as Bootle, Leeds, Newcastle upon Tyne and Swansea. However, the private sector appears reluctant to decentralize office uses to regions distant from London and the South East.

The office market is inextricably linked to the financial services sector, which plays a dual rôle as financier and occupant. Financial deregulation in 1986 led to a rapid growth in office rentals levels and subsequently to a spate of new construction. By the end of 1988, prime office rents in the City of London were reported to be nearing £70 per sq. ft (Valuation Office

1988). Five years later, the substantial overdevelopment of office floor-space in the City of London had caused prime office rents to fall back to only £27–30 per sq. ft (Valuation Office 1993).

Industrial market

As much as 40 per cent of Britain's industrial floor-space was constructed before 1945. A substantial legacy of Victorian factory buildings remains. Some 44 per cent of factories still have multi-storey production (Fothergill et al. 1987). As companies grow, they prefer to expand on their existing sites. If this is not possible, a move up the property ladder may be necessary. The foot of the ladder consists of small workshops (from 50 m^2) and nursery units (from 250 m^2). Standard terraced units on industrial estates, commonly known as sheds, are normally constructed at between 1,000 and 3,000 m^2. At the top of the ladder, units of 10,000 m^2 and above are constructed on self-contained sites.

Business space market

The appearance of the business market in the 1980s reflected a perception that the traditional demarcation between office and industrial activities had broken down, particularly in the high-technology manufacturing sector. The success of the Cambridge Science Park, which became a focal point for local high technology growth in the early 1980s (Brindley et al. 1989), led to a plethora of proposals throughout the country for science parks, research parks, business parks and campus developments. A change in the Town and Country Planning (Use Classes) Order in 1987 responded to this pressure by creating the B1 Business Class. This abolished the planning distinction between most office and light industrial uses. A spate of out-of-town business developments then followed, particularly in the South East. However, much of the new business space has been high quality office accommodation, constructed on what would previously have been considered traditional industrial locations. A new generation of buildings, with innovative design reflecting flexible use, has still to emerge in any quantity. Indeed, the business market has fast become the upmarket campus component of the office sector.

Leisure market

Growing affluence and more leisure time in the 1980s helped create a specialist leisure market. The market includes squash clubs, multiplex cinemas, golf courses and theme parks. Many new shopping proposals were accompanied by a leisure element. The leisure market is highly volatile and, in comparison with other sectors, the value of the property is more closely linked to the profitability of particular occupier's business.

Market imperfections

In a perfectly competitive market, rapid changes in price balance the quantity demanded with the quantity supplied and ensure equilibrium. Such markets eliminate surpluses and overcome shortages quickly. In practice, the perfectly competitive market does not exist. All markets, including the much-quoted Covent Garden Fruit Market, contain imperfections. However, some markets are much closer to meeting the conditions of perfect competition than others. Land & property markets are riddled with imperfections, since the conditions of perfect competition are violated extensively within these markets. Indeed, the widespread nature of such imperfections makes property markets among the least efficient of all (Balchin et al. 1988). This section therefore sets out the five most important conditions of perfect competition and examines how far land & property markets depart from these conditions.

A large number of buyers and sellers

The first condition requires that the number of buyers and sellers in a market is large enough to ensure that no one buyer or seller is able to influence the market price. This may be true in the market for semi-detached houses, but the market for other types of property is often dominated by few buyers or sellers. For example, there may be many willing buyers of potential development land at the urban periphery, but only a few sellers, each with considerable land holdings. In the inner city, there may be few buyers and few sellers. In six wards in inner Manchester, one vendor, the city council, accounted for over half the development sites sold between 1978 and 1983 (Adams et al. 1988). However, the most extreme example of monopoly power in the land market is provided by ransom strips. This is where a small strip of land, in places no more than a metre in width, lies between a development site and the public highway, and no alternative access to the highway can be obtained. In such cases, it is common for the monopoly owner of the ransom strip to claim up to one-third of the value of the development site.

A homogeneous product

The second condition requires that, in all respects apart from price, products exchanged in the market should be identical in order that purchasers should not prefer the qualities of any one product above another. Land and property are almost at the other end of the spectrum. Every transaction is unique since the location is different. However, some products offered in land & property markets are close substitutes. One newly completed office block in a city centre available to let may be only marginally different from another. In contrast, an office block 20 years old offered for sale in a suburban high street is a very different product. Substitutability may therefore diminish with age, location and tenure.

31

Ease of entry and exit

The third condition requires that buyers and sellers should be free to enter and leave the market at will. There are two barriers to this in land and property. First, high transaction costs are involved on transferring (or conveying) ownership rights. Dubben & Sayce (1991) estimate that the total bill from solicitors, surveyors and agents, combined with stamp duty and VAT amount to 4 per cent on top of the purchase price. Secondly, most property users display a remarkably strong preference for their existing location. Prior investment in the site and premises, combined with potential costs and disruption involved in relocation, often deter movement even if the original location is no longer suitable or efficient.

Frequent transactions

The fourth condition requires that transactions should be frequent enough to allow the market quickly to eliminate surpluses or overcome shortages. Land and property are bulky capital goods, acquired infrequently. Despite recent attempts to create a unitized property market (see Ch. 3), land and property cannot normally be acquired in small chunks or gradually over a period of time. In land & property markets, the frequency of transactions varies according to the type of land or property traded and the state of the market. For example, in the six wards in inner Manchester previously mentioned, only 92 transactions in land occurred during the whole of the period 1978 to 1983, giving a mean of 2.5 transactions per ward per year (Adams et al. 1988). In contrast, sales of semi-detached house may be plentiful in a good year, although a subsequent steep rise in interest rates may substantially reduce market activity.

Full information

The fifth condition requires that buyers should be aware of all the prices asked by sellers, and sellers aware of all the offers made by buyers, in order that both can make rational market choices. Furthermore, since prices paid in previous transactions influence vendors' supply prices, rational market behaviour would be fostered by full disclosure of recent transactions in, and the ownership of, land and property. Some purchasers, such as developers who buy sites through third parties, have a vested interest in keeping transactions secret. Although information on the ownership of land has long been available in Scotland in the Register of Sasines, open access to the Land Registry in England and Wales was granted only in 1990. Only 13 million of the 22 million properties in England and Wales are included, since compulsory registration of title was introduced only gradually from 1937. Although ownership rights in England and Wales are now much easier to discover, no details of transaction prices are available. This information circulates haphazardly around the traditional network of surveyors and valuers, with the most important transactions published in such journals as

Estates Gazette. The paucity of information on prices actually paid means that unusually high transactions can be quoted in support of unrealistic asking prices.

In recent years there has been a growing interest in good property research. Most financial institutions now undertake property forecasting themselves or commission it externally. Many leading firms of chartered surveyors have set up research departments. Independent research firms have also grown in stature, such as Investment Property Databank (IPD) and Property Market Analysis (PMA). A Society of Property Researchers has been formed. Despite these moves forward, "The absence of centralized market place means that comprehensive data on property performance is difficult and costly to collect" (Morrell 1991: 35).

Market failure

A resource-efficient allocation is considered in welfare economics to be one in which it is impossible to make one person better off without making someone else worse off. This is known as **Pareto optimality**. Neoclassical economists believe that markets are able to achieve Pareto optimality automatically, provided that the conditions of perfect competition are satisfied and that no external distortions exist. Market imperfections occur when the conditions of perfect competition are violated within the market. Market failure happens if the functioning of the market is distorted by external influences. Such imperfections and failure are characteristic of land & property markets and produce inefficiencies in land and property use. This section explains the three main ways in which land & property markets are subject to failure.

Externalities

An externality arises when the production or consumption of a commodity creates social costs or benefits which market mechanisms are unable to transmit into private costs or benefits. Externalities therefore create beneficial or harmful effects, for which no payment is either made or received by producers and consumers. For example, if the owner of a derelict site undertakes reclamation and landscaping, it may enhance the value of the neighbouring properties. However, if the site is subsequently brought back into use for car dismantling, property values in the neighbourhood may decrease. Since an individual owner takes no account of such social costs or benefits, land & property markets tend to produce an underprovision of beneficial externalities and an overprovision of harmful ones.

Pearce et al. (1978) define three types of externality which may affect the value of land and property. Producer–producer externalities occur, for example, where a riverside brewery is dependent upon the quality of the water supply. If another firm up stream begins to dump waste into the river, then the brewery will be faced with the additional cost of water purification. A factory chimney that pours black smoke on the washing of nearby residents provides a classic example of a producer–consumer externality. Consumer–consumer externalities often occur in the housing market. A substantial extension built on one house may shade a neighbouring house and cause its value to fall. Developers compare the private costs of development with the private benefits. Unless unusually altruistic, a developer is not particularly interested in the social costs that a development may inflict on the community, or the social benefits that it may be create. Areas already highly congested may therefore be subject to intense development pressure, while less congested but economically depressed areas strive to attract substantial new development.

Public goods

A public good, once produced, can be enjoyed by more than one consumer at the same time, without diminishing the utility derived by any other consumer. Indeed, no consumer who wishes to benefit from a public good can usually be excluded. Since it is not possible to control access to public goods, no charges can be levied at the point of consumption. This makes it impossible to organize the supply of public goods through normal market mechanisms. A lighthouse is the classic example of a public good. Although public goods are normally supplied by the public sector, the definition of a public good is dependent on its distinctive qualities rather than on the means of supply. Many urban goods, such as roads, parks and the external environment of the city, display elements of public-ness. Even when supplied by the public sector, public goods tend to be heavily used but underproduced.

Lost opportunities

Opportunities to use land and property more efficiently may be lost if individual action is dependent upon collective confidence. All the householders in an older area may be keen to spend time and money in renovating and modernizing their own properties. However, no single householder will want to be the first to start, unless there is a guarantee that others will follow suit. On that basis, no one would take any action and the area would continue to deteriorate. All the householders are trapped in what is known as the prisoner's dilemma (Harvey 1987), since each is unable to act in their own best interests, without knowing the intentions of the others.

The impact of imperfections and failure

As a result of imperfections and failure, land & property markets are in a perpetual state of disequilibrium. A balance is never achieved between supply and demand. Such markets move from shortages to overprovision and back to shortages. Pareto optimality in land & property markets is an illusion since a resource efficient allocation of land & property as a whole cannot be achieved by consideration only of the private costs and benefits applicable to each plot of land. Nevertheless, the impact of market imperfections and failure varies from one type of property to another. For example, particular markets may be categorized as either weak, semi-strong or strong, according to their informational efficiency (Baum & MacGregor 1992, Rutterford 1993).

The marketing of semi-detached suburban houses, for example, takes place in conditions nearer to perfect competition than that of vacant inner-city land. As Chisholm & Kivell (1987: 52) consequently point out, in respect of the inner-city land market: "There seems little doubt that there are structural characteristics, applying to the transactions of both private and public vendors, which systematically raise vendors' expectations above realistic market levels, and encourage the speculative holding of land against the possibility of better future offers." Where market imperfections or failure are prevalent, as happens in many inner cities, "urban land economy" is more accurate and preferable as a term than "urban land market". The extent to which market imperfections and failure justify urban planning is taken up in detail in Chapter 4.

The market impact of urban planning

At one time, the impact of urban planning on land & property markets was discussed by reference to floating and shifting values. This is well explained by Reade (1987). If a steadily expanding city is surrounded on all sides by agricultural land, all owners within the surrounding area may hope one day to be able to sell land for development at a price higher than its value in agricultural use. In fact, only a relatively small proportion of owners would actually find their land in demand for development, even no planning system existed. Development value thus **"floats"** over an extensive agricultural area, but ultimately settles on only a relatively small part of it.

When urban planning is introduced, planning permission will be granted in some locations but refused at others. As a result, any potential development value on land refused planning permission is considered to **"shift"** to land granted planning permission. However, since the past expectations of all owners in the wider area had been unduly raised by floating value, any value gains on sites granted planning permission are felt to be outweighed by the value losses which landowners refused planning permission all perceive. However, it was considered in theory, that planning had a neutral impact on land & property markets since the actual rather than the perceived gains and losses cancelled each another out. Yet, although the concept of floating and shifting value has been used to justify statutory attempts to appropriate development value for the community, it represents a static rather than a dynamic understanding of the impact of urban planning on land & property markets. For planning in practice does not simply shift values around a city but critically affects the utility or profitability of the uses from which the demand for land is derived.

Indeed, if bad planning produces a less efficient allocation of land-uses by making users locate sub-optimally, thus reducing utility and profitability, users will lower bidding prices for land and value will be lost not merely shifted. In contrast, if good planning produces a more efficient arrangement of land-uses, and improves accessibility and complementarity within a city, it will increase utility and profitability and enable users to make higher bids. Furthermore, if planning overcomes market failure by regulating negative externalities, encouraging the smooth provision of public goods and opening up opportunities that would otherwise be lost, resources will again be allocated more efficiently. Urban planning can cause higher or lower bidding prices to be made for land, depending on whether it increases or decreases overall welfare.

Urban containment has been a central feature of postwar planning in the UK. Much debate has surrounded its impact on residential land & property markets. It was long held that land prices cannot push up housing prices, since the price of land is determined by the price of housing and not vice versa (Grigson 1986). This view has now been subject to sustained criticism. Cheshire & Sheppard (1988) argue that urban containment will increase the price of new houses, if it reduces their supply. If builders can sell houses for more, they will pay more for land. Although high land prices do not cause high house prices, both are caused by development restrictions.

Empirical evidence shows that, nationally housing land prices rose by twice the rate of house prices between 1968 and 1988, or 350 per cent above inflation (DOE 1992a). Although the relationship between incomes and house prices has remained stable over time, Evans (1986b) contends that house buyers have responded to rising real land and house prices by purchasing smaller quantities of housing and, in particular, by economising on land. Urban containment policies have therefore induced powerful substitution effects in the housing market. Evans (1991b) argues that, by raising the real price of land, urban containment has resulted in a gradual shift towards more intensive forms of development. Apartments, flats and maisonettes have become much more significant as a proportion of new dwellings, but bungalows have become much less significant. Rooms in new houses have became smaller. Plot sizes have been reduced, resulting in smaller gardens. Over time, house purchasers therefore received less space for every pound spent. Furthermore, rising real land prices have served to increase pressure for the development of allotments, sports grounds and back gardens within existing urban areas and for the demolition of houses with large gardens for redevelopment at much higher densities. Suburban cramming, which Whitehand & Larkham (1991) investigate in detail, has thus been encouraged by urban containment.

Cheshire & Sheppard (1988) estimate that the urbanized area of the South East would increase from 19 to 28 per cent of the region, if all planning restrictions were to be abandoned. House prices would only fall by 3 to 5 per cent, but plot sizes would increase substantially, possibly by as much as 65 per cent. Earlier analysis of the impact of urban planning on the commercial and industrial markets (Cheshire et al. 1985) revealed the much higher land costs faced by British businesses in comparison with those in similar cities in the United States. Evans (1991a) considers that, by raising the price of land, urban containment constrains economic growth. Simmie et al. (1992) argue that the facilitation of economic growth should long ago have replaced urban containment as the main objective of British planning. Whether or not this is accepted, the market outcome of urban containment is now evident is ways that were never considered when the policy was first adopted.

Conclusion

Despite urban planning, market processes retain great power to determine how land is used and developed. However, as this chapter has shown, such processes are far from perfect and are unable to deliver a resource efficient allocation of land and property. Although the case for urban planning is thus based on market imperfections and failure, it cannot be substantiated without further evidence that urban planning produces better outcomes that does the market on its own. After more detailed examination of the development process in the next chapter, this challenge for urban planners is therefore taken up and discussed more fully in Chapter 4.

Notes

1. In this chapter, the term "interests in land" is used in its strict legal sense. As Chapter 4 explains, the term is used in subsequent chapters in a broader theoretical sense to describe the relationship between an individual or organization and an object.

CHAPTER THREE

Land & property development processes

Continuous change has always characterized the urban environment. Existing buildings are adapted to new uses. Obsolete buildings fall vacant and may be demolished. New buildings are constructed on sites where demolition has taken place and on land not previously in urban use. Whether change occurs slowly and is almost unnoticed, or happens rapidly and is highly disruptive, a production process is creating a finished product: the built environment. This form of production is known as the land & property development process.

There are many similarities between land & property development and other production processes, such as car assembly. Successful production demands complex organizational systems to bring the necessary inputs together at the correct time. This complexity may not be immediately apparent from a visit to a building site or a car assembly plant. Members of the public therefore often equate the process of construction with the process of development, remaining unaware of earlier preparations. This chapter seeks to unravel the development process from inception to conclusion, to examine how it is generated and to explore why it is so uneven and volatile. The chapter begins with the story of an important site on the River Thames at Greenwich.

Greenwich Reach

Approximately 400 m to the west of Greenwich Town Centre, the A200 crosses Deptford Creek Bridge at a point about five miles southeast of Central London. The River Thames is visible at the mouth of the creek some 200 m to the north. In the early 1990s, the then tallest building in Europe could be seen rising at Canary Wharf, across the river. The immediate view in that direction was much less spectacular. The scene to the west of the creek (see Fig. 3.1) was dominated by a disused power station (site A) overlooking scrapyards and small industrial premises mostly in poor condition (sites B and C). To the east of the creek (see Fig. 3.2) an aggregates processing works occupied site D, while a smaller area nearer the

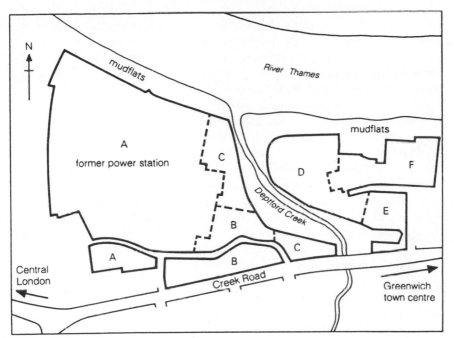

Figures 3.1 & 3.2 Greenwich Reach.

bridge (site E), previously occupied by another scrapyard, was vacant. Beyond site E, across a poorly maintained access road, four small companies traded from another group of older industrial buildings (site F). The surrounding area to the east and west which experienced severe social stress, was occupied mainly by local authority flats.

A visitor to Greenwich Reach (the collective name for sites A–F) in the summer of 1990 may have had great difficulty in believing that a planning application for the comprehensive redevelopment of the entire 12 ha for 32,000 m² of business space, 8,000 m² of retail space, 400 m² of leisure space, 600 dwellings and a 150 bedroom hotel with passenger ship facilities, was under consideration by the borough council. The visitor would certainly not have known of events "behind the scenes" that led up to this proposal.

Greenwich Reach had witnessed a process of gradual but continuous change since the end of the Second World War. In 1947, for example, the town gas works which had occupied site D closed, and was replaced by an aggregates business that eventually became part of the multinational corporation, ARC. Boatbuilders and other water-based users dwindled in number. Scrapyards and more noxious industries began to appear, giving rise to frequent complaints from 1976 onwards. The power station closed in 1983. Only 3.7 ha of the site was owned freehold by the then Central Electricity Generating Board (CEGB). The remaining 3 ha was held on a long ground lease from the City of London Corporation and Trinity House. The lease was due to expire in 1990. Although the CEGB wished to dispose of its site, it undertook no active marketing and no potential purchaser appeared. At the other end of Greenwich Reach, business was slack for the welding company that owned site F. Surplus space was first rented out, but in 1986, the entire site was sold to Arena Industries Ltd, subject to four existing tenancies. The purchaser was not in fact a manufacturing business, but a family investment company with property interests. Residential and commercial redevelopment was successfully under way over the river on the Isle of Dogs and the potential for similar schemes at Greenwich had been spotted.

The acquisition of site F by Arena Industries coincided with the growing diversification of the freehold owner of site C, London Iron and Steel, from scrap metal dealing into property development. The company had previously acquired redundant power stations purely for scrap, but later participated in subsequent redevelopments. In West London, in partnership with a national house-builder, it successfully redeveloped the site of a former power station for 250 houses for sale and 75 housing association dwellings for rent. This encouraged both partners to consider a second scheme, elsewhere in London. Naturally, at Greenwich Reach, London Iron and Steel kept a very close watch on the adjoining CEGB site. However, its first move at Greenwich was to purchase site E from another scrap metal dealer in 1987. This latter company, which had owned the freehold for almost ten years was pleased to move to a more suitable site in Dagenham, where fewer complaints could be expected from local residents. The company received what it considered to be a good offer from London Iron and Steel, partly reflecting the site's development value. For London Iron and Steel, the purchase represented an important investment which increased its stake in the redevelopment of Greenwich Reach. Shortly afterwards, London Iron and Steel acquired another site elsewhere in Greenwich for the eventual relocation of the scrap metal business from Greenwich Reach.

At this time, a new local plan for Greenwich was in preparation (see Ch. 8). The deposit plan had been published in May 1986 and the local plan inquiry held in the spring of 1987. The deposit plan included the whole of Greenwich Reach within an industrial improvement area and envisaged no immediate change, apart from the possibility of tourist related uses, such as coach parking, to the east of the creek. Although the redevelopment potential of Greenwich Reach was not debated at the inquiry, since no formal objections were made, by mid-1987 the local planning authority had become increasingly concerned about the future of the power station site. Following discussions with the CEGB, the authority therefore prepared a planning brief for Site A to encourage redevelopment. This indicated that the western half could be redeveloped for housing, provided that at least 50 per cent of any dwellings built were offered for rent to persons on the local authority waiting list. The eastern half was deemed suitable for industrial development.

Meanwhile, tentative redevelopment proposals east of the creek had already been prepared by both Arena Industries and London Iron and Steel and discussed informally with the council. The noise, dust and flying metal generated over the years from sites D and E, had led to more and more complaints from adjacent residents. The council decided that industrial relocation was essential to secure an acceptable residential environment. However, since the council's own resources were severely constrained, it could neither fund relocation itself nor consider compulsory purchase. Ground conditions were known to be highly contaminated at Greenwich Reach, particularly by heavy metals and organic generating gases at sites D and E. Expensive foundations were likely to be required in several places, owing to the presence of made ground and silt clay. The local authority concluded that only a substantial and comprehensive private-sector redevelopment would be able to cover the expected costs of relocating existing businesses and tackling problematic site conditions. This would necessitate the replacement of lower-value industrial activities by higher-value business and residential uses and thus channel the expected spill-over of development pressure from the Isle of Dogs to where it was most advantageous to Greenwich.

A planning brief for the whole of Greenwich Reach (including the site of the power station) was therefore approved by the local authority in early 1988. The brief suggested a mixture of new uses, including housing, retailing, business space, leisure activities and a hotel. A new station on site E to serve a possible extension to the London Docklands Light Railway was recommended. A riverside path with public access was also proposed. The local plan was modified to incorporate these proposals which have since formed the basis of planning policy for Greenwich Reach. The preparation of the planning brief provided an opportunity for the local authority to contact all remaining landowners at Greenwich Reach to investigate their willingness to relocate. Although Arena Industries and London Iron and Steel had both identified redevelopment potential at Greenwich Reach prior to the planning brief, its publication encouraged ARC to review the future of the aggregate processing works on site D. Although the site was operated by ARC South Eastern, the planning brief aroused the interest of ARC Properties Ltd, which had been formed in 1984 as a separate subsidiary of the parent company.

Events then moved quickly. In July 1988, at the height of the development boom, Arena Industries, London Iron and Steel and ARC Properties entered into partnership, forming a new joint venture company, Greenwich Reach Developments Ltd, to redevelop the entire area. The new company controlled the ownership of sites C, D, E & F. Over the following few months, London Iron and Steel managed to acquire the freehold of the whole of site B, as a result of separate negotiations with the various owners. At the same time, Greenwich Reach Developments Ltd invited the CEGB to incorporate site A in the overall scheme, but found that, as a nationalized industry with little experience of commercial property development, it was reluctant to become involved. A professional development team was appointed, with Sheppard Robson as lead architects and Grimley J. R. Eve as chartered surveyors and planning consultants. The team included an American architectural practice with previous experience of waterfront development, landscape architects, environmental specialists, highway consultants, specialist commercial property advisers and a firm of public relations consultants. The search began for occupiers of the commercial floor-space and for potential development partners, able to take responsibility for separate parts of the scheme.

In June 1989, London Iron and Steel restructured and rationalized its business activities and withdrew from the development partnership. Its interests in Greenwich Reach were acquired by the two remaining members of the joint venture company. In October 1989, a draft strategy for the entire seven miles of the Greenwich Waterfront was published as a consultative document by the local authority. The strategy sought to capitalize on the area's maritime past, by identifying key opportunities for imaginative waterfront development. At Greenwich Reach, it was suggested that a permanent high water level could be retained in the creek by constructing lock gates or a cill across its mouth with the Thames. This would facilitate the mooring of historic ships with associated shore-based maritime history displays and encourage a mixed waterside development around the creek. At the same time, the local authority pressed hard for the London Docklands Light Railway to be extended to Greenwich and sought to make Greenwich Town Centre more attractive for tourists and residents alike.

When the preliminary redevelopment proposals for Greenwich Reach were presented by the professional team to the local authority, during a lengthy series of meetings prior to the submission of planning applications, they were well received in principle. However, the council suggested that the proposed business development should not be devoted exclusively to office use but should include significant industrial use. It also indicated that the proposed housing density should be reduced. In early 1990, Greenwich Reach Developments Ltd submitted two schemes for outline planning permission, one of which included the power station site, allowing for the involvement of the CEGB, while the other excluded it. The applications were subject to widespread consultation within the local community and many comments were received from local groups and businesses. One of the boatbuilders who occupied part of site F, for instance, drew attention to the very active nature of his business, commenting on "its immense potential as an attraction of tourists to a living maritime Greenwich" and emphasizing the need "to find a place for us in this venture". The Greenwich Society welcomed the overall land-use proposals, but commented that they reinforced the need to tackle traffic congestion in the nearby town centre. The Meridian Action Group which represented local residents, supported the removal of bad neighbour industries but disliked several aspects of the new development, including the possibility that pedestrian users might take a short cut through the Meridian Estate to Greenwich Town Centre.

For almost eight months, negotiations between the professional team and the local planning authority took place to secure a mutually acceptable development. In the end, the joint venture company agreed to provide a series of community benefits, to be specified in a planning agreement. The company consented to make 25 per cent of that part of Greenwich Reach designated for residential use, available to a local housing association for the development of low-cost rented accommodation, and to contribute financially towards the extension of the Docklands Light Railway to the Greenwich side of the river. Greenwich Reach Developments Ltd agreed to provide several other community benefits, including a riverside walkway for public use, a small building for a creche and day nursery, replacement workshop premises for the traditional boatbuilders and up to 200 car parking spaces, specifically for short-stay visitors to the town centre. A marginal shift in emphasis from business to residential development was also negotiated. The local planning authority dropped any demand for significant industrial development on the site and resolved in October 1990, to grant outline planning permission, subject to the planning agreement.

However, by this time the national economy was moving rapidly into recession. Further partners and potential occupiers had still to be attracted. Rapidly rising interest rates meant that the funding of such developments became increasingly expensive. Market conditions thus militated against an early start, despite successful planning negotiations. The developers explored whether a central government subsidy by way of a city grant, might be available from the Department of the Environment to make the scheme viable, if suitable occupiers and development partners could be identified. Discussions took place between Greenwich Reach Developments Ltd and various house-builders, hotels chains and cruise liner operators to explore the possibility of their participation in the development. When the deposit version on the new unitary development plan for Greenwich was published in November 1991, the whole of Greenwich Reach was allocated for the approved mix of development. Greenwich Reach Developments Ltd and Powergen, which had replaced the CEGB on the privatization of the electricity industry, discussed the possibility of a joint development. In 1992, Powergen demolished the power station. Greenwich Reach Developments Ltd began preliminary work to clear redundant structures and deal with the contamination on site D, in the expectation that, in due course, confidence would improve and development could commence. However, in the meantime, the outlook from Creek Road Bridge remains bleak.

Models of the development process

In the Greenwich case, a variety of activities have taken place over several years in anticipation of eventual development. Land has been bought and sold. A development partnership has been formed and a search instigated for potential occupiers and other partners. Site conditions have been investigated and contamination has begun to be treated. On the basis of preliminary designs, applications have been made for outline planning permission. Financial appraisals have been undertaken and potential funding sources examined. These activities will enable development to happen more rapidly, once market conditions improve. Yet, many residents of Greenwich may remain unaware of all these preparations, and of the lengthy and often hectic negotiations involving landowners, developers, investors and the local planning authority. Indeed, any member of the public standing on Creek Road Bridge still sees no more than another under-used and poorly maintained part of inner London.

If urban planning is to intervene effectively in the development process, it is essential to understand what happens behind the scenes. An attempt must therefore be made to conceptualize the development process in order to assess the contribution of particular actors, the significance of specific events, and the complexity of relationships that make development happen. For example, Cadman & Austin-Crowe (1983) suggest that the development process can be divided into four distinct phases: evaluation, preparation, implementation and disposal. Yet, this implies a rigid sequence of events that moves with inevitability towards its outcome. Moreover, it represents the perspective of only one actor – the developer – and concentrates on only one site in the whole of the urban area. Far more sophisticated models of the development process are reviewed by Healey (1991a) and by Gore & Nicholson (1991).

According to Healey (1991a), four different types of model can be identified:

(a) equilibrium models, deriving directly from neoclassical economics
(b) event-sequence models, reflecting an estate management preoccupation with managing the development process
(c) agency models, from a behavioural or institutional perspective, that concentrate on actors and their relationships
(d) structure models, grounded in urban political economy, identifying forces that determine relationships in, and drive the dynamics of, the development process.

Gore & Nicholson (1991) acknowledge the final three types of model but commend a further approach that seeks to identify the particular institutional, financial and legislative framework or "structure of provision" for each type of development. A separate model would thus be produced for each development sector. Gore & Nicholson (1991) maintain that any one model can be only partially representative of the complexity and variability of the land & property development process.

Healey (1991a) and Gore & Nicholson (1991) together detail fifteen different models of the development process. Subsequently, Healey (1992) suggests how an institutional model of the development process could be constructed that both describes events and agencies and explains how they relate to broader structural forces. For a thorough understanding of the merits of various alternative models of the development process, readers are recommended to consult both reviews. However, in examining the relationship between urban planning and the development process, models that focus on the sequence of events and on the variety of actors in the process are of particular interest. Two particular models will therefore be used as a basis to structure discussion in this chapter, the first of which concentrates on events and the second on actors.

Event-based models

One of the best event-based models of the development process employed the concept of a development pipeline to categorize relevant research (Barrett et al. 1978). As Figure 3.3 shows, the model reduces the multiplicity of activities in the development process to three broad sets of events, each

45

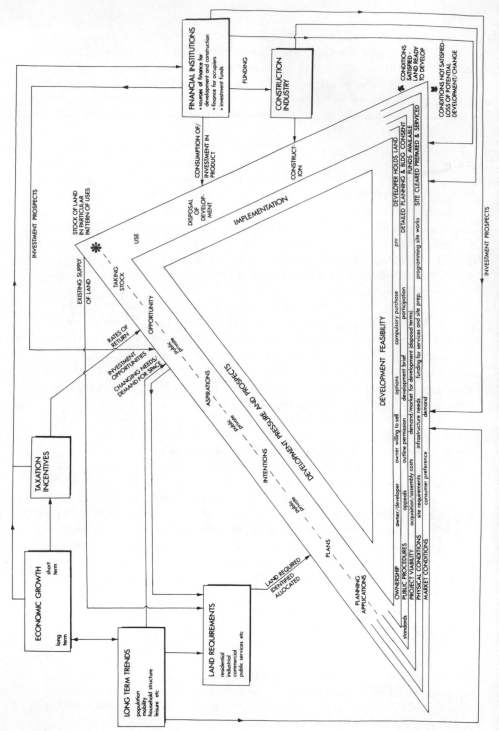

Figure 2.2 An event-based model of the development process (Source: Barrett et al, 1978)

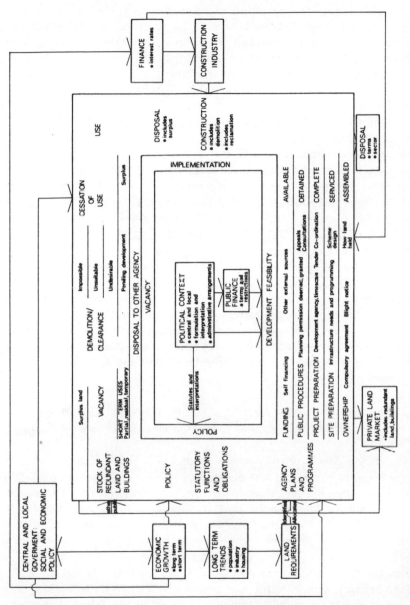

Figure 3.4 An event-based model of the public-sector development process (*Source*: Gore & Nicholson 1985).

of which forms one side of the triangular pipeline. External factors shown in "black boxes" generate development pressure and prospects in the first side, culminating in the identification of particular sites. Development feasibility, which covers the spectrum of subsequent events up to the commencement of construction, is tested in the second side. The third side, implementation, includes both the process of construction and the transfer of the completed development into new use and occupation. Particular events within each side may happen in a different order from that shown. However, the necessary events in each side must be completed before moving to the next.

Although the model is shown as a triangle, in practice, it operates as a spiral, producing a fresh pattern of land-use at the end of each cycle. This highlights the dynamic nature of the development process in which the relationship between factors such as taxation and viability may change from one cycle to the next and produce different outcomes in the built environment. The speed at which sites progress round the triangle also varies. At any one time, each site with development potential may be at a different point in the pipeline. With sufficient information, the progress of every site in an urban area could be plotted, showing the operation of the development process on a city-wide basis. Gore & Nicholson (1985), who undertook this exercise for vacant sites in South Wales, extended the triangular model by incorporating a fourth side within the public-sector development process, to allow for vacancy to occur between the end of implementation and the start of development pressure. Although discussion will now concentrate on the triangular model, where appropriate, it will make reference to the extended rectangular model, produced by Gore & Nicholson (1985) and shown in Figure 3.4.

Development pressure and prospects in event-based models

Activity in the development pipeline begins only when it is triggered by broader economic, political and demographic factors. These external influences are depicted in boxes outside the pipeline. Economic growth, taxation incentives and the impact upon land requirements of long-term trends in population growth, household formation and associated factors, may all create development pressure and prospects. In the rectangular model, the social and economic policy of central and local government is identified as an important external influence in its own right. Such external influences begin to generate activity within the pipeline as the private sector responds to demand and as the public sector seeks to meet needs. When such opportunities arise, aspirations may give rise to firm intentions and appropriate development sites are sought. Whether or not suitable land is allocated in a development plan, by the end of the first side of the model, a site is identified and a planning application is submitted. Only the next side will determine whether development can proceed.

The first side of the model warns planners not to assess development potential superficially. It is incorrect, for example, to allocate land for specific uses such as sheltered housing or for high-technology industry simply because sites are ideal in physical terms. Rather, it is essential first to consider whether relevant external factors, working through development pressure and prospects, are likely to generate sufficient need or demand for these particular types of development in the locations identified.

Development feasibility in event-based models

Development feasibility is tested in five specific ways. These are shown as five parallel streams in the second side of the model, each relating to a particular set of influences or constraints. All five streams must be successfully negotiated, if development is to occur. The model neither implies a particular sequence of events within or between streams, nor infers that any one stream is more important than another. Such factors vary from one development to the next. Each of the five streams is now examined.

Ownership

As Chapter 2 explained, a variety of ownership rights may exist in the same land. A developer must either acquire or respect all such rights. For example, rights of way across a development site must not be infringed, without consent. A site that has no single owner, but is divided between two or more freehold owners, is said to be in multiple ownership. In some cases, problems can arise in identifying or tracing absentee owners. Such constraints particularly affect the feasibility of urban redevelopment. Options or conditional contracts are frequently used to reserve the right to purchase land, once planning permission is secured (see Ch. 2). If owners of land with development potential are unwilling to sell (see Ch. 5), passive ownership may also become a serious constraint to development. Although local planning authorities may initiate compulsory purchase action in such circumstances, many are reluctant to do so for administrative, political or financial reasons. This is explained in detail in Chapter 7. If the feasibility of private-sector development is threatened by ownership constraints, assistance from the local authority is therefore rare. For development to prove feasible, the developer must hold the land by the end of the second side.

Public procedures

The first side of the model ended with an application for planning permission. If permission is refused, there may be grounds for appeal. Approval may have been sought in the first instance for the principle of development, in which case an outline planning application would have been submitted. If granted, subsequent application(s) for detailed approval of design, layout and other reserved matters will be necessary. For substantial developments such as Greenwich Reach, the local planning authority may issue a planning or development brief to guide the submission of planning applications. As in Greenwich, the local community may be consulted when the brief is prepared and at the time of a planning application. Such participation may encourage the local authority to seek changes to submitted schemes.

Although not mentioned in the two models, a variety of other consents, apart from planning permission, may be necessary before development becomes feasible. Approval under buildings regulations, which deal with matters such as the standard of construction, building safety and energy conservation, will be required. If roads and sewers are to be adopted on the completion of development, their designs will need to be approved by, and agreement reached with, the highway authority and water company respectively. If it is intended to build across an existing public highway, an application will need to be made for a street closure order. A fire certificate may be required from the fire officer and, in the case of a public house, restaurant or place of entertainment, a licence is needed from the magistrates. By the end of the second side, all necessary consents must be obtained.

Project viability

For private-sector development, a viability study will be undertaken to determine whether expected revenues are likely to exceed expected costs by enough to produce the desired rate of profit. Costs can usually be forecast with much greater accuracy than revenues. Account must be taken not only of land acquisition and building costs but also of professional fees, marketing and advertising costs and significantly, of the interest charges payable during construction (Darlow 1988). Revenue depends on market demand at the time of completion which may be up to four years ahead. Design work is undertaken alongside viability studies, since such studies may highlight the need for design modifications to maximize uses likely to produce most revenue and minimize those likely to produce least revenue. Each time the design is refined, viability is reassessed.

Significant changes may take place in economic activity, interest rates or the availability of competing accommodation between the commencement and completion of development. Unless a prospective occupier is secured in advance, it is therefore a matter of risk whether demand at the time of completion will be strong enough to make development viable. When a lease is signed before development has commenced, it is known as a pre-let. Development is unlikely to commence in fragile markets without a pre-let. Even in a robust market, a prudent developer with no pre-let will normally allow for a void period of at least six months (during which the development may remain unoccupied following completion) and will assume no increase in rental levels or selling prices above those existing at the time of the viability study.

If development appears viable, external sources of funding will be sought, unless a developer has sufficient internal reserves. Short-term finance will be needed to provide working capital during construction and long-term finance will be required on completion. The main sources of private development finance are discussed later in the chapter. In the public sector, projects compete for the limited funds available from government sources and feasibility thus depends on inclusion within a capital programme. Spending priorities have traditionally been determined not by market-orientated approaches to viability but by political assessments of need, backed up by such techniques as cost–benefit analysis. However, in the 1980s, viability studies became increasingly important in the public sector, as target rates of return were set for certain public bodies. By the end of the second side, the developer must secure the necessary funds, whether from private or public sector sources.

Physical conditions

A developer must ensure that the site identified can accommodate the proposed development in physical terms. Site surveys will be undertaken to record ground levels, investigate soil structure and check for the extent and severity of contamination. In some areas, subsidence from past mining activity may need to be considered. Any restrictions that prevent connection of the site to foul or surface water sewers, water supply pipes or to gas, electricity or telephone services must be identified.

A distinction should be drawn between the existence and the impact of physical constraints. For as Gore & Nicholson (1985: 187) point out: "Physical constraints . . . do not necessarily *prevent* development, as they can normally be expressed in terms of extra preparation or construction costs." Such costs may be eligible for a derelict land grant or other public subsidy. Any delay to the development timetable caused by physical constraints can be as serious as the cost of treatment. Completion may have to be postponed, revenue will be lost and interest charges on working capital will mount up. By the time the development is eventually finished, the market may have moved into recession and demand may have evaporated. Merit therefore exists in programming preliminary site works well in advance of the expected start of construction. Indeed, as at Greenwich, early treatment of contamination may be essential to establish development feasibility. By the end of the second side, site clearance, preparation and servicing must be complete, with the site ready in physical terms, for development to start.

Market conditions

Market conditions need to be monitored right up to the start of development. If consumer demand changes, the development mix may be altered. For example, if two-bedroom houses on the first phase of a residential estate sell more quickly than three-bedroom houses, the developer may reduce the latter and increase the former in the second phase. Similarly, if the latest information identifies a shortage of small office suites in the commercial sector, last-minute design alterations may be made to target development to the identified shortage. In the public sector, consultation takes place to confirm or modify earlier assessments of need. For example, a new health clinic will be built only after detailed discussions between the Regional Health Authority, the Family Practitioners Committee and the Community Health Council.

Macroeconomic conditions can change rapidly, casting doubt on the feasibility of proposed developments. For example, between May 1988 and October 1989, interest rates doubled from 7.5 to 15 per cent. Many development schemes in an advanced state of preparation, including Greenwich Reach, were abandoned. Developers in the private sector pay such careful attention to current market conditions that they tend to behave in concert. As subsequently discussed, this leads to an overproduction of built space at the height of a development cycle and underproduction in the years that follow. By the end of the second side of the model, market conditions must be such to encourage early construction.

Implementation in event-based models

Despite all preparatory work, the third side of the model, spanning the period of construction and subsequent occupation of the completed development, is rarely trouble-free. Only implementation reveals whether the risks taken by the developer have been justified.

Construction

Although house-builders usually undertake their own construction work, most commercial developers rely instead on building contractors. There are two main forms of building contract (Cadman et al. 1991). Under the first, the developer instructs a professional team of architects, quantity surveyors, engineers and associated consultants to design the development. Tenders are normally invited from six to eight different contractors, on the basis of the drawings and specification prepared by the professional team. The lowest tender is usually selected, unless there are particular reasons for not doing so. A standard form of contract, prepared by the Joint Contracts Tribunal (known as the JCT contract) is common. The professional team is responsible for the supervision of the contract, and for ensuring that the development is constructed in accordance with the approved drawings and specification.

The second form of contract is the design and build package, in which the contractor takes responsibility for all design and construction work. A performance specification is drawn up which sets out the quantity and quality of the accommodation required by the developer. On this basis, firms specializing in design and build packages are invited to tender. The firm chosen is responsible for the way in which the performance specification is achieved and for obtaining all necessary statutory consents. In many ways, a design and build package is comparable with the purchase of existing property. It is normally cheaper and quicker than a JCT contract and is particularly advantageous for simple or standard forms of development.

In the public sector, substantially reduced development activity has combined with competitive tendering to diminish the rôle of traditional direct works departments in local authorities and other public bodies. Construction projects may be offered for tender under either of the two main forms of contract, depending on the nature of the project.

The fortunes of the construction industry are particularly susceptible to the development cycle. Tenders may be unexpectedly low for any development commenced during a slump. In contrast, contractors may be unable to cope with the volume of work offered in a boom. At such times, lengthy delays may occur in obtaining materials and considerable difficulties may be experienced in recruiting and retaining skilled labour. Any discovery of unexpected ground conditions or any late alterations to the design can render the construction process highly problematic.

Transfer into new use and occupation

Development not built for owner-occupation will be available for sale or lease, following its completion. Every effort will normally be made to secure tenants or purchasers before the development is finished. Residential developers usually employ their own sales personnel, operating from a show house and on-site sales office. Commercial and industrial developers tend to use estate agents, particularly if rental levels or selling prices are subject to negotiation. For major developments outside London, both a local firm of agents and an national agency in London would normally be instructed.

Once the development is constructed, marketed, disposed and occupied, a full cycle in the development process has been completed. In due course, the property may become obsolete, fall vacant and be demolished, with the site again entering the first side of the development pipeline. Demolition and replacement of commercial property is induced primarily by external economic pressure rather than by physical deterioration or obsolescence (Bourne 1967). Buildings are likely to be sold for redevelopment once they are worth more as cleared sites. Redevelopment will occur sooner in areas where rents are rising than in areas where they are falling (Evans 1985).

The triangular model therefore indicates that the development process is circular as well as dynamic. However, the model does not directly address the period which may exist between the cessation of one use and the commencement of redevelopment pressure for another use. To examine this period, we need to turn to the fourth side of the Gore & Nicholson (1985) model.

Urban land vacancy

Vacancy arises on the fourth side of the model produced by Gore & Nicholson (1985), primarily because the continuation of a given use becomes impossible, unsuitable or undesirable. Demolition and clearance of vacant buildings may take place and short-term uses may be found for vacant sites. Although land and buildings therefore pass into the redundant stock, Gore & Nicholson (1985) suggest that few sites remain there for any length of time. Most start to make their way once more round the development pipeline. Such progress can be mapped on the model, although it will not be evident to members of the public, until construction actually begins. Gore & Nicholson (1985) therefore argue that land vacancy is a transient feature of the urban environment since sites move into, and then out of vacancy in response to economic, political and social change.

Urban land vacancy is an emotive issue, both politically and environmentally (Civic Trust 1987, Chisholm & Kivell 1987, Kivell 1993). It has attracted a widespread literature, reviewed comprehensively by Cameron et al. (1988), who applied analysis from the labour market to land markets and development processes. This was further refined by Couch & Fowler (1992) who drew a distinction between frictional vacancy, regarded as the normal product of the development process, demand-deficient vacancy, arising principally from cyclical changes in the level of demand, and structural vacancy, defined as land rendered permanently surplus to requirements by changes in technology or in the nature of demand.

Land that is frictionally vacant may be making its way round the development pipeline, only to be blocked by planning, physical, ownership or valuation constraints which stop it from achieving development feasibility. If land is vacant simply for frictional reasons, supply-side policies seeking to unblock development constraints may be effective. Such policies alone are unlikely to overcome demand-deficient or structural vacancy since they assume that potential demand exists and can be turned into effective demand simply by removing supply-side constraints. Land which is vacant for either demand-deficient or structural reasons can remain permanently in the redundant stock, never even beginning the journey round the development pipeline. Only policies which seek to stimulate demand for land-using activities are likely to succeed in tackling demand-deficient vacancy. If vacancy is caused by structural changes, policies need to transform the structural character of either the vacant land or its surrounding area.

Agency-based models

Although the models produced by Barrett et al. (1978) and Gore & Nicholson (1985) concentrate on the sequence of events in the development process, they draw attention to the importance of certain rôles (such as owners and developers) and of particular institutions (such as central and local government and the construction industry). Indeed, at Greenwich Reach, decisions taken by owners, developers and the planning authority proved turning points in the case study. However, the exact relationship between events, rôles and institutions is not easy to discern in event-based models. This highlights the need for an agency-based model of the development process, such as that produced by Ambrose (1986) and shown in Figure 3.5.

According to Ambrose (1986), the development system consists of three main fields: the state, the finance industry and the construction industry, each of which contains several elements. The general public and informal pressure groups seek to influence these fields from outside. The model identifies separate rôles or functions in the development system rather than individuals or organizations. Indeed, any particular individual or organization may undertake more than one rôle or function. For example, planning officers in local government are also members of the public and may invest their savings in the finance industry.

Ambrose (1986) compares his model to the wiring system of a house which produces no light or heat until it is switched on. The development system is energized only as money, political influence or some other form of interaction flows along the linkages that connect the various elements. These flows, which are often stronger in one direction than the other, are produced by contractual, statutory or informal relationships. At critical switch points, the flows are liable to be interrupted or diverted into other forms of investment or economic activity. The model emphasizes that the production of the built environment results from the control that particular actors exercise over powers and resources and from bargaining and negotiation between actors which enable such powers and resources to be activated. An agency-based perspective, although very different from an event-based one, complements it well. The rôles of particular actors are therefore examined in detail in subsequent chapters.

From the models of Barrett et al. (1978), Gore & Nicholson (1985), Ambrose (1986) and others, we can understand more clearly what is involved in the process of development, and better appreciate the strategies, interests and actions of various actors. However, we cannot readily identify what drives or generates development activity in the first place, and cannot thus explain

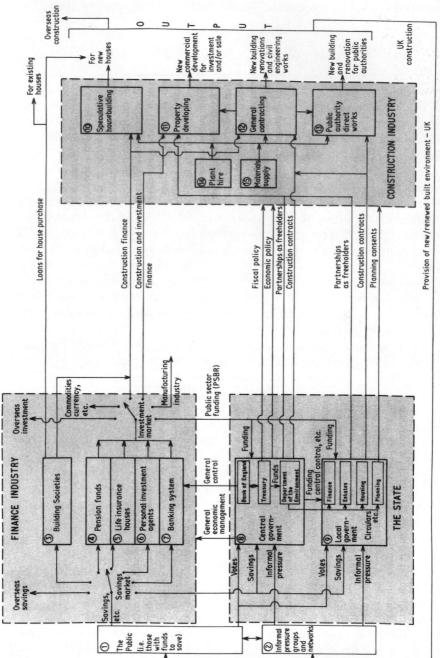

Figure 3.5 The development system in the UK (*Source*: Ambrose 1986).

thus explain why the production of the built environment varies continuously in form and quantity from place to place and over time. Barrett et al. (1978) contend that the development process is triggered off by external factors, such as economic growth, but the precise means by which such factors initiate development remains unclear. Ambrose (1986), who reveals the rôles or functions of particular actors, suggests that broader contextual processes condition the flow of resources and other forms of "energy" between the state, the finance industry and the construction industry.

The flow of private finance from insurance companies, pension funds, banks, and building societies to property development is therefore considered in the next section. This is not intended to provide a comprehensive account of development finance, but rather to explore how the development system is energized by powerful resource flows from finance capital to the construction sector. Readers who require a more detailed explanation of the great variety of development funding techniques, many of which are highly complex, are advised to consult sources such as Darlow (1988), Cadman et al. (1991) or Adair (1993). The uneven and volatile nature of development activity, evident in the discussion of development finance, is then considered in more detail in the following section. Alternative explanations for this are explored in the penultimate section of the chapter which investigates how structure and agency relate in land and property development.

Development finance

Most development is financed, usually to a substantial extent, from external sources. If funding is raised for a specific development, it is called **project finance**. If development funding is raised by a public company but not necessarily tied to a specific project or projects, it is called **corporate finance**. "Although this distinction is often blurred, it is useful in differentiating developers who have the financial muscle to raise corporate finance from those who rely solely on project specific finance" (Adair 1993: 59). The distinction between debt and equity in development finance, which cuts across that between project and corporate finance, is equally important.

Those who lend **debt finance** have the right to be repaid with interest, but normally have no entitlement to share in development profits. Three main types of debt finance are identified by Adair (1993). These are bank loans, mortgages and debt corporate paper. Debentures or corporate bonds are a good example of the latter type. These are issued for 10 or more years, pay a fixed rate of interest, can be traded on the capital markets, and are effectively long-term loans to development companies. Those who lend **equity finance** participate in the risks and rewards of development, and are entitled to share in development profits. Five main types of equity finance are identified by Adair (1993). Two of these, sale & leasebacks and disposals, are subsequently discussed in more detail. The third type involves various forms of joint-venture, such as partnerships between a local authority and a development company (see Ch. 7). Equity corporate paper is the fourth type. This includes, for example, company shares issued on the Stock Exchange. The final type of equity finance, securitization and unitization, which emerged in the 1980s, involves various devices to break up the ownership of a very large development into shares suitable for individual investors, but has yet to be widely adopted.

Developers who rely too heavily on equity finance may lose control of particular projects to the equity partner or even face hostile takeover bids, if too many voting shares are issued on the Stock Exchange. However, in troubled times, equity finance may be more advantageous to a developer, since equity lenders share the risks of development and may have no automatic right to payment. In contrast, developers who rely too heavily on debt finance, in particular on bank loans, may face a financial crisis, if interest rates rise steeply or unexpectedly. Banks require to be repaid with interest, whether or not it suits the borrower. Developers with a high proportion of debt to equity finance are said to be highly geared.

Many developments are therefore funded by a mixture of debt and equity finance. **Short-term finance** is required for the development period, and is normally arranged for a maximum of five years to cover the costs of site acquisition, construction, fees and marketing. On completion, when **long-term finance** is raised, short-term finance is repaid. If a completed development is sold rather than let, long-term finance will be arranged by the purchaser rather than the developer. Short-term finance is usually more expensive than long-term finance since an unfinished building provides the lender with less security than a completed development. At one time, debt was mainly used as short-term finance, and equity reserved primarily for long-term finance. Such a clear distinction has long since broken down.

In the first place, short-term development finance and long-term investment finance are sometimes both provided by insurance companies and pension funds, who traditionally acted as long-term financiers (Cadman et al. 1991). More significantly, the development boom of the late 1980s was fuelled by a massive growth in lending by the traditional short-term financiers, such as high street and merchant banks. During this period, such innovations as revolving short-term credit were introduced to bridge the gap between short- and long-term finance. Indeed, a host of novel but highly complex financial devices emerged in the 1980s which encouraged developers to expand their debt finance, either through raising money on the capital markets or more typically, by bank borrowing (Adair 1993).

Banks, for example, most of which had previously restricted property lending to 75 per cent of development cost, commonly began to offer top-up loans, known as mezzanine finance, which enabled developers to borrow up to 95 per cent of development cost. Of course, banks required a higher rate of interest for mezzanine finance and imposed more stringent conditions. Developers were encouraged to hedge against subsequent steep rises in interest rates through a variety of techniques, such as those colourfully described as caps and collars. The capital markets become an important source of debt finance for the larger development companies. For example, sterling commercial paper (essentially a form of IOU able to be traded) was extensively used from 1986 as a form of short-term finance by larger companies. Many such companies also raised long-term loans in foreign currency of up to £100 million at a time (known as Eurobonds) on the European capital markets.

The development boom of the late 1980s would therefore not have happened without rapid expansion of debt finance through such innovative funding mechanisms. However, once the boom collapsed, many, but not all, such innovations quickly disappeared and extreme caution returned to development finance. The specific rôles of the insurance companies, pension funds, banks, and building societies in development finance will now be examined in turn.

Insurance companies and pension funds

As Chapter 2 explained, the most significant investors in commercial property are insurance companies and pension funds. Several such investors have built up considerable shares in property companies, some even taking a majority holding. Although institutional investors who decide to extend their property portfolios normally first seek to buy additional standing investments, from time to time, they may make funds available for new development. However, most institutions who have invested in development have sought to minimize their own exposure to direct development risk.

Until the late 1950s, the involvement of institutional investors in development was restricted to the provision of conventional mortgage finance to developers (Cadman 1984). Since this did not allow investors to benefit from the rising capital values that were evident from the early 1960s onwards, forms of equity sharing in development such as "sale and leaseback" were devised instead. Under such an arrangement, once a development is completed, the investor buys the freehold and immediately grants a long lease back to the developer, who sublets individual units to tenants. The developer in a sale and leaseback is essentially a middleman between investor and user. As rents payable by tenants to the developer rise over time, so the rent received by the investing institution from the developer also rises. The exact distribution of such growth is determined by the increasingly sophisticated nature of sale and leasebacks (Darlow 1988). Through sale and leaseback, institutions became increasingly involved in design and construction in order to control development quality at an early stage. As a result, the present form of many city centres owes as much to the demands of investors as to the influence of planners.

The property market crash of 1974 provided financial institutions with the opportunity to acquire prime new investments at bargain prices. Many had been built by speculative developers who had subsequently run into financial difficulties. Between 1975 and 1977, insurance companies, pension funds and property unit trusts purchased £2,381 million of commercial property, effectively mopping up the surplus created in the "Barber boom" of the early 1970s (Cadman 1984). This was encouraged by central government in order to help stabilize the financial system. By the beginning of the 1980s, some institutions had already built up their property holdings to their earlier long-term target levels (Nabarro 1990).

For most of the 1980s, many institutions were reluctant to fund new development for the same reasons that they chose to switch investment from property into gilts and equities (see Ch. 2). However, a few institutions, such as Norwich Union, contradicted this trend and moved significantly into direct development, setting up their own development teams to eliminate the need to partner a developer. This is examined in detail in Chapter 6. Nevertheless, institutional funding for development as a whole did not significantly increase until 1989 and 1990, by which time the development boom was ending. Although institutions spent more than £2 billion on new development during these two years (IPD 1991), it was evident that some funds were again beginning to pick up bargains from developers in difficulty. For example, Scottish Widows, subsequently paid Rosehaugh (see Ch. 6) £27 million in 1991 for the award-winning Fleet Walk Shopping Centre in Torquay, a development originally valued at £40 million.

Indeed, institutions who now invest in new development are more likely to buy projects directly from developers either before, during or immediately after construction. Sale and leasebacks have therefore become less popular as a method of equity finance than direct disposals by developers. The precise arrangement for sharing development risks and returns between the investor and developer in such a disposal will vary according to the particular type of funding (Adair 1993). For example, if the development site is acquired before construction, and the institution provides development finance, the developer's rôle may be reduced merely to that of project manager. This is known as forward funding. In contrast, in forward commitment, the institution merely undertakes to purchase the development, once it is fully let. However, as institutions significantly reduced the flow of funds to property development during the 1980s, the more innovative sources of finance became essential to the development system.

Banks

Banks traditionally provided developers with working capital or short-term finance to cover costs prior to sale or letting. In the 1980s, banks became the main lenders of not only short-term development finance, but also of new types of medium-term finance and, by default, of long-term finance as well, when loans failed to be repaid. As a result, total bank lending to property companies soared from approximately £10 billion in 1986 to a record £41 billion in 1991 (Debenham Thorpe 1993). By 1992, this had fallen back to £40 billion, but of this, only £1 billion was advanced to the largest 15 UK property companies. So much had been lent at the height of the boom to relatively inexperienced developers that by 1992, a quarter of all debts owed by the property sector to UK clearing banks alone (equivalent for the banks to three years' annual profits) were expected to be written off (Kynoch 1992). Barclays, the most exposed clearing bank, which had lent £8.8 billion to the property sector, recorded an 87 per cent fall in pre-tax profits in the first half of 1992, owing to bad debt provisions on property of £1.07 billion. Although total bank lending to property companies was subsequently cut back to £36 billion by 1993, even this lower figure still accounted for 11 per cent of the banking sector's commercial loan portfolio.

The "aggressive inter-bank competition" (Darlow 1987: 616) to lend money for property development in the mid- to late 1980s was attributable to both greater competition and entrepreneurship in the domestic banking sector after financial deregulation and the globalization of international capital markets (Flender 1990, Adair 1993). Between 1988 and 1992, almost £9 billion was invested from overseas in the UK property market, mainly from American, Swedish and particularly Japanese banks (Debenham Thorpe 1993). As a result, UK clearing and merchant banks accounted for only 57 per cent of property loans outstanding in 1992, with overseas banks responsible for 43 per cent, compared to their much lower share of 18 per cent in 1980.

The rapid expansion of bank lending in the 1980s affected the nature of development in three specific ways. First, in making loans, banks appeared to place greater importance on the creditworthiness of the borrower than the characteristics of the proposed development. In contrast, pension funds and insurance companies are much more interested in the long-term investment value of any development. Bank lending freed those developers considered creditworthy from the conservatism of pension funds and insurance companies, enabling them to move into fringe locations such as London Docklands which many traditional institutions initially considered too risky for long-term investment. Secondly, the willingness of banks to form syndicates, combining with each other to fund developments beyond the resources of any one bank, allowed developers to contemplate "mega-projects" that would not previously have been financed. Rosehaugh Stanhope's Broadgate Centre, for example, was funded by a consortium of 21 separate Japanese banks. Thirdly and perhaps most significantly for the whole development system, the excess enthusiasm of British and especially overseas banks to lend and lend again, explicable only by their collective failure to understand the development cycle, inevitably created a substantial over-supply of commercial property, especially in London. Indeed, Goobey (1992) comments that banks were almost falling over themselves to lend on property during this period. The banking sector therefore carries heavy responsibility for the "boom and bust" development crisis of the late 1980s and early 1990s.

Building societies

Although building societies remain the most important source of finance for owner-occupied housing, banks and other lenders have eroded their market share of the mortgage business. In the past, house-builders aimed to secure mortgage allocations from particular societies for new estates, but this practice has diminished with the greater competition between mortgage lenders to attract borrowers. The Building Societies Act 1986 recognized their growing significance within the national economy, and allowed both their participation more directly in the development process and their diversification into a wide variety of financial and investment services.

Building societies have responded to such new opportunities in a variety of ways. Many, like National and Provincial, now provide extensive insurance and foreign exchange services, and offer loans for non-house purchase, enabling borrowers to buy cars, boats, caravans, etc. Abbey National has formally altered its legal status from a non-profit making society into a public limited company. The Nationwide Anglia has invested £600 million to establish a development company known as Quality Street, building private rented accommodation with a high standard of service. As the Building Societies Act 1986 allowed societies to invest up to 10 per cent of their portfolio in non-residential sectors, the Alliance and Leicester has moved into commercial development finance. In 1990, for example, it provided equity mortgages of £7.7 million and £9.8 million respectively to two development companies, to fund new office schemes in Banbury and Milton Keynes.

As Ball (1983) commented, the cosy life building societies enjoyed as monopoly providers of owner-occupier mortgage finance has gone forever. Instead, since 1986, most building societies have established links with other property developers and investors or the wider financial community. However, it was perhaps fortunate for their savers, that building societies had undertaken only limited diversification into commercial development before the boom collapsed in the late 1980s.

The uneven and volatile nature of development

The incremental production of the built environment depends primarily on the identification and realization by the private sector of short-term opportunities for profit, rather than on any assessment by the public sector of social and economic needs for built space in the long term. As Edwards (1990: 177) comments: "Property development processes are an integral part of the mechanism of uneven development – whereby differences in income, wealth, investment and production are reproduced and changed, but never evened out either between places or people." According to a survey of two-thirds of the top financial institutions in the UK, all but six of the 22 locations most favoured by investment managers were in the South East. Considerable disparities existed even within this region. The list was headed not by Haringey, Brent or Camden but by Guildford, Reading, Crawley and St Albans.

However, uneven development cannot be explained by a simple north–south divide, since Chester and similar northern locations were also highly regarded by investment managers. Developers and investors have usually been keener throughout the UK, to build shops and offices than factories. None of the 22 most favoured locations had a high percentage of employment in traditional manufacturing. Indeed, at the average annual rate of construction between 1974 and 1984, it would take 75 years to renew the industrial building stock (Fothergill et al. 1987). This suggests that uneven development of land and property is both geographical and sectoral.

As Edwards (1990) further remarks, the land & property development process is boom-prone and crisis-prone, experiencing much more dramatic fluctuations than the economy as a whole. Developers tend to delay construction until rapidly rising rents indicate an acute shortage of existing accommodation. By this time, property users are already experiencing difficulty and inconvenience in finding suitable premises. This encourages more and more developers to start building, without paying heed to the overall amount of development commenced at the same time. Of course, once these developments are all finished, available accommodation is greatly in excess of user demand and rents stabilize or even fall until the excess supply is soaked up.

Commercial development activity is therefore characterized by lengthy periods of slump followed by rapid and short-lived booms. Barras (1984 & 1985) investigated office development cycles in London and identified three postwar booms, peaking respectively in 1962, 1973 and 1979. A fourth and more spectacular boom subsequently peaked in 1989. By 1992, sufficient office floor-space was estimated to be available or under construction in London to meet demand for the following 12 years at the average rate of take-up experienced between 1983–90 (Simmons 1992). The later development is commenced, the riskier it thus becomes, since by its completion, supply is likely greatly to exceed demand. Residential development responds in a similarly unstable way to movements in mortgage rates, although the reliance of most residential developers on their own workforce makes it essential to maintain minimum production, even in times of severe slump. As the term cycle has almost natural connotations in mainstream economics, Edwards (1990) describes the land & property development process not as cyclical, but as highly volatile.

Significant innovations in development activity were initiated in the boom of the late 1980s. The lifespan of buildings was shortened, as it became profitable to demolish offices less than 25 years old and rebuild better-quality accommodation at higher densities. At London Wall, windswept blocks dating from the 1960s were demolished precisely for this purpose. More significantly mega-projects of a scale not seen for many years were intended to transform whole areas on the fringes of commercial centres. Some such as Broadgate on the northern edge of the City of London, commenced in good time. Others, such as Spitalfields, Paddington and Kings Cross, were still in preparation when the boom ended. In the residential sector, all the main house-builders came together to form Consortium Developments, a company specifically established to promote the development of new country towns, funded entirely by the private sector. However, none of the proposed sites gained planning permission and the consortium eventually suspended operations.

In inner urban areas, the state took advantage of the development boom to promote flagship redevelopments, such as Salford Quays in Greater Manchester. At Canary Wharf in London Docklands, the combined power of finance capital, property development and central government launched the most significant commercial development in Europe in the 1980s (Daniels & Bobe 1993). At a cost of £1.4 billion, the first phase of Canary Wharf contained 420,000 m² of prime office floor-space. However, Canary Wharf provided a telling epitaph to the development boom (Merrifield 1993). In 1992, its Canadian–based developer, Olympia and York, was forced to file for bankruptcy protection, owing $12 billion to 100 banks worldwide, with interest payments at Canary Wharf alone mounting at the rate of £40,000 an hour. Since so much competing development was simultaneously on the market in a recession, it became impossible to attract tenants to Canary Wharf at the rental levels envisaged when the project was commenced. Although encouraged by central government and finance capital, one of the most highly respected development companies in the world thus initially reinforced and later fell victim to the volatile nature of the development process.

Structure and agency in the development process

As the development process is so volatile, it is relevant to ask whether it is controlled by people or whether it is driven by powerful forces beyond the control of individuals and organizations. According to Healey & Barrett (1990), if we wish to discover why development takes particular forms in particular places and at particular times, we need to set the strategies, interests and actions of individuals and organizations within the context of broader social, economic and political processes. Drawing on the work of Giddens (1984), Healey & Barrett (1990) therefore suggest that we need to explore how "agency" and "structure" relate to each other in land and property development. They contend that this can best be done by connecting actor-based or institutional forms of analysis (extensively used, for example, to investigate the behaviour of particular types of developer) with relevant perspectives from neoclassical and Marxist economics. The components of this more holistic approach will now be examined.

Agency

Agency is a term used to embrace the entire manner in which actors in the development process define and pursue their strategies, interests and actions. Actors who play important rôles include landowners (see Ch. 5), developers, investors and professional advisers in the private sector (see Ch. 6) and developers or development facilitators in the public sector (see Ch. 7). Particular individuals or organizations may well play more than one rôle. For example, apart from their statutory planning responsibilities, local authorities may act as landowners, developers and development facilitators. These strategies, interests and actions are critical to the production of the built environment. For instance, as Chapter 5 reveals, the motives of particular landowners may determine whether they take an active or passive approach to making land available for development. Yet actors in the development process never define and pursue strategies, interests and actions entirely on their own. To a greater or lesser extent, the performance of each actor is linked to that of others. More importantly, the way in which particular actors behave is set within a broader context, known as structure.

Structure

Structure is a term used to describe the socioeconomic and cultural framework within which actors define and pursue their strategies, interests and actions. Structure consists of the organization of economic and political activity, and of the prevailing values that frame individual decision-making. Two opposing views of structure have traditionally existed: the neoclassical and the Marxist.

The neoclassical view contends that individual decisions are made within a market framework. According to this approach, development activity is initiated by demand, to which supply responds to produce development at the right time, in the right place, and at the right price (Lichfield & Darin-Drabkin 1980). Actors therefore define and pursue their strategies, interests and actions within a context set by market signals, in particular by the price mechanism through which supply and demand are brought into equilibrium.

Yet, actors in the development process are not always free or even willing to respond to market signals. Development may be impeded by supply-side constraints (such as land contamination or green belts) even if demand exists. Complex negotiations between those involved in development may break down. Some actors, such as particular types of landowner, may be wholly motivated by non-financial interests and may not respond at all to markets signals. In any event, since land & property markets are riddled by imperfections and failure and exist in a perpetual state of disequilibrium, such signals may never be properly transmitted in the first place. Indeed, Fainstein (1994) contends that, in view of the time it takes to organize major forms of construction and to mobilize the necessary resources, developers cannot respond immediately to market demand. She suggests that they formulate their strategies on the basis of financial availability, government incentives, community acquiescence and anticipated demand. As Healey & Barrett (1990) suggest, the neoclassical assumption that actors in the development process behave rationally and can negotiate unproblematically, is mistaken.

A very different structural framework is found in Marxist thinking. Marxists consider that society's resources are distributed not by the market, but by the class struggle between capital and labour. In this context, the capture of rent by landowners is often portrayed as a parasitical activity that saps the ability of capitalists to accumulate and removes even more of the full product of labour from the workers. More recent work in the Marxist tradition identifies the restless nature of finance capital which is constantly on the move in a global search for the highest rate of profit (Harvey 1982 & 1985). Finance capital moves into development activity for only so long as particular forms of development in particular locations offer the highest returns. Once this ceases to be the case, finance capital moves on elsewhere. The production of the built environment is therefore driven not by user demand but by the global search of finance capital for the highest investment returns. As a result, development activity is highly volatile with enormous sums of money flowing into favoured areas for short periods of time, while locations unattractive to finance capital remain permanently neglected.

Although neoclassical and Marxist economics relate agency behaviour to the broader socioeconomic framework in different ways, they are both too abstract to pinpoint the precise manner in which structure and agency interact. Resource flows are certainly a powerful influence on development activity, but Healey & Barrett (1990) maintain, the strategies, interests and actions of individuals and organizations are not automatically determined by such dominant social and economic forces. People can choose simply to accept and respond to powerful forces or instead, they can begin to challenge and transform them. Moreover, as institutional analysis has therefore discovered, agency behaviour is highly variable and is influenced not merely by resource flows, but also by rules and ideas prevailing in society.

Resources, rules and ideas

Healey & Barrett (1990) therefore contend that the structural framework for land & property development is neither fixed nor free from challenge but rather that continuous interaction takes place between structure and agency. People are not simply driven by powerful forces wholly beyond their influence or control. Although actors define and pursue their strategies, interests and actions in the context of a structural framework, structure itself is established, re-established or replaced as the resources, rules and ideas by which it is constituted are deployed, acknowledged, challenged and potentially transformed through agency behaviour. What people can achieve is not simply determined by powerful forces, since over time, such forces themselves are continuously shaped and changed by what people achieve.

Land & property development therefore takes place within a threefold structural framework which is continuously influencing, and being influenced by, agency behaviour. This framework consists of:

(a) *Resources* and the economy. Resources for development derive from both the private sector, as finance capital searches for profitable investments or supply interacts with demand, and the public sector, as spending priorities determine capital programmes. Public sector resources may also be used to lever private sector development through grants and incentives. In the 1980s, innovative methods of development finance changed the resource framework for development.

(b) Politico-juridical *rules* and the state, which control economic and political activity and limit development opportunities. Urban planning comes under this heading. The state is under pressure to deliver environmental quality, social facilities and economic opportunities, to reduce pollution and to safeguard the natural and built environment. Politico-juridical rules for development seek to reconcile these often conflicting objectives. In the 1980s, enterprise zones were introduced, in which normal fiscal and planning rules were relaxed. This changed the politico-juridical framework for development.

(c) Cultural *ideas and values* people hold about what they should build, what they would like to occupy and what kind of environment they seek. Such ideas and values emanate from a wider debate, to which well informed environmental groups may make as articulate a contribution as the development industry and its professional facilitators. In the 1980s, heightened environmental concern captured people's attention, locally, nationally and internationally. This changed the cultural framework for development.

Although resources, rules and ideas set a framework which drives or generates development activity, agency behaviour is diverse and always capable of challenging and transforming whatever constitutes the structural framework at any time. Such continuous interaction between structure and agency, in which each influence the other, helps explain why the production of the built environment varies continuously from place to place and from one year to the next.

Conclusion

In the immediate postwar years, the state began to participate powerfully and directly in land development. However, in the decades which followed, the state retreated from such strong interventionist measures (Ambrose 1986). This trend accelerated in the 1980s, when the private sector came increasingly to dominate development activity in the UK. Development by the public sector was scaled down as central government sought to exert tight control over capital expenditure, especially by local authorities. Significant types of development activity, such as council house-building and school construction, were substantially reduced or even eliminated. New town development corporations, which had embarked on extensive programmes of direct development from the 1950s onwards, were wound down. In contrast, urban development corporations, established during the 1980s, concentrated on facilitating private sector development. Once the public sector withdrew as an active participant in the development process, except as landowner and facilitator (Healey 1991b), the direct control that it exercised over the type of development constructed and the level of development activity, was substantially reduced.

Although the production of the built environment remains regulated by the state, it is neither driven nor controlled by the state. Urban planning provides an opportunity to intervene in land and property development in order to influence the form of towns and cities. This chapter has shown how the production of the built environment involves a variety of actors in a complex sequence of events. The planner is only one actor, and by no means the most powerful, and planning permission is only one event, and by no means the most significant. As a result, urban planners have tended to react to new development products after their launch, rather than anticipate and influence them. The rapid growth of superstores in the 1970s and the emergence of business parks in the 1980s, typifies such reactive planning.

However, many urban planners, equipped with a better understanding of the development process and a more realistic assessment of their ability to influence it, have begun to redefine their rôle in relation to development. This is evident, for example, in the growing importance of both planning gain and development promotion, discussed respectively in Chapters 4 and 7. Urban planners now seek to influence the various other ways in which development feasibility is tested, as well as planning permission. They may aim, for example, to tackle problematic site conditions or improve market conditions through public investment. Barras (1985: 99) even suggested that: "The crucial question as far as the planning system is concerned is whether or not development control policy should be used to counter the instability created by the booms and slumps of the development cycle. The arguments in favour of such an objective are that it would reduce the volatility and uncertainty of market conditions, to the benefit of developers, investors and occupiers, and minimize the negative externality effects created by cleared sites and vacant buildings which are left at the end of each boom." However, urban planning at present has no responsibility to counter the volatile nature of development activity.

Over the next few years, the planning profession as a whole is likely to face an immense challenge in reflecting how best it can influence the production of the built environment in a market economy. As planning and development move closer together, this fundamental concern deserves greater theoretical attention, more empirical research and innovative types of practice. Furthermore, as planners try more effectively to influence development, developers and other important actors will increasingly seek to influence plans to their particular advantage. The next chapter therefore considers the true nature of urban planning in a market economy, while strategies, interests and actions of landowners, developers and other important actors are examined in subsequent chapters.

CHAPTER FOUR

Urban planning in a market economy

Earlier chapters have contended that markets in land and property are riddled with imperfections and failure which occur respectively because, within them, the conditions of perfect competition are extensively violated and, beyond them, external factors arise that distort market operations. As a result, the ability of market mechanisms to allocate land and to organize development efficiently is far from perfect. Indeed, market imperfections cause mistaken signals to be sent to market operators, creating perpetual disequilibrium between the supply and demand for land and property. Such imperfections help explain the volatility of the development process, which causes new buildings to be underproduced during lengthy periods of slump but to be overproduced during short-lived periods of boom.

Market failure can be traced to the intrinsic nature of land as a social rather than a private commodity. It is evident in the overprovision of negative externalities but the underprovision of positive ones, in the market's lack of interest in the creation of public goods and in its propensity to let slip opportunities to use land resources more efficiently. The potential use and value of any one parcel of land is thus directly constrained by harmful activity taking place on neighbouring land. This makes a resource-efficient allocation of land and property impossible to achieve through the market alone. Although land & property markets are well equipped to handle private costs and benefits, they are unable to take account of social costs and benefits, such as the congestion costs imposed throughout a neighbourhood by the excessive development of one site or the environmental benefits produced for neighbouring owners by derelict land reclamation.

Developers may well seek to minimize private development costs at the expense of social development costs (e.g. by refusing to provide sufficient play-space for children on a new housing estate) and to maximize private development benefits at the expense of social development benefits (e.g. by building in greenfield locations where houses are easier to sell than on brownfield sites where new development could make use of vacant land). Profit maximization for the individual developer may thus be achieved only at the expense of the wider community. Indeed, the built environment, once produced, lasts for many years, but the availability of development finance normally depends on the returns from development in the first few years of a building's life exceeding the costs of development by sufficient to ensure the desired profit. Costs and benefits that occur over a much longer period are substantially discounted in conventional methods of development appraisal. The market's exclusive concern with private rather than social costs and benefits is therefore reinforced by the higher priority it accords to short-term rather than long-term returns. Furthermore, even if land & property markets were to operate under the conditions of perfect competition and without any external distortions, no market mechanism exists to ensure an equitable distribution of land resources between different social groups. It would be perfectly possible for a resource-efficient market to allocate the best development land to the rich and the worst to the poor.

This chapter therefore explores the nature of urban planning in a market economy where the development process creates a built environment that is not the most efficient, equitable or sustainable in the long term. It examines whether market imperfections and failure provide sufficient justification for state intervention through urban planning or whether, as some critics argue, the failure of grandiose planning indicates that the state is unable to do any better than the market and should therefore leave well alone. The chapter contends that the relationship between the state and the market in urban planning must be reconsidered in order to identify more sophisticated and specific ways for urban planners to intervene effectively in the development process.

Indeed, the potential contribution of urban planning to promoting equity, efficiency and sustainability in the built environment of a market economy can be readily articulated without relying for its justification on the vague and elusive concept of the public interest. The chapter therefore commences by examining the rôle of urban planning as a process of mediation between the variety of often competing interests that exist in land and property. Attention is subsequently given to exploring which of these interests gain and which lose from planning and development. This helps concentrate concern on the social distribution of development costs and benefits, exemplified in practice by planning gain, which, in seeking to capture a greater share of the financial benefits of development for the local community, highlights the true nature of urban planning as a form of state intervention in the development process.

Beyond the public interest

According to the Department of the Environment (1992b: para. 3), "The town and country planning system is designed to regulate the development

71

and use of land in the public interest". The concept of the public interest has long been held up as justification for the intervention of urban planning in the development process. Yet, as McAuslan (1980) contends, the public interest is but one of three distinct and competing philosophies or ideologies of law that dominate or conflict at different points in the planning system. The first of these, the traditional common law approach, maintains that the law exists and should be used to protect private property and its institutions. The second, the orthodox public administration and planning approach, suggests that the law exists and should be used to advance the public interest, if necessary against private property. The third, the radical or populist approach contends the law exists and should be used to advance the cause of public participation (see Ch. 9) against the two previous ideologies.

Despite central government's reliance on the second ideology, McAuslan (1980) demonstrates the significance of the two other ideologies in establishing the legal basis for urban planning. He argues that unresolved conflict between all three ideologies in planning law, in particular between the ideology of public participation on the one hand and the ideologies of private property and public interest on the other hand, is an important cause of disarray in, and disillusion with, the planning system.

The public interest: an elusive concept

As Sorauf (1957) originally pointed out, the public interest lacks a neat and precise formulation, but has acquired a pragmatic and functional definition. He compared five different ways in which the public interest has been defined, each of which he considered unsatisfactory. These have variously sought to identify the public interest with a common or widely held set of values, with a superior rationality, with a moral imperative or higher ethic, with the process or product of compromise between competing interests, and with a highly personalized view of wisdom that defies consensus or agreement. Indeed, Sorauf (1957: 618) maintained that: ". . . by becoming all things to all people, the public interest has found at best a superficial acceptance and achieved only the survival of the innocuous." Most pressure groups, he warns, seek to capture the public interest for their own ends and to achieve special priority for their own concerns by equating them with the public interest.

Ross (1991) considers that the notion of a public interest appeals to politicians and planners precisely because it is capable of manipulation to cover any occurrence. Although the public interest is often applied as a rationale for planning, it is abstract almost to the point of irrelevance. Moreover, Ross (1991) contends that widespread and indiscriminate reference to the public interest in planning practice actually serves to disguise the costs and benefits of the planning system to particular interests. As the public interest is impossible to pin down, it is best considered a figment of administrative imagination. A strong theoretical tradition has therefore emerged in recent years which sees urban planning as a process of mediation between competing interests rather than as the elusive pursuit of the public interest.

Conflict mediation between interests

Within this tradition, Healey et al. (1988) explain in detail how specific interests relate to the planning system. They define the concept of interest as the relationship between an individual or organization and an object. If the object is a particular development site, for example, several organizations and individuals may have an interest in its future. Apart from the owner of the site, local residents may well be interested in its amenity value and house-builders in its development value. These interests may be immediately apparent, but others may be less noticeable, such as the future occupiers of any houses constructed on the site and the building societies or mortgage companies who would lend them money.

Although certain interests are more apparent in the planning process than others, Healey et al. (1988) contend that neither positivist nor Marxist approaches can fully reveal how interests in land actually arise. On the one hand, positivist approaches, which assume that people know and express what they want, neither explain how individual interests are influenced by society nor account satisfactorily for those interests not always articulated in the planning process, such as ethnic minorities in inner cities. On the other hand, Marxist approaches, which consider that interests are imposed on individuals by a given mode of production, present a simplistic view of the relationship between capital and labour in an advanced society and ignore sociocultural factors such as gender, religion and attachment to location, each of which may determine attitudes to land-use. Healey et al. (1988) consequently prefer a more sophisticated post-structuralist approach to interests which acknowledges that people may value land for the use to which it can be put, for the sum which could be obtained if it were to be exchanged and as a source of wider social and cultural values. Conflict occurs when competing interests who value land in different ways, such as house-builders and amenity societies, seek to promote or prevent development of the same site. The task of urban planning becomes to mediate in such conflicts, without necessarily having to identify a public interest. A variety of groups can therefore be considered potential clients of the planning service (Kitchen 1990). In particular circumstances, planners may give priority to certain client groups above others.

Healey et al. (1988) argue that the contemporary planning system is biased in favour of certain powerful interests. Specifically, they identify the agriculture industry, the mineral extraction industry, certain types of industrial firms, knowledgeable property developers, well organized community and environmental pressure groups, and land and property owners interested in the appreciation of their property holdings as interests that have gained most from the planning system over the years. Such an approach sits uneasily with the official line that the system is designed to regulate the development and use of land in the public interest and that all interested parties benefit equally from the planning process. In effect, as Reade (1987) points out, urban planning alters the distribution of financial and environmental resources between interests, causing some to gain but others to lose. This is explored later in the chapter.

Modern challenges to urban planning

Urban planning originated as a response to the appalling living conditions widespread in 19th-century cities. Early planning pioneers promoted an alternative vision of well ordered, healthy and attractive settlements, comprehensively designed from the start. They advocated a relentless attack on the squalor and degradation of existing cities through direct physical action taken by the state, legitimized in national legislation. Early planning concepts were influenced more by architecture, engineering and surveying, in each of which the physical rather than the social or economic nature of development was emphasized, than by urban or welfare economics, where the necessary level of sophistication developed much later.

In the 20th century, the growth of urban planning matched the expansion of the public sector as a whole. This reached a high point with the creation of the welfare state in the late 1940s, which established the universal provision by the public sector of health, education and other social services. The introduction of a comprehensive and centrally directed planning system in the Town and Country Planning Act of 1947 was seen as an important component of the creation of the welfare state. At the time, the public sector was thought likely to dominate construction activity as new towns were built and old ones were reconstructed. For example, new housing starts in the public sector exceeded those in the private sector up to the late 1950s and remained only marginally below private sector output throughout the 1960s.

During this period, urban planning stuck rigidly to its physical roots, long after the social and economic causes of urban problems had become apparent. For instance, when the Ministry of Housing and Local Government (1955) first encouraged local planning authorities throughout the country to designate green belts, their purpose was defined purely in physical terms as checking the further growth of large built-up areas, preventing neighbouring towns from merging, and preserving the special character of particular towns. This statement of purpose reflected both continued faith in the roots of urban planning in architecture, engineering and surveying, and an unwillingness to justify urban plans instead in social and economic terms. Indeed, the potential contribution of green belts to social and economic regeneration in inner cities was not formally recognized by central government (Department of the Environment 1984) until many years later.

Although urban planning does not replace the market but works through it, affecting the value of land as it is bought and sold and creating potentially lucrative development opportunities for others to implement, many urban planners are reluctant to explain and define their activities in relation to market processes. As a result, the potential of urban plans to confront market imperfections and failure remains poorly articulated and insufficiently developed. Yet, from the mid-1960s, as the impact of urban plans came under challenge from two markedly different perspectives, the continued reliance of urban planners on a philosophical basis and mode of operation grounded in architecture, engineering and surveying, helped generate a crisis of confidence in planning, to which the profession had no fresh intellectual response. For these challenges, mounted first by community activists and then by New Right theorists, overturned the political consensus that had long sought to promote the public interest in the development and redevelopment of land through a centrally directed planning system.

The challenge from community activists

Community activists were among the first who criticized comprehensive urban redevelopment, as both a product and a process. As a product, it was alleged that the new urban environment, consciously planned and developed across entire neighbourhoods, lacked interest and vitality, was dominated by the public sector, and provided a fertile breeding ground for crime and vandalism. The complete destruction of older street patterns, with their lively mixture of uses, buildings and ownerships, however obsolete, was regretted. Such intense criticism reflected the conviction, most clearly articulated by Jacobs (1961), that the rich variety of urban life and culture present in densely developed cities was best preserved and fostered through the retention and gradual renewal of mixed land-uses and conventional streets, rather than by their wholesale replacement with planned redevelopment.

At the same time, it was further alleged that, since the process of urban redevelopment was driven forward by the state with little or no consultation, it was inherently paternalistic. Community activists explicitly rejected the view that elected politicians and their expert advisers could readily determine what was in the best interests of those most directly affected. The urban planner was thus caricatured alongside the local housing officer as an "evangelical bureaucrat" (Davies 1972). When comprehensive redevelopment fell from favour, urban planners were no longer able to initiate major restructuring in such areas, and market processes instead resumed control of urban change.

The challenge from New Right theorists

New Right theorists, who led the attack on urban planning in the 1980s, contended that the likelihood of government failure was far stronger and more dangerous than that of market failure. Drawing on Hayek (1960), Friedman (1962) and other libertarian writers, Sorensen (1982), for example, suggested that the crisis of confidence in urban planning was due to misplaced idealism and over-ambition. Markets, he contended, stimulate innovation and facilitate its application and are "the only effective way to harness the dispersed knowledge of the community to maximize the quantity, range and quality of services produced at the lowest possible prices" (p. 185). According to Sorensen (1982), by failing to understand and acknowledge the dominant market order, urban planning had reduced consumer choice of alternative lifestyles, ossified land-use patterns, stifled commercial competition, produced dull uniformity in urban design, increased urban blight, raised housing costs and thus ensured a negative redistribution of wealth from the poor to the rich. He further argued that the true rationale of development control was principally economic and was to be discovered in the preservation of property rights, the enhancement of property values, the provision of lower-cost infrastructure, the quicker and cheaper resolution of land-use conflicts, the conservation of scarce resources and the avoidance of costly environmental disaster. Sorensen (1982) explicitly rejected any rôle for urban planning in tackling social inequality or promoting the social redistribution of land resources.

Subsequently, Sorensen (1983) set out a manifesto for implementing a market theory of planning. On the basis that market solutions were preferable to state intervention, he suggested that urban planning should concentrate on problems that government had a good chance of solving in a cost-effective way. The state should avoid the protection of vested interests, encourage entrepreneurship, decentralize power and establish competing centres of advice in order to generate more information and ideas. Adverse planning decisions should entitle those affected to full compensation. Individual rights and freedoms should be valued, with individuals given greater recourse to legal action to protect themselves from harmful externalities. However, the manifesto proved internally inconsistent in seeking both to uphold the rule of law through publicly known and consistently applied planning laws and regulations and to encourage flexibility, diversity and innovation "by abandoning rigid zoning or building standards in favour of performance standards and more subtle policing of externalities" (p. 79).

Response to New Right theorists

Subsequent writers sought to expose the questionable intellectual validity of New Right thinking in urban planning. As Pike & Warren (1983) contend, rational behaviour in the market is apparent only in profit maximization and the pursuit of self-interest, motives of doubtful relevance to the

76

allocation of a social commodity such as land. Government failure can be tackled directly, for example by expanding public participation and by eliminating paternalistic attitudes in the bureaucracy. Furthermore, within a just society, the excessive inequalities created by market processes are unlikely to be tolerated for ever. Pike & Warren (1983) therefore believed that urban planning could help achieve social justice through improving the accessibility of lower-income groups to services, activities and decent housing.

It is apparent that New Right thinking fails to acknowledge extensive monopolies in land and property ownership or to recognize that secrecy in transactions reinforces such power in the market place. Urban information systems, seen by Klosterman (1985) as an essential part of urban planning, can enhance market choice by making relevant information on land and property widely available. This would otherwise be difficult or expensive to collect, and its absence would be likely to cause costly locational mistakes. Such action helps diminish the imperfections inherent in land & property markets.

More generally, Klosterman (1985: 9–10) argues that "Specific government actions to reduce conflicts between incompatible land-uses, co-ordinate private development and public infrastructure, preserve open space and historic buildings, and examine the long-range impacts of current actions can similarly be justified as needing to correct market failures revealed in the physical development of the city." Low (1991) contrasts monetary values, with which markets are exclusively concerned, with the broader sociocultural value that most people attach to countryside, coastline or mountains or indeed to buildings of high quality or places of historic or aesthetic significance. No guarantee can be given by the market that such broader values will be respected and such environments will be preserved. Indeed, "The decisions we make today we may well regret tomorrow; or our successors on the planet may well regret them. The preferences of the unborn do not enter market transactions." (p. 185).

Yet, collectivism is on the decline, socially, economically and politically. Mass industrial production, with its associated social and economic structures, pioneered in the motor industry by Henry Ford, is giving way to flexible manufacturing. This involves, for example, team production, decentralization of decision-making, and greater contracting out of work to small firms. The replacement of "Fordism" by "post-Fordism" typifies the postmodernist era. Goodchild (1990) contends that postmodernism involves a rejection of totality, whether present in economic concentration, aesthetic standardization or comprehensive planning. He further suggests that the arrival of postmodernism has fundamentally changed the nature of planning, design and development. The greater emphasis on the local context in urban design and the renewed preference for mixed-use development thus reflect the diversity inherent in the postmodernist era.

According to Goodchild (1990), deregulation, deconcentration and decentralization characterize public administration in postmodernist planning. Nevertheless, postmodernism in a political context does not correspond merely to New Right thinking, but strikes a chord with those on the left who argue in favour of democratic decentralization and press for policies which better cope with social diversity. As Goodchild (1990: 134) concludes: "The strength of postmodernism is to express a sense of dissatisfaction with the institutions of the recent past in a way which cuts across the strategies of the liberal Right and the collectivist Left". Whether or not the post-modernist model is accepted, the state is increasingly seen as setting the context or framework for action by, or in association with, the private and voluntary sectors, rather than taking direct action itself. This is well illustrated by the replacement of local authorities with housing associations and societies in the much reduced provision of social housing.

In the 1980s, New Right thinking certainly captured the political high ground (Thornley 1991), causing the frontiers of urban planning to be rolled back. This was reflected by the fragmentation of urban planning (Brindley et al. 1989) into several market-led and market-critical styles, variously pursued in different locations. Brindley et al. (1989) contend that market-led styles of urban planning became dominant by the end of the decade, with planning retained by central government primarily to stimulate and support market processes. Yet, New Right thinking proved unable to meet renewed concern in the early 1990s about environmental quality and sustainability and about social and community welfare (Healey 1992b).

This new agenda provides urban planning with both a fresh opportunity and a critical test of its ability to influence market processes rather than merely respond to them. This calls for a new conception of urban planning to close what Klosterman (1985) calls the tremendous gap between planning potential and its performance. Any such conception requires a realistic recognition of the capacity of both markets and governments to fail. Active and dynamic intervention in market processes may therefore become far more important than the routine administration of excessively rigid and conservative development regulations, which Klosterman (1985) considers exemplify the planning performance gap. In this context, planners could facilitate the renewed search for better planning by grasping the value of the market as a working tool, without abandoning their activities or completely subordinating them to the market (Low 1991). The market might indeed provide a standard against which to evaluate and justify the outcomes of planning policy (Willis 1988). The challenge for urban planning in the next decade is thus to develop understandings and methods "which neither blindly follow the market nor naively seek to 'structure' it" (Healey 1992b: 420).

Urban planning as shaping market behaviour

Social, economic and political realities are now fundamentally different from those dominant in the heyday of the welfare state in the late 1940s. For example, in the political arena, the state is no longer seen as a controller and a provider but rather as a regulator and an enabler. As Blacksell et al. (1987: 1) explain: "In a market economy, the function of town planning is to *regulate* rather than *control* the timing, form and location of development in order to promote the efficient allocation of resources, minimize negative externalities and ensure the conservation of valued environments". Such an approach could successfully enhance urban design and amenity as a by-product of good planning rather than as an end in itself. Indeed, in the context of the urban form debate identified by Yiftachel (1989), good urban planning, through shaping market behaviour, enhances equity, efficiency and sustainability in the built environment to an extent that improves and is seen to improve upon the outcomes that would otherwise be generated by the market alone. This approach acknowledges that, in a market economy, state intervention in the development process needs to be fully justified by evidence of market failure and government success. Moreover, it contends that urban plans should not be market-led but rather that markets should be plan-influenced.

Efficiency

Urban planning has traditionally sought to reduce negative externalities through direct regulation and to promote positive ones through direct action. More recently, the policy emphasis has shifted to making the polluter pay and theoretical attention has concentrated on the potential contribution of user, product and pollution charges, balanced by subsidies, to the creation of quasi-markets in externalities (Sunman 1990). Yet, as Reade (1987) notes, urban externalities do not always come from a single or easily identifiable source that can be readily charged. Indeed, as Sunman (1990) acknowledges, quasi-market instruments are still in their infancy and are likely to be best deployed in association with traditional regulations. A continuing rôle for urban planning in regulating urban externalities and thus promoting the more efficient use of land resources can therefore be articulated.

In the past, urban planning has been further justified in relation to public goods and lost opportunities but such justifications have tended to be underdeveloped in practice. The provision of roads, parks and other public goods is certainly important, but it is misleading to consider these goods in isolation from their potential to shape market behaviour. A good urban plan will therefore consider road construction, for instance, in the context of the development opportunities that it is likely to create, and will seek to organize the timing and location of public investment in order to extract maximum public benefit from subsequent development opportunities. The multiple ownership of land with redevelopment potential is a serious barrier to urban regeneration and a prime reason why inner-city land often remains vacant (Adams et al. 1988). In welfare economics, it presents a helpful example of a lost opportunity, which a good urban plan should attempt to address. Indeed, good urban planning should encourage active landowners and confront passive ones (see Ch. 5). These illustrations demonstrate the clear rôle for urban planning in improving the efficiency of market outcomes.

Equity

Markets breed social polarization by distributing their resources unevenly between rich and poor. As Eversley (1990) demonstrates, cities are increasingly characterized by an urban underclass who experience multiple deprivation by virtue of low income, restricted employment opportunities and poor access to education, housing and other services. The underclass is almost invariably dependent on means-tested benefits, finds it impossible to save, and relies for survival on the informal economy. The elderly, chronically sick, disabled, one-parent families, young single homeless and ethnic minorities are all disproportionately represented. Although evident on peripheral housing estates and in older industrial towns, the underclass is concentrated in inner metropolitan areas. Such multiple deprivation is characteristically transmitted down the generations, since "The underclass consists largely of people who have no prospect, whatever the state of the national economy, of breaking out of that class . . . " (Eversley 1990: 15).

Many types of development favoured by the market are irrelevant to the underclass and indeed to others on low incomes who do not suffer such intense deprivation. As Ambrose (1986) contends, those without cars and whose incomes are low, are likely to have far greater need for a local chemist than for brand new shopping centres, full of relatively expensive supermarkets and trendy boutiques. For such groups, the process of urban redevelopment is disproportionately disruptive and the product regressively redistributive.

Redevelopment is disruptive because its profitability depends primarily on the replacement of low-value uses, such as cheap housing or workshops, by higher-value uses, such as expensive flats or air-conditioned luxury offices. The urban poor experience not merely the dust and noise of urban redevelopment but also the stress and disruption of finding cheap replacement accommodation. It is regressively redistributive because those who gain from such redevelopment are already better off than those who lose (Ambrose & Colenutt 1975). The gains are substantial and can be quantified, but accrue to a limited number of people. The losses are non-quantifiable, take several forms and impinge on many more people. As Ambrose & Colenutt therefore warn, urban redevelopment tends to benefit the rich at the expense of the poor.

Urban planning seeks to correct the unequal distribution of costs and benefits from development for both practical and philosophical reasons. As Ambrose (1986: 107) points out, practically: "If the state is to play *no* redistributive or protective rôle, the result is bound to be increasing inequality, costly health and welfare problems and probably a degree of social dissent that will require heavy expenditure on law-and-order enforcement. These costs are soon likely to outweigh the money saved by not funding social support policies." Many have argued philosophically that urban planning should have a bias to the poor. Self (1989: 21), for instance, suggests that: "The only feasible planning strategy is one which combines overall substantive gains for society generally with a special emphasis on improving the position of the poor and relatively disadvantaged."

However, as Self acknowledges, planning policies for the preservation of charming villages and protection of green views enhance property values for the already better off, while urban containment raises the housing costs of first-time buyers and the urban poor. Indeed, Blowers (1980) argued that urban planning in practice has often reinforced the existing pattern of resource distribution by widening the gap between rich and poor. As Ross (1991) contends, urban planners have until recently been reluctant to identify winners and losers, hiding instead behind the fiction of the public interest. This, she believes, must be abandoned if urban planning is to make any real contribution to the social redistribution of resources.

In the 1980s, urban planning thus began to target particular policies towards those groups most disadvantaged by market processes, such as the elderly, disabled, and ethnic minorities. This reflected the desire to promote equality of access and opportunity for all groups to urban services and facilities. The People's Plan for Greenwich, one of the first to pioneer such an approach in inner London, is evaluated in Chapter 8. Yet, as Chapter 10 reveals, the statutory planning process itself is inherently inequitable, allowing those who can afford professional representation a better chance to influence plan formulation.

Sustainability

Sustainability achieved international prominence in the 1980s, reflecting worldwide concern about the deterioration of the global environment. Sustainable development has been defined by the Brundtland Commission (1987: 43) as development that meets the needs of the present without compromising the ability of future generations to meet their own needs. This concept has been widely applied to the natural environment and to farming and forestry but its applicability to the built environment remains to be tested in detail (Green 1990).

The UK Government (1990) responded to such widespread environmental concern by preparing the first national strategy for the natural and built environment, published as a White Paper, entitled "This common inheritance". This favoured the application of market mechanisms, wherever possible, to encourage producers and consumers to behave in an environmentally friendly way. Green (1990) comments that the use of such mechanisms in the development process may require a developer to meet the long-term environmental costs associated with a development. As well as charges for related infrastructure, these could include contributions both to community and transport services and to the unforeseeable costs of cumulative growth or economic decline. This would produce greater costs and lower profits for developers in already congested areas, and the reverse elsewhere. The principle of sustainable development, applied through urban planning, would thus challenge the entrenched power of short-term costs and benefits in conventional methods of development appraisal, requiring longer-term costs and benefits to be given equal consideration.

Although the White Paper acknowledges that land-use planning can help preserve the best of the present environment for future generations, Begg (1991) contends that sustainable development may prove difficult to implement through the planning process. He identifies three reasons for this. First, the complexity of environment issues makes it hard to place any realistic value on environmental damage or improvement. Secondly, the strength of the pro-growth lobby is reflected in the greater priority that economic growth is accorded over environmental protection. Thirdly, the channelling of general public concern about the environment into specific political will is likely to be undermined by the reluctance of politicians to place environmental protection for future generations above matters of immediate electoral interest.

Nevertheless, Begg (1991) suggests that, as an integrative concept linking economic and environmental management, the notion of sustainable development marks a watershed in the evolution of town and country planning which potentially represents the greatest move forward since the Town and Country Planning Act of 1947. Acceptance of sustainable development, he argues, provides an opportunity to challenge the market-led dominance of the 1980s, precisely because the concept of sustainability incorporates an understanding of market processes. As a result: "The concept of sustainable development will help overcome what has perhaps been the greatest inhibition to good town and country planning: the chasm between short-term sectoral economic policies and the longer-term visions of urban and regional planning" (Begg 1991: 8). However, Blacksell et al. (1987) consider that, for urban planners to take full advantage the new environmental politics and of the concept of sustainable development, the narrow concentration of urban planning on land-use allocation now needs to be broadened into a concern for the environment as a whole.

Land-use planning and land policy

Land policy is a term applied to all the ways in which the state seeks to intervene in the use, exchange, value, ownership, management and development of land. Lichfield & Darin-Drabkin (1980) identify three broad types of land policies, extending from those that exercise most control over specific developments to those that exercise least. The first type, with which urban planners are most familiar, involves either direct control over development, with or usually without taking land into state ownership, or direct state participation in a particular development. The second type seeks to influence development by fiscal measures, of either a general nature (such as development land taxation) or a specific nature (such as capital taxation allowances for new development in enterprise zones). The third type operates through influencing development more generally, for example by providing information and guidance to the land market. As Healey et al. (1988) demonstrate, the British planning system has sought primarily to control development without taking land, and to provide supporting guidance and information to those involved in development. Although significant in particular locations and at particular times, other measures have generally been less important.

Although the comprehensive planning system conceived in wartime was originally intended as an active means of state intervention in the development process, when eventually implemented in 1947, it became primarily a passive response to development proposals initiated by the private sector. Lichfield & Darin-Drabkin (1980) in part attribute the relegation of active planning to the demise of successive attempts by Labour administrations to establish general fiscal policies for development land. Each of these attempts sought to tax a proportion of the value of land attributable to its development potential rather than its existing use. The subsequent repeal of each scheme by succeeding Conservative governments highlighted the intense antagonism between the two main political parties over the taxation of development land value. For a detailed account of the Central Land Board and the development charge established in 1947, of the Land Commission and the betterment levy established in 1967 and of the Community Land Act and Development Land Tax Act of 1975 and 1976 respectively, readers are recommended to consult Leung (1979), Cox (1984), Parker (1985) and Grant (1986).

By the mid-1980s, the separation of land-use planning from land policy had been reinforced by this tradition of adversarial politics in land (Cox 1984). Although the use, value and ownership of land are never separated in the minds of landowners, developers and investors, planners were required artificially to concentrate on land-use and ignore both value and ownership. Yet, once urban planning is conceived as a means of intervention in the development process, such an artificial distinction is untenable, as use creates value which owners can capture. The essential relationship between use, value and ownership in policy terms can be readily recognized without needing to reopen past debates. As the next chapter shows, the more efficient use of land, for example, may be best achieved by tackling an ownership constraint to development. Effective intervention may therefore require urban planners to possess knowledge of land law and valuation. Moreover, almost by stealth, urban planning itself has found a way to reconnect use, value and ownership in order to shape market behaviour more effectively. This is known as planning gain.

Planning gain

Planning gain is a term commonly applied to the provision by a developer of some additional benefit, not necessarily related to the immediate development, offered to, or more usually requested by a local planning authority. Other popular names include community benefits, developers' contributions and planning advantages (Healey et al. 1992b). The term has no statutory significance and is not found in legislation. No direct linkage yet exists to ensure that any benefits received at least cover the social costs of development. If this fails to happen, it can be argued that the term "gain" is strictly inaccurate. Indeed, the Department of the Environment (1991a) considers the term planning gain to be imprecise and misleading, and refuses to use it in policy guidance. Section 50 of the Town and Country Planning (Scotland) Act 1972 refers to planning agreements. However, in England and Wales, when Section 106 of the Town and Country Planning Act 1990 (previously Section 52 of the Town and Country Planning Act 1971) was amended by the Planning and Compensation Act 1991, planning obligations replaced the term planning agreements, south of the border. Yet, as Fordham (1991) comments, planning gain as a term is now so well entrenched in practice that there is little likelihood it can be eliminated by the Department of the Environment.

Local authorities were first empowered to enter into planning agreements in the Housing, Town Planning etc. Act 1909. This power was repeated in succeeding legislation, but until 1968 each agreement had to be approved individually by the Minister. The use of planning agreements grew rapidly as a result of both the removal of this restriction and the development boom of the early 1970s. A survey of 225 local authorities by Dennison (1988) revealed that they had concluded over 4,000 planning agreements between 1981 and 1985. Dennison (1988) found from a more detailed sample of 46 local authorities that, although planning agreements were most frequently used to secure infrastructure provision, they were also significantly employed to ensure the dedication of land for public use, minimize environmental impact, extinguish existing user rights, and restrict the activity allowed within a development. However, the extent to which the latter can be considered planning gain is a matter of debate.

Of course, the most outrageous forms of planning gain have always attracted the greatest publicity. For example, one planning application in the London area for sand and gravel extraction was met by officers of the local authority with a request for a £25,000 contribution to the local hospice or a £50,000 contribution to restoring a local clock tower (Franzini 1988). Yet, despite some unease among developers that planning gain is a form of bribery, blackmail or sweetener (KPMG 1990), research commissioned by the Department of the Environment (1992e) showed that the vast majority of planning agreements concluded in the late 1980s concerned the regulation and control of development rather than the achievement of wider planning or community objectives. The research revealed that between 6,500 and 8,000 agreements were reached each year. Of the 852 that it investigated in detail, most sought either to regulate the use or occupancy of development or to secure on-site infrastructure. Only 12 per cent involved financial contributions and very few indeed required off-site infrastructure provision. The Department of the Environment was pleased that the guidance it had originally issued to local authorities in 1983 to prevent abuse of planning agreements appeared to be working well.

Subsequently, Healey et al. (1992b) have suggested that the nature of planning agreements changed markedly and that their number increased significantly. They identified three reasons for this. First, the development boom of the late 1980s created greater opportunities for planning gain, in much the same way as had that of the early 1970s. Secondly, the power of local authorities to influence infrastructure provision was diminished by privatization (particularly that of the water industry in England and Wales) and by cutbacks in their capital spending. Thirdly, central government itself encouraged the provision of social, educational, recreational, sporting or other community facilities, and the promotion of nature conservation (including tree planting and the creation of wildlife ponds) by planning obligations (Department of the Environment 1991a). This allowed local authorities to secure community development and achieve environment quality through explicit bargaining with the private sector.

The scope for planning gain was further widened by the Planning and Compensation Act 1991 which enabled developers in England and Wales (but not in Scotland) to enter into a planning obligation by unilateral undertaking rather than by agreement with the local planning authority. This could help developers win planning appeals, if permission has been refused after failure to reach agreement with the authority. Furthermore, the Department of the Environment (1992c: para. 5.25) encouraged local authorities to include policies on planning gain in local plans, stating that: "Where a planning authority expect developers to enter into planning obligations on a regular basis, in relation to similar types of development, they should set

...eir policy in their local plan." This will make planning gain more open to scrutiny and challenge during plan preparation, not only from members of the public but also from landowners, developers and, of course, the Secretary of State.

In Scotland, structure plans have increasingly sought to ensure that the private sector helps fund collective infrastructure provision (Rowan-Robinson & Durman 1993). Healey et al. (1992b) discovered reference to planning gain in all but one of the 16 English plans they investigated. Contributions expected by local authorities varied from the provision of road infrastructure, environmental improvements and public open space in Salford to subsidizing the costs of childcare and training in Harlow. The latter example supports concern expressed by Gill (1991: 36) that: "planning gain can be used to replace the sources of local government funding that are not as free-flowing as in the past." However, in extending Bailey's (1990) distinction between policies that promote urban efficiency by reducing social costs and those that enhance urban equity by meeting social needs, it is clear that the justification for planning gain is now grounded in both efficiency and equity.

Nevertheless, the potential for planning gain is highly dependent on the strength of the local economy. As Rowan-Robinson & Lloyd (1988) point out, local authorities in prosperous areas can expect the private sector to contribute more to the provision of infrastructure than those in declining areas, who indeed may prefer to meet infrastructure costs themselves in order to attract inward investment. As Fordham (1993) therefore maintains, planning gain should not be regarded as a modern form of land or betterment tax, since it is negotiated on a site-by-site basis rather than applied at a uniform rate. As a result, it is best considered a variable development cost rather than a standard claim on development land value.

However, the earlier that the precise cost of planning gain is known, the greater the likelihood that it will be reflected in a lower residual land valuation and, on purchase, pass from the developer to the original landowner (Rowan-Robinson & Lloyd 1988, Hodge & Cameron 1989). At the time when agricultural land in Berkshire was valued at only £4950 per ha but prime residential land at £1,850,000 per ha, the county council published precise requirements for infrastructure, amenities and services contributions to encourage this to happen (Williams 1989). Such clear guidance may help reduce the delay that developers fear in protracted negotiations on planning gain. Rowan-Robinson & Durman (1992) suggest that in Scotland, such negotiations may add between two and six months to the development control process.

Although standard development impact fees or charges are commonplace in Canada and the United States (Bailey 1990, Dawson & Walker 1990, Delafons 1991), the British preference for a more discretionary approach to planning gain remains strong. Yet, for significant developments that substantially increase traffic on motorways or trunk roads, a standard system of developer contributions to highway improvements has already been suggested by the Department of Transport (1992). Indeed, experience in the United States, which Delafons (1991) considers has much to teach planners in Britain, confirms that, in a market economy, good urban planning not merely regulates land-use but ensures that the social costs of development are reimbursed to the community.

Conclusion

Most people have some expectation of the kind of ideal environment in which they would like to live. These expectations reflect a mixture of personal preference and social influence, with the exact balance differing from one society to another. Although such expectations may be expressed initially at a domestic level (in the desire, for instance, of some people to live in houses rather than flats or apartments) they certainly do not stop at the doorstep. For example, in their immediate neighbourhood, people prefer particular shopping centres to others, demand that roads are safe to cross, and expect parks to be provided for their recreation. At a wider level, they may wish to see the local heritage and countryside preserved, and interna tional action taken, for instance, to protect threatened rain forests. Such expectations reflect diverse individual interests and cannot readily be subsumed by a wider public interest.

Despite New Right theory, market mechanisms are unable to allocate environmental resources in the most efficient, equitable or sustainable way. When markets fail to respond to individual environmental expectations, people usually demand action by central or local government on their behalf. As Young (1993) shows, the styles in which such environmental protest is expressed range from the moderate and conventional to the radical and populist. Yet, the failure of comprehensive redevelopment planned in the 1960s and 1970s reminds us to seek government success and not merely market failure. This chapter has therefore identified more sophisticated and specific forms of intervention in the development process which, in shaping market behaviour, aim to enhance equity, efficiency and sustainability in the built environment. Planning gain, if properly used, provides a good example, since it brings together the use, value and ownership of land in a way that is essential to the success of urban planning in a market economy.

PART 2

ACTOR PERSPECTIVES

CHAPTER FIVE

Perspectives from the landowner

According to the Guinness Book of Records, the largest landowner in the UK is the Forestry Commission, which owns approximately 1.13 million ha. The largest ever private landowner was the 3rd Duke of Sutherland (1828–92) who owned 550,000ha, an estate more than three times that of the largest private owner today, the Duke of Buccleuth, who holds 136,000ha (Matthews 1993). Even now, extensive land ownership remains a source of wealth, status and power (Shoard 1987, Sutherland 1988). Yet, as Chapter 2 pointed out, the property rights of a single old person, living alone in a poorly maintained house, are accorded equal respect in law to those of the most powerful landowning families in the country.

Despite public fascination with the ownership of land, the contribution of the landowner to the development process has been relatively neglected. Two reasons account for this. First, in neoclassical theory, the supply of land is considered to respond to demand pressure, enabling land to move into its most profitable use. As a result, the individual preferences of particular landowners merited little attention from economists who believed such preferences were incapable of general analysis and perhaps ought not to exist at all (Wiltshaw 1985). Secondly, a widespread misconception exists that urban planning has diminished the rôle of the landowner in the supply of land.

In some countries, the state allocates land for development in a plan, acquires the land from the owner and undertakes the development itself. This has never been the case in the UK, apart from in very special circumstances, such as the development of new towns or the reconstruction of obsolete or war damaged city centres. Although the allocation of land is a public decision taken by local planning authorities, the bringing forward of land to implement that allocation is normally a private decision left to landowners and developers. Since it is assumed that land allocated by the planning system will usually be made available for development, the ownership of land is rarely considered a legitimate issue during plan preparation. Yet, as Goodchild & Munton (1985: 9) reveal: " . . . the motives and circumstances of landowners are extremely varied and as a consequence owners do not respond uniformly to the development opportunities open to them."

This chapter explores the land management and development strategies pursued by various types of owner. It draws on case studies from research into the rôle of landowners in urban planning and the development process. Two particular studies are referred to in some detail. The first examined the involvement and influence of landowners on local plan preparation in Cambridge, Greenwich and Surrey Heath (Adams & May 1991 & 1992). A full account of these three plans and of the statutory planning process is subsequently given in Chapter 8. In the second study, the contribution of landowners and other actors to making land available for industrial development in the Cheshire–Wirral corridor in North West England was investigated (Adams et al. 1994).

Such research reveals that the strategies pursued by individual owners are highly diverse. The chapter therefore explores the extent to which earlier approaches to landowner classification account for such diversity. This reveals that both the behaviourist approach, which concentrates on owner **characteristics**, and the structuralist approach, which classifies owners by their **function** in the process of production, can only part explain the individual strategies pursued by particular landowners. Moreover, neither fully recognizes the diversity of landowner behaviour as a whole. This makes it essential to investigate empirical **outcomes** of landowner strategies, rather than concentrate purely on characteristics or functions. The chapter therefore concludes by exploring the empirical distinction between active and passive landowner behaviour in planning and development.

Land management and development strategies

All owners of land with development potential pursue **land management and development strategies**, either consciously or unconsciously. These strategies are produced by the way in which owners respond, or fail to respond, to three basic decisions: if and when to develop land or sell for development, whether and how to relate to other actors, and how to manage land prior to development. These are called respectively the financial, operational and management decisions. Those who own land with development potential but never consider these matters, unconsciously pursue strategies that may affect the development process as much as those pursued by owners who energetically seek to exploit such potential.

The concept of land management and development strategies represents an extension of Goodchild & Munton's (1985) decision model, which itself draws on earlier work at the University of North Carolina (Chapin & Weiss 1962, Weiss et al. 1966, Kaiser & Weiss 1970). As Figure 5.1. shows, Goodchild & Munton (1985) contend that landowners reach financial, operational and management decisions as a result of interaction between contextual factors (over which they consider individual landowners have little or no influence) site characteristics and owner characteristics.

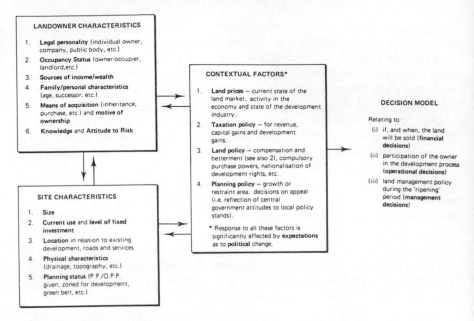

Figure 5.1 Landowner behaviour: constraints and the development process (*Source:* Goodchild & Munton 1985).

Figure 5.1 appears to be a static model in which landowners react to contextual factors on the basis of given site and owner characteristics. In practice, all three types of variable interact dynamically. For example, Goodchild & Munton (1985) suggest that owners may apply for planning permission to improve site characteristics. Moreover, Adams & May (1991) show that many landowners seek to influence planning policy to enhance contextual factors. In the latter case, the structural framework for development (see Ch. 3) may be challenged and potentially transformed by the actions, interests and strategies of particular landowners. This possibility is fully reflected by the term land management and development strategy, which seeks to refine the distinction between financial, operational and management decisions. This distinction will now be considered further.

The financial or development decision

An owner who recognizes that land has development potential must decide if and when to undertake development, or if and when to sell for others to develop. Goodchild & Munton (1985) maintain that virtually every owner of development land will eventually sell for capital gain. Although this may be true of farmland suitable for housing development, notable exceptions otherwise occur to this general rule. Manufacturing companies may keep development land vacant for many years, before eventually bringing it into use for their own purposes. For example, an international chemical company that has extensive holdings of land at Bromborough in the Wirral owned one site of 15 ha since 1850. This has been gradually developed the decades, and even now, one hectare still remains fallow (Adams et al. 1994). Landowners who change direction may also decide to develop rather than sell. Several former textile companies in the North of England, for example, switched from manufacturing to property development, a move often initiated by the demolition and successful redevelopment of their own mills. However, Adams et al. (1988) suggest that most such brownfield development is preceded by a change in ownership.

According to Goodchild & Munton (1985), an owner who wishes to maximize the financial gain from land investment should accept the highest offer, once planning permission is granted, unless at least one of four particular circumstances justify a delay. These include the likelihood of a favourable change in the rate of tax on the proceeds of sale, or a significant increase in the value of development land in the short term. Alternatively, there may be a lack of alternative investment opportunities in circumstances where compulsory purchase would be unlikely, or the possibility of rapid growth in the income accruing from the land's existing use. Of course, development land may be offered for sale for reasons other than to maximize financial gain. This may happen for non-pecuniary reasons, such as illness or retirement, or if property on site becomes functionally obsolete.

The operational decision

Operational decisions concern the relationship between landowners and other actors in the development process, particularly planners and developers. Most landowners in areas with the highest development potential and the best connections to existing services, try to have their land allocated for development during local plan preparation (Adams & May 1992). Those who do not may entrust the task to developers, with whom they conclude an option or conditional contract. Owners who seek the release of land for future development through the statutory planning process appear more likely to succeed if professionally represented. Operationally, a landowner may therefore appoint a lawyer, chartered surveyor, planning consultant or other professional representative, or indeed a team of such representatives, in order to pursue a land management and development strategy more effectively. Unless an option or conditional contract has previously been granted, when the time to sell eventually comes, the owner must decide whether to do so by private treaty, formal tender or public auction (see Ch. 2).

The management decision

Once development potential is apparent, an owner must decide how best to manage land prior to sale or development. Owners may be tempted to minimize their financial and legal commitments to any pre-development use, while seeking to maximize their opportunities for short-term earnings. However, as Goodchild & Munton (1985: 108) point out "The intensity of farming activity falls close to the urban edge, but acquiring evidence on the extent to which this is a deliberate management strategy aimed at hastening the development of the land, rather than an understandable reluctance to invest in a difficult and uncertain farming situation, is difficult." In such cases, when tenanted farmland is surrendered, it may not be re-let by the landlord, except on a short-term basis for uses such as horse grazing. If the land were included in the green belt, owners may be persuaded to take a longer-term view of land management.

Owners of urban sites and buildings with redevelopment potential may be equally reluctant to commit resources to maintenance. Buildings thus decay and are demolished, creating vacant sites, either used for temporary purposes such as open storage or which remain unused. Urban planning has found it harder to control the interim management of such sites than their eventual development. According to Moss (1981: 104) urban wasteland leads to progressive deterioration in the city environment: "Unkempt, overgrown and rubbish strewn, these areas of urban wasteland have now become a depressingly familiar characteristic of the inner city. Offensive to the eye, dulling to the spirit and dangerous to all who stray within its boundaries, urban wasteland has an insidious and innate ability to spread." Such wasteland was often originally created in the 1960s and 1970s, when municipalities acquired swathes of land for ambitious new highways or bought and cleared whole areas of substandard housing, only to discover that the necessary resources for road construction or new public-sector house-building, no longer existed.

Diversity characterizes the financial, operational and management decisions of landowners, reflecting both their varied experience of development and their individual motives for ownership. Since the contribution of owners to the development process is critical but often unpredictable, we next examine the extent to which two alternative approaches to landowner classification explain the diversity inherent in land management and development strategies.

A behaviourist approach to landowner classification

Goodchild & Munton (1985) contend that individual owners perceive land management and development in a way that relates significantly to their own particular characteristics and circumstances. They suggest that variety in owner behaviour is explained primarily by the specific characteristics and circumstances of each landowner rather than by any differences in contextual factors or site characteristics. This is essentially a process-orientated or "behaviourist" approach which explores how the events that culminate in urban change can be traced back to the behavioural characteristics of particular landowners. Six important types of landowner characteristic, which Goodchild & Munton (1985) identify, will now be considered in turn.

Legal personality

The individual landowner can be distinguished from the company and the public body as different legal personalities owning land. However, not all individual owners, companies or public bodies behave alike in planning and development. For example, some individual owners participate enthusiastically in local plan preparation, but others ignore the process altogether. Company behaviour also varies. In Greenwich, one manufacturing company battled continuously through planning applications and at the local plan inquiry to have its site reallocated for retail warehouse use, so that it could sell up and move elsewhere. Another company who owned and operated a car showroom in a nearby high street and had no immediate desire to move, was quite surprised to be informed when interviewed for research, that its site had already been reallocated for office development (Adams & May 1991).

Diversity certainly characterizes owner behaviour in the public sector, since the responsibilities of statutory agencies vary enormously. According to Gore & Nicholson (1985), statutory agencies whose participation in the development process is central to their existence (such as the Land Authority for Wales) are likely to be far more active in managing their land than agencies whose involvement in development is peripheral to their main business (such as British Coal). To an extent, this distinction broke down in the 1980s, when many public bodies found themselves under intense pressure from central government to identify surplus land and property for sale to the highest bidder. For example, sales and lettings of redundant railway land by the British Rail Property Board in 1988 contributed £335 million to British Rail's total income, effectively preventing BR itself recording a deficit. As a result, the Financial Times described BR as "not so much a railway as a property company with an irksome mass transit sideline".

In contrast, central government itself is often less than entrepreneurial in the management of its own land holdings. For instance, the Comptroller and Auditor General (1988) suggested that the National Health Service could save up to £500 million a year in running expenses, by selling surplus land and empty property. Subsequently, the House of Commons Public Accounts Committee (1989) severely criticized the Ministry of Defence for delay in releasing surplus land and buildings. This followed an admission by Sir Clive Whitmore, the Permanent Under-Secretary of State, that no overall strategy existed for the management of the 220,000 ha Defence Estate. In Greenwich, the Ministry of Defence own substantial areas of vacant and under-used land, including the Royal Arsenal, which the borough council wish to see opened up for tourism and related residential, retail and employment development. After several years of persuasion, the Ministry eventually announced that the site would be released in 1995.

In practice, landowner behaviour may therefore vary as much within the various types of legal personality as between them. This highlights the need to investigate not merely legal personality, but factors that lie behind legal personality. For example, it has been suggested that the corporate owner most likely to dispose of surplus land appears to be a single company, having some expertise in property management and development, holding land recently acquired and valued at open market prices, but in some financial difficulty (Adams et al. 1988). Such detailed knowledge may be essential to explain why landowners with the same legal personality relate very differently to urban planning and the development process.

Occupancy status

Owners of land or property that is tenanted are more likely to sell what they regard as an investment, than owner-occupiers who use land or property themselves. However, the presence of tenants may delay commercial redevelopment since they will be entitled to remain at least until the expiry of any existing lease or tenancy agreement. In Ellesmere Port, a specialist steel manufacturer acquired the freehold of an adjacent building in 1984, which had been leased by the previous owner to a charity for a youth training centre. The manufacturer wanted to refurbish the building and convert it to offices and laboratories, but could not begin to do so until vacant possession was obtained. This took three years (Adams et al. 1994). Furthermore, under landlord and tenant legislation, tenants may be entitled either to renew a lease or tenancy agreement when it expires, or to receive compensation, if required to move for redevelopment. Owner-occupiers who sell and wish to stay in business must find suitable replacement accommodation and meet the full costs of relocation themselves. However, when land prices rise, owner-occupiers and landlords are both likely to be more aware of the exchange value of their assets and as a result, more willing to sell for the right price.

Sources of income and wealth

Landowners may be influenced in their behaviour by the extent of any associate wealth, beyond their immediate land assets. Wealthy landowners with substantial income from a variety of assets are better placed to hold out for higher prices than impoverished landowners in need of cash. The prospect of substantial development gains provides the main impetus for landowner representations during local plan preparation (Adams & May 1992). Such representations relate not to **current** income and wealth but to **future** income and wealth generated through the reallocation of land to a higher-value use. Indeed, landowners are rarely deterred from such involvement by a low but realistic assessment of their chances of success. As

a result, local plan preparation often encourages many landowner representations, which may vary in their degree of seriousness but which must each
be accorded equal respect by the local planning authority.

Particular family and personal characteristics

Family and personal characteristics may determine whether or not land is
made available for development. This is illustrated by the case of a single
dwelling in large grounds, owned by an elderly widow and located in a village in Surrey Heath. The property had been bought many years earlier by
her husband and it held special memories of their married life. Despite its
obvious development value, she had many numerous approaches from
developers and had no intention of selling. As a result, the site was left
unallocated in the local plan, despite its development potential (Adams &
May 1991).

In the mid-1980s, a major employer in Cheshire wished to expand a substantial manufacturing plant onto four hectares of adjacent agricultural land.
This was owned by a family trust. Although the site was then in the green
belt, planning permission was granted in 1985. However, negotiations to
acquire the site eventually broke down in 1988. Although the average value
of industrial land in the area was estimated to be £125,000 per ha, the
manufacturing company offered only £75,000 per ha, as the four hectares
alone had no access to the public highway, other than through the existing
industrial plant. Moreover, since the manufacturing company knew that it
would have to relocate a foul sewer crossing the land, it reduced its overall
offer by a further £50,000, to reflect the cost of this work. Vendors keen to
sell might have been willing to resolve such a valuation dispute by compromise. However, since the beneficiary of the trust was still young, the
trustees were in no rush to accept what they considered a low offer for the
land. Instead, they decided to wait, if necessary for many years, until they
can persuade the local authority to allocate a more substantial area for
development, with its own direct access to the public highway (Adams et
al. 1994).

Knowledge of and attitude to risk

Uncertainty characterizes the development process. Landowner behaviour
is conditioned by knowledge of, and attitude to risk. Involvement by landowners in the local planning process is part of a risk-reducing strategy.
Owners who achieve a higher-value allocation through making representations on a local plan confine the risk involved in subsequent planning
applications primarily to matters of detail.

Means of acquisition and motive for ownership

Land management and development strategies are significantly affected by
the motive for ownership. Indeed, for many landowners, this is the single

most important characteristic influencing behaviour. According to Good-child & Munton (1985), the main motives for ownership are occupation, investment, making land available for others on a non-profit basis, and control. Owner-occupiers are primarily concerned with use value, but may be tempted to sell by high exchange value. Investors who purchase land and property are likely to behave more consistently than those who inherit it. This suggests that the means by which land is acquired may affect how owners respond to subsequent development opportunities. Benevolent owners, usually with extensive holdings, may be willing to make land available for non-profit making organizations such as sports clubs.

Some owners, such as manufacturing companies, may acquire land to control its future development. If land or property next door to an existing factory comes on the market, acquisition ensures that it will be readily available, if needed for future expansion. For example, in 1986, a month after a concrete-batching plant in inner Birkenhead closed and before it was formally advertised, the site was acquired by an adjacent and long-established marine and chemical engineering company, employing over 300 people. This company had no immediate plans to use the site at the time of purchase, but kept it vacant for two years, by which time business had substantially expanded. Since the site was immediately available and could be quickly developed, production was increased with the minimum of delay (Adams et al. 1994).

Relevance of the behaviourist approach

The strength of the behaviourist approach is that it begins to explain why the land management and development strategies pursued by individual owners are so diverse. However, it fails to provide a sound theoretical framework for categorizing landowners or predicting their behaviour. Moreover, their varied behaviour clearly reflects a greater range of characteristics than the six identified by Goodchild & Munton (1985). For instance, land management and development strategies at least in the public sector, are significantly influenced by political and institutional factors (see Ch. 7). A more comprehensive statement of landowner characteristics is therefore needed before this approach can account for the diversity of landowner behaviour as a whole. This may prove difficult without a stronger theoretical base. In this respect, the behaviourist approach contrasts sharply with the structuralist approach which is richly grounded in theory.

A structuralist approach to landowner classification

Massey & Catalano (1978) regard land ownership in Great Britain as a capitalist institution. From a Marxist perspective, they investigate the effect of private land ownership on the structure and development of capitalist society. As a result, they identify three distinct types of private landowner differing from each other in their rôle within the overall structure of social formation and critically, by their function in the process of production. These three types are former landed property, industrial land ownership and financial land ownership. Massey & Catalano (1978) estimate that various state agencies own about 19 per cent of land in Great Britain, but do not consider statutory land ownership in any depth. Instead, a structuralist analysis of local authority land ownership undertaken by Montgomery (1987), could be extended to statutory land ownership as a whole. These four types of land ownership will now be considered in turn.

Former landed property

Former landed property consists of the remaining holdings of the landed gentry and aristocracy, the church and the crown. In each case, extensive and predominantly rural estates are retained not purely for investment purposes, but as part of a wider social rôle. As Massey & Catalano (1978: 79) contend: "For the landed aristocracy (as for the gentry) landownership is not simply a question of owning land, but of owning specific tracts of land with which they have a historical and/or social connection." They acknowledge that former landed property could also include other historic landowners such as Oxbridge colleges, who they excluded for lack of sufficient information.

In certain locations, former landed property can still have a significant influence on urban development. For example, in Morley, a growth area in West Yorkshire five miles south of Leeds, substantial areas in and around the existing town have been owned by the Earls of Dartmouth since the early 18th century. Dartmouth Park, the largest in Morley, was given to the town by one of the present Earl's ancestors. When a new local plan was proposed for Morley in the early 1980s, it became inevitable that significant areas of Dartmouth land would be proposed for new residential or industrial use. However, successful representations made by the Earl's agents ensured that when the plan was finally adopted in 1986, the extent of Dartmouth land allocated for development was much higher than originally proposed by the local planning authority. Indeed, 54 per cent of land on major sites allocated for residential development by the adopted plan, and 31 per cent of that allocated for industrial development, turned out to be in Dartmouth ownership (Adams 1987).

Two examples from Cambridge illustrate different attitudes that may be held by landed gentry towards development. An owner of a 1,400ha estate east of Cambridge had little desire to see further change in the estate village and therefore regarded future development as a very low priority. Any builder seeking options on the land was despatched with considerable speed. In contrast, family trustees of an equally large estate to the south of Cambridge commented in detail on the consultation local plan and submitted a series of planning applications to secure the release of land for a major hotel and shopping development (Adams & May 1991).

Industrial land ownership

Industrial landowners consist of owner-occupier farmers and manufacturing industrial capital, both of whom need to own land as condition of production. Land usually represents the bulk of capital invested by owner-occupier farmers. Although the value of such land is greatly enhanced if sold for development, not all owner-farmers welcome such an opportunity. Three examples were found in Cambridge and Surrey Heath, where owner-occupier farmers argued strongly for their land to be released for development. By way of contrast, one nursery gardener in owner-occupation actually objected when the local authority proposed to allocate part of the land for housing development, since it would undermine the viability of the remaining business. Most manufacturing companies own the land on which actual production takes place. Major manufacturing companies are more likely to hold extensive reserves of land for future expansion, while minor manufacturing companies tend to purchase land only when needed for immediate development (Adams et al. 1994).

Although Massey & Catalano (1978) include the construction sector within industrial land ownership, they suggest that the largest contractors and developers not only hold land as a condition of production, but in many cases have a financial stake in rising land values. Ball (1983) argues that the well established house-builders are able to act as both industrial and financial landowners, making profit from both construction turnover and land dealing. Subsequently, Short et al. (1986) found in Central Berkshire, an area of rapid growth, that a much greater proportion on profit was likely to derive from turnover than from land dealing, owing to intense competition among builders to acquire development sites. Indeed, if planning consent is likely, most landowners will be reluctant to sell for below full development value.

Financial land ownership

The main financial landowners are property companies, pension funds and insurance companies, to whom land ownership provides an opportunity to profit from development or from holding land as a long-term asset. Financial land ownership is as much the product of the capitalist mode of production as industrial land ownership, but in contrast to industrial landowners, financial landowners are motivated by the investment potential of land and property. Financial land ownership has expanded substantially since 1945, especially in value terms. This expansion has been concentrated on office and retail property in established commercial centres (see Ch. 2). Financial landowners demonstrate the most consistent approach to planning and development of any of the four categories in the structuralist classification. Since they are concerned almost exclusively with maximizing the exchange value of their holdings, financial owners are likely to seek the highest-value use for which planning permission can be obtained, or for which land might be allocated in a local plan.

Statutory land ownership

In the 20th century, statutory land ownership expanded significantly as the state became more involved in social and economic life. Central and local government, nationalized industries and statutory undertakers all became important landowners. Municipal land ownership grew rapidly from the 1950s to the late 1970s as slums were cleared, new houses built and new roads constructed. By 1982, for example, almost 58 per cent of land in Manchester was owned freehold by the City Council, with a further 7.5 per cent owned by other public bodies (Kivell & McKay 1988).

Montgomery (1987) contends that statutory land ownership can best be explained as means to achieve the potentially contradictory purposes of the state rather than as a end in itself. In particular, he identifies five main functions for which local authorities hold land. The first two may be considered as production functions: to make development land available to the development industry and to make industrial land and premises available to manufacturing and service firms. The third function, that of consumption, involves making land available for uses such as housing, education, health, recreation and social services. Within the fourth function, that of circulation, land is provided for general interest uses such as conservation and for more specific purposes like transport and public utilities. Finally, local authorities also hold land as investment, securing the full market returns on sales and leases. Within this final function, local authorities may also acquire land in anticipation of future development.

Local authorities and statutory development agencies are often involved in buying land suitable for economic development, undertaking servicing and reclamation and making it available to industrial users or developers. Ellesmere Port & Neston Borough Council, for example, has gained considerable experience in purchasing derelict or despoiled land and recycling it for new industrial development. In one notable case, it bought a contaminated tip of 1.4 ha for £25,000 in the early 1980s. Over the next two years, it cleared and levelled the site at a cost of £450,000 and put piled foundations in for £78,000. In both cases, the work was fully funded by derelict land grant. Construction of 19 small industrial units then began. These were funded mainly by a European regional development grant and £200,000 from the urban programme, topped up by money from the council's own resources. All 19 units were successfully let, verifying how reclamation and development by statutory landowners can help meet the accommodation needs of small businesses (Adams et al. 1994). The significance of such development promotion is explored in more detail in Chapter 7.

As Montgomery (1987) points out, conflict over the use and exchange values may occur internally within local authorities, if a proposal to sell municipal land to the highest bidder undermines planning policies. The example of a school site owned by Cambridgeshire County Council on the edge of a village east of Cambridge, demonstrates that such proposals do not always succeed. The County Council's Director of Land and Buildings, attempting to maximize the site's development potential, objected to its inclusion within the green belt in the consultation local plan. The Director of Land and Buildings unsuccessfully sought to persuade planning officers that the natural boundary of the green belt should follow the external perimeter of the school. This would have enabled development to take place on the school playing fields, if the school were ever declared surplus. No subsequent representations were made by the Director of Land and Buildings, owing to the lack of any immediate prospect of development and to the remote possibility of winning political support.

In other circumstances, financial pressures, or the immediate prospect of substantial development gains, may persuade local authorities to view such opportunities differently. Montgomery (1987) contends that Sheffield City Council became a property speculator in the early 1970s, taking advantage of conditions created by the national property boom. Despite the variety of reasons for which local authorities own land, he suggests that "At its crudest, the land acquisition and disposal strategies of local authorities are locked into the structure of capitalist societies, the operation of the capitalist land market and the institutional structure of property relations" (p. 50).

Relevance of the structuralist approach

The structuralist classification is based on the function of the landowner in the process of production and is not easily extended to the processes of planning and development. Apart from the particular case of financial land-owners, diversity in landowner behaviour is as evident within the structuralist categories as between them. For as Healey et al. (1988) point out, interests in land are multifaceted and conflict-ridden rather than necessarily class-based. Alliances may be formed between fractions of capital and fractions of labour. In the West Midlands, for example, new employment development in the green belt, in the vicinity of the National Exhibition Centre, was supported in the late 1970s and early 1980s by an alliance of capital interests, who wished to make profits, and labour interests expressed through local political leaders, who needed to establish new places to work. Moreover, certain actors possess a multiplicity of interests. For example, owner-occupier farmers may have stewardship interests as landowners as well as production interests as land-users. As a result, the structuralist approach cannot easily account for the complexities of land-use, land ownership and land development.

Active and passive behaviour

Although neither the behaviourist approach, which concentrates on owner **characteristics**, nor the structuralist approach, which classifies owners by their **function** in the process of production, fully recognize the diversity of landowner behaviour as a whole, they each reveal important factors that motivate individual landowners. Such motives encourage certain land-owners to pursue more active land management and development strategies than others. From a practical perspective, the distinction between active and passive behaviour is important, since it turns the spotlight from characteristics and functions to the empirical **outcomes** of their strategies.

As Cameron et al. (1988: 124–5) contend: "Major owners of urban land appear to utilise their land holdings in a variety of ways. In both the public and private sectors, some seek to maximize revenue by active participation in the land market releasing and buying surplus land as appropriate conditions arise. Others hold excess land as a measure of coping with future growth without the accompanying need for future land acquisition or relocation of production elsewhere. And others appear to have no explicit policy for their surplus land." The rest of the chapter therefore examines the distinction between active and passive behaviour in order to highlight typical contributions that landowners make to urban planning and the development process.

Active landowners

Active landowners are those who develop their own land, enter into joint venture development or make their land available for others to develop. Active landowners may try to overcome site constraints to make land more marketable or suitable for development. This could involve applying for planning permission, appealing against a planning refusal, or tackling problematic physical or infrastructural constraints. Active behaviour may be motivated by political concerns, or the prospect of financial reward, or the desire by land-users such as manufacturing companies to meet their own land needs. Active owners who obtain planning permission, tackle development constraints or offer their land for sale without undue influence from developers, make a significant contribution to the development process.

Historical patterns of urban development owe much to active behaviour by landowners in the past. As Kivell & McKay (1988: 170) state: "there is a small, but impressive, body of literature within the mainstream of urban geography which stresses the importance of land tenure in determining the timing, direction and nature of urban morphology." However, such influences are not merely historic since active landowners continue to shape the development of towns and cities. In Cheshire, for example, one active owner of agricultural land on the edge of Crewe has already started to prepare some 14 ha for the eventual extension of the adjacent business park.

An agricultural tenancy on the site was terminated with full compensation in 1989. Discussions have been held with prospective developers. In due course, it is intended to submit a planning application or seek the allocation of the site for business development in the next review of the Crewe local plan. In the 1980s, many such owners made proposals for entire new settlements on their land (Lock & Shostak 1985, Lock 1989, Hall 1989a) Few were actually successful in obtaining planning permission. In the Cambridge area, eight such proposals were refused permission by the Secretary of State for the Environment in 1992, following a lengthy public inquiry. Nevertheless, landowners active in the development process tend to be closely involved during the preparation of statutory local plans (see Ch. 11). Active landowners who achieve land allocations to their own advantage, help to determine the pattern of future urban development.

Passive landowners

In contrast, passive landowners take no particular steps to market or develop their land, even though they may intend to do so in the distant future. They may respond, or fail to respond, to offers from potential developers, but otherwise they retain land without development. They rarely attempt to overcome constraints in order to make land more marketable or suitable for development. Passive owners therefore contribute little to the development process, and nothing at all, if they refuse to sell land that has development potential. Indeed, as compulsory purchase is rare, owners of land with development potential who refuse to sell, act as constraint in the development process. Some owners who are willing to sell, but only on restricted terms and conditions (for example, by offering limited leaseholds but not freeholds) may also impede development, if potential purchasers are discouraged from making offers (Adams et al. 1988).

Passive ownership may arise for various reasons. Chisholm & Kivell (1987) draw attention to the low holding costs of keeping land vacant, and to the use of such land as loan collateral. Howes (1989) suggests that owners may keep land off the market if they are uncertain about their future needs or unaware of the likely marketability or value of the land. An owner may retain land for development in the distant future or may have acquired land in the expectation of a substantial rise in its value. Some owners may be under no immediate pressure to sell, while others may prefer the amenity value of land in its undeveloped state to the monetary receipts from sale. The Civic Trust (1988) highlights the apathy of many owners, both public and public sectors, which allows urban sites to become vacant and unsightly. where economic decline and restructuring has been most intense, passive attitudes to land management and development are particularly evident among those major manufacturing and other production interests who no longer require the extensive areas of land, on which their prosperity previously depended (Adams et al. 1994).

Although government policy has concentrated almost exclusively on passive behaviour in the public sector, research reveals the existence of widespread passive ownership in the private sector. For example, many large manufacturing companies maintain historic land reserves, often substantially in excess of likely future needs. Indeed, national and international companies with a substantial portfolio of land holdings in many locations, tend to ignore the potential of relatively small areas alongside existing factories. Such land may eventually be released following corporate restructuring, internal reappraisal of future space needs, or, in the case of former nationalized industries, as a result of privatization. A rapid rise in land prices, as occurred in the late 1980s, will provide greater incentive for passive owners to sell.

On landed estates, inheritance may activate ownership. In mid-Cheshire, for example, redundant farm buildings on one large agricultural estate owned by the same family since 1850, remained derelict until the son took over on the death of his father in 1989. While the father was alive, the estate continued to be run as a traditional agricultural venture. However, the son is keen to diversify, and intends to redevelop the redundant farm buildings for commercial or industrial use to generate income for new agricultural plant and buildings (Adams et al. 1994). Passive owners may therefore be activated by a change in circumstances.

Conclusion

This chapter has emphasized that urban planning and the development process is centrally concerned with the ownership, as well as the use of land. Development prospects are significantly influenced by the motives and behaviour of owners, particularly as the state undertakes compulsory purchase only as a last resort. Whereas active landowners may welcome or indeed initiate development, passive owners can undermine development potential. Moreover, as explored in more detail in Part 3, most active landowners participate enthusiastically in local plan preparation in order to seek the most beneficial allocation for their land. Active and passive behaviour thus represent the empirical outcomes of land management and development strategies, which themselves may be shaped by specific landowner characteristics or functions, identified in the behaviourist or structuralist classifications.

CHAPTER SIX

Perspectives from the developer, investor, and development professions

In the British context, the term "development plan" is a misnomer. Statutory plans do not plan development, but primarily allocate land for housing, employment and other uses. Whether and when development actually takes place depends almost exclusively on the private sector, since development by the public sector (low-cost housing, schools, industrial estates, etc.) is now much reduced. Yet, by building roads, servicing sites, undertaking reclamation, selling land in its ownership, and by other similar types of action, the public sector influences the viability of private-sector development.

Apart from landowners, the most important actors in the private sector are those who undertake speculative development, those who invest in it and their professional advisers. The strategies, interests and actions of each of these actors are explored in this chapter. Attention is first given to residential development and subsequently to commercial development. The chapter examines how development products reflect the growth and present structure of the industry. This is illustrated by case studies. It suggests that, despite popular misconception, property development is not necessarily a licence to print money, but a highly competitive and risky business. Indeed, three of the development companies examined in the case studies experienced severe financial difficulties.

Although planners and developers have different priorities, the chapter contends that they are locked together in a state of mutual dependence. Unlike developers, urban planners do not seek to profit from development, but aim instead to promote efficiency, equity and sustainability through intervention in the development process. It is therefore ironic that planners rely so heavily on the unpredictable and volatile nature of speculative development for implementation. As a result, urban plans tend to incorporate market criteria implicitly or explicitly into their preparation, while private developers expect the state both to exercise "strategic market management" of land-use change (Healey 1992b), and to protect them from unreasonable behaviour by other actors, such as environmental groups or landowners. In this context, it is not surprising that the chapter reveals keen participation by developers, investors and their professional advisers in the planning system.

The residential development sector

Growth and present structure

The growth of speculative residential development can be traced to the early-19th century, when industrial methods of building replaced traditional craft production (Clarke 1992). Speculative house-building for rent, dominant throughout the 19th century, declined sharply in the decade before the First World War. After 1920, social and economic benefits encouraged the rapid expansion of speculative house-building for sale. Four of the five top building contracting firms in the 1980s (Wimpey, Laing, Costain and Taylor–Woodrow) originated as speculative house-builders between the wars. Each subsequently diversified into civil engineering and general contracting (Ball 1983).

In the postwar period, owner occupation increased from 26 per cent of households in 1946 to 68 per cent in 1993. The speculative house-building industry underwent rapid expansion. Small local builders (such as William Leech founded in the North East in 1932) grew into national companies. Barratts, which started in 1958, again in the North East, became at one time the largest UK house-builder. The house-building industry still contains many small builders, but is now dominated by a few very large builders. Ball (1983) shows that house-builders with an output of over 250 units a year increased their market share from 25 to 50 per cent during the 1970s. He contends that the relative growth in importance of larger producers can be explained by their extensive access to finance capital, often made available by parent companies. By 1979, four of the twenty largest firms were owned by major independent contractors (such as Wimpey and Taylor–Woodrow) and eight were subsidiaries of large conglomerates (such as Broseley and Bovis). Some of the eight independent companies, including Barratts, had raised substantial capital on the Stock Exchange.

In contrast, Ball (1983) explains the relative decline of small and medium-size builders by their dependence for capital on banks, which restrict the availability of credit, particularly in a downturn. Small and medium-size house-builders are therefore unable to profit from booms and slumps in the same way as large house-builders who, by arranging their own finance, can buy land cheaply during slumps and are well placed to sell houses early in a boom.

By 1985, capital in the house-building industry had become highly concentrated, with the top three builders (Barratt, Wimpey and Tarmac) then accounting for 18 per cent of all output and the top 12 for 36 per cent. Concentration of capital has subsequently increased. For example, Beazer, who acquired Second City, Monsell Youell, William Leech and French Kier, replaced Barratt in the top three in 1991. Tarmac merged with McLean, while Trafalgar House, the parent company of Ideal Homes, bought Comben. In the early-1990s, several medium-size builders fell victim to the recession.

Davis Build, for instance, a specialist inner-city builder, which had grown from humble beginnings in 1974 to reach a £60m turnover by 1989, went into receivership in 1990.

Yet, the severity of the recession affected even the largest house-builders. In 1991, Barratts, the most rapidly growing house-builder in the 1970s and early-1980s recorded its first ever pre-tax loss, at £106 million. This led to the departure of the group chairman and chief executive and the recall of the founder, Sir Lawrie Barratt, from retirement. In the same year, Lovells recorded a pre-tax loss of £46 million. As a result, the company pulled out of Spain and the United States, sold its Scottish operations, and closed down Lovell Urban Renewal, which had previously gained a reputation for innovative inner-city development. To survive, Lovells negotiated a major restructuring of its banking facilities, under which the value of its land bank was written down to more realistic levels. Beazer, which had expanded so rapidly in the 1980s, ran into difficulties in 1991, and agreed to a £351m takeover by the Hanson Group to enable its debt to be refinanced, while keeping the company together.

Land supply for residential development

House-building is thus an increasingly concentrated but highly turbulent industry, whose fortunes are inextricably linked to the national economic cycle. Earlier studies (Ball 1983, Rydin 1986, Short et al. 1986) not only demonstrated the economic and financial instability of the industry but also emphasized the importance to house-builders of land supply. As Goodchild & Munton (1985: 69) point out: "The developer needs to acquire land regularly to maintain a production flow of dwellings and other properties, and to retain the full employment of his labour force and other factors of production . . . the sites must either have planning consent already or the developer must anticipate that planning consent will be granted before he wants to commence development." Urban planning is perhaps of greater importance to house-building than to any other corporate sector, since it regulates the supply of land, which house-builders regard as an essential raw material.

According to Smyth (1984), the minimum period from the purchase of a residential development site to completion is generally three years. For larger estates, constructed in phases, it may be longer. Sites therefore need to be held in a land bank for at least two to three years. Land banking can be viewed as a strategic response to uncertainty in the house-building industry (Bramley 1989). According to Ball (1983: 148): "A useful way of conceptualizing the nature of a house-builder's land bank is to treat it as a portfolio of land just as a commercial bank or other financial institution has a portfolio of assets. In both cases, the portfolio consists of a spread of high-yielding but potentially risky assets (in the builder's case these will usually be sites of white land[1]) and safer but less profitable assets that can ensure a steady cash flow and corporate stability. Portfolios also have a temporal profile consisting of assets with different dates of maturity and profit realization. In general, a land bank portfolio spreads risks and takes the pain out of speculation." House-builders usually have many times the area under option or conditional contract (see Ch. 2) than owned freehold. For example, Ball (1983) discovered one company that had 15 times as much capital invested in options as it had in directly purchased land.

Land banking and urban planning

Few companies now tie up land indiscriminately through options and conditional contracts, relentlessly pursuing its release through applications and appeals. Although such an unsophisticated strategy may well have been pursued in the past, successful house-builders now use the planning process to their own advantage by seeking to influence policy formulation. The more sophisticated house-builders target their options and conditional contracts on land that they are confident will be released in future statutory development plans, if necessary as a result of their own representations at the appropriate time (Adams et al. 1992). This approach was encouraged in the 1980s by central government policies for housing land release in the 1980s. According to Rydin (1986), these represented a new form of corporatist decision-making that aimed to offer house-builders some control over the release of house-building land. For example, at local level, the House-Builders Federation became heavily involved on its members' behalf in land availability studies undertaken jointly with local planning authorities.

Sophisticated use of the statutory local planning process (see Ch. 8) is illustrated by the involvement of two house-builders, Brinson and Pelican[2], in the preparation of the first and second reviews of the Ashford Local Plan in Kent. This revealed clear attempts to influence the planning of future residential development in the town. Brinson Developments, commented during the preparation of the original Ashford Local Plan in 1982, and made three site-specific representations on the first review of the plan in 1987. These sought to promote two sites in which it held interests, and to prevent the development of a third site, owned by its competitor, Pelican Homes, and initially favoured by the local planning authority.

In 1987, a late representation to the first review was also made by Brinson on an area of land, known as Willesborough Lees. This land had just been bought by the company, having been previously identified by the local authority in a policy choices report in 1985. Two other residential developers with contiguous interests in land also made representations. At the first review, the inspector adjudged that the development was acceptable in principle, but that environmental problems prevented its release at that time. However, in the second review in 1992, approximately half of the Brinson land together with that of the two other developers was allocated for housing, subject to the approval of a development brief.

Pelican acquired 130 ha of land at Park Farm, Ashford, after it was identified as suitable for development by the local planning authority in the first review consultation plan. Despite objections from many local residents, Pelican supported the authority at the local plan inquiry, offering to prepare a development brief for the site. This was intended to demonstrate how arrangements for servicing, infrastructure and open space could benefit the local area. In the second review of the local plan, Pelican Homes sought to have its land at Park Farm, not previously allocated, added to the designated site. Four hectares were subsequently included by the local planning authority, with the balance of land reserved as a green wedge. The preparation of statutory local plans thus presents well informed house-builders in an area with an opportunity to influence the supply of development land for some years to come. One of the first house-builders in the South East to recognize this was Charles Church.

Charles Church: a case study of a residential developer

In 1966, Charles and Susanna Church built and sold one house in Camberley, Surrey. They invested the proceeds in four more houses. In the next 21 years, they created a company with an annual turnover of £74 million and an annual output approaching 700 houses. Charles Church Developments, then the eighteenth largest house-builder in the UK, was floated on the Stock Exchange in 1987, with the Church family retaining a majority holding. According to Chartered Surveyor Weekly (1987: 13), the formula which had guaranteed the company's success in the past remained the same: Charles Church " . . . builds houses in the prosperous South East and goes for the top end of the market with an average price of over £110,000. The emphasis is on quality and interestingly, on sites that have special appeal – often with mature trees, for example."

In the 1980s, Charles Church Developments devoted considerable energy to ensuring a continuous supply of building land. In 1987, the company strengthened its land and planning group with the appointment of several new staff, including four new regional land directors. It took on more chartered town planners to identify sites, influence plan preparation, and monitor plan implementation. As Figure 6.1 shows, between March and September 1987, the company's planning staff achieved considerable success in improving its land supply position.

The company's immediate target was to build up a land bank of over 20,000 plots as quickly as possible. In the interim report in May 1988, Charles Church stated that: "We have consolidated our hold on building land within the South East with several purchases on very good terms and we have won six planning appeals, three of them of major importance. Given that demand is reaching new levels assisted by low interest rates and low income tax rates, and that the planners and politicians appear to want to stifle further housing growth in the South East, our strong land bank assures us of a very important share of housing production for a long time to come." (Charles Church Developments plc 1988).

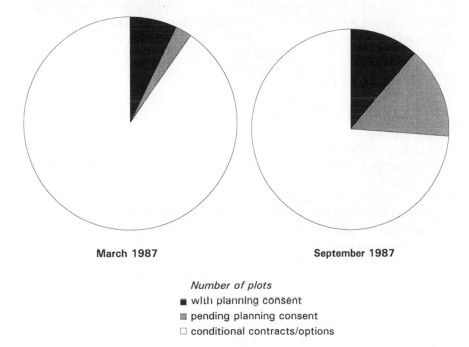

March 1987   **September 1987**

Number of plots
■ with planning consent
▨ pending planning consent
☐ conditional contracts/options

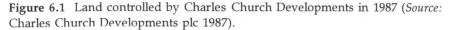

Figure 6.1 Land controlled by Charles Church Developments in 1987 (*Source:* Charles Church Developments plc 1987).

The 1980s saw a rapid expansion in pre-tax company profits from £2.41 million in 1982/3 to £6.26 million in 1984/5, £11.9 million in 1986/7, and £18.5 million in 1987/8. However, the company retained much of its pre-tax profits to finance the programme of expansion, and consequently paid relatively low dividends. On earnings per share of 3.9p after tax in 1985/6, no dividend was paid, while the following year, earnings per share of 9.5p produced a dividend of only 1p per share. In 1987/8, a dividend of 4p per share was paid on earnings per share of 13.4p.

In May 1989, Charles Church, disappointed with the company's stock market rating and believing that he could achieve better results for share-holders and employees, repurchased the company from the Stock Exchange. Shortly thereafter, Charles Church himself was killed in a flying accident and his wife took over as chairman. Subsequently, the company was hit extremely hard by the recession, recording pre-tax losses of £50.3 million in 1989/90 and £18.1 million in 1990/1. By early 1991, the company owed a total of nearly £130 million to its 65 banks.

A new chief executive was appointed in January 1991 and a far-reaching restructuring package agreed with the banks in August 1991. This effectively saved Charles Church Developments from receivership and laid the basis for the company's eventual return to profitability. Under the restructuring, the Church family shares were surrendered and its loans written off by the banks. In turn, the banks swapped their loans for almost 80 per cent of the equity of the company, with the remaining equity divided between existing preference shareholders and the new management team. A new independent chairman was appointed to replace Susanna Church. All regional offices were closed and staff numbers reduced from 350 to about 100.

Although the company retained its large land bank which, at the beginning of 1992 still stood at approximately 10,000 plots, the value of the land was substantially written down to below market levels, providing a useful investment for the future. Charles Church Developments was thus saved from receivership by the patience of its bankers and their trust in the quality and marketability of its product. In mid-1991, Charles Church Developments again started to acquire land, and by early-1992 had 21 different sites under construction. The founder's emphasis on environmental and construction quality was retained. The new management team expected that the company would soon return to profitability and would thereafter expand again.

The involvement of Charles Church in the Surrey Heath Local Plan Between 1981 and 1985, during the preparation of the Surrey Heath Local Plan (discussed in detail in Ch. 8) which covered the area where Charles Church had first started in business and where his head office was still located, the company was among the most rapidly growing house-builders in the South-East. Surrey Heath Borough Council initiated debate on a new local plan in 1981 by publishing an issues report that identified 12 possible locations to help accommodate 6,200 new homes over the plan period. Through consultants, Charles Church Developments submitted detailed written comments on 11 of these sites. The representations sought to highlight the advantages of any land already under option to Charles Church, and to demonstrate that provision could easily be made for 7,000 dwellings or, indeed, for a considerably higher figure.

Following the issues report, the company attempted to acquire as many options as possible on the 12 sites. When the draft local plan was published in 1982, Charles Church had already obtained options on five areas of land totalling 55 ha, either within or immediately adjacent to the original 12 sites. The company submitted planning applications on all these sites in 1981 or 1982 and, to press its case further, made informal representations on the draft plan in early 1982. However, since these applications were considered premature by the local planning authority, none was approved and, in the deposit plan, published later in 1982, only the site owned by the company at Bagshot was proposed for development. Charles Church Developments responded by submitting both planning appeals and a series of formal objections to the local plan.

For the local plan inquiry, the company appointed a formidable professional team. A national firm of planning consultants, instructed to challenge the council's approach to housing land availability, was supported with specialist highway advice by the senior partner of a London-based firm of chartered engineers and, with knowledge of the local housing market, by a well known local estate agent. A barrister was appointed to co-ordinate the presentation and act as advocate at the inquiry. The professional team submitted representations not only to uphold the merits of sites already under option to the company but also to cast doubt on the feasibility of developing one of the major sites preferred by the council in which competitors of Charles Church had begun to take an interest.

The local plan inquiry was held in the middle of 1983 and the inspector reported to the local planning authority early in 1984. Of the six sites on which Charles Church Developments had submitted formal objections, the company was supported by the inspector on three. Nevertheless, only one of these sites (discussed below) was allocated for development in the adopted plan in 1985, and that was shown only for reserve housing. This was despite further protestations from the company when the proposed modifications to the plan had been published by the local planning authority in May 1984.

However, the adoption of the Surrey Heath Local Plan never acquired the sense of finality with Charles Church that it may have done with the local planning authority. A 7 ha site, owned freehold by Charles Church, illustrates this well. The site lay in an area of scattered dwellings and farms just beyond the built-up edge of Lightwater. In 1981, Charles Church Developments submitted two planning applications for residential development. When both were refused, the company appealed to the Secretary of State for the Environment. Although the appeal inspector felt on balance that permission should be granted, the Secretary of State did not accept this recommendation and dismissed the appeals.

Meanwhile, in order to strengthen its position, the company had submitted a formal objection against the failure of the local planning authority to allocate the site for residential development in the Surrey Heath Local Plan. The inspector at the local plan inquiry, taking account of the recommendations made by the previous inspector at the planning appeal, recommended that the site should be allocated for reserve housing in the local plan. This recommendation was accepted by the local planning authority and the site was withdrawn from the green belt when the local plan was adopted in 1985.

Any belief that the local planning authority may have held that reserve housing meant much longer-term development was certainly not shared by

Charles Church Developments. Two years after the adoption of the local plan, a further planning application was submitted and, on its refusal, an appeal was again made to the Secretary of State for the Environment. Despite the short period since the adoption of the plan, both the inspector at this appeal and subsequently the Secretary of State for the Environment, agreed with Charles Church that an insufficient supply of housing land remained available. The appeal was therefore allowed. The local authority attempted to overturn this decision in the High Court, but without success. The well researched and professionally backed submissions that the company had made over several years, at both appeals and local plan inquiry, therefore reaped significant dividends in enabling the site to move forward from the speculative to the immediate part of the company's land bank.

Statutory local plans have since become a more important part of the planning system (see Ch. 8). The early example of Charles Church, whose traditional attempts to secure the release of land through the development control process were supplemented by extensive involvement in local plan preparation, has now been followed by many medium-size and most large house-builders throughout the UK.

The commercial development sector

Growth

Although speculative residential development was well established before the Second World War, speculative commercial development remained rare (Whitehouse 1964). Most manufacturing companies owned rather than rented their factories and head offices, in many cases custom-built to their particular requirements. Commercial and industrial development was undertaken by individual entrepreneurs or by companies building for their own occupation (Ambrose & Colenutt 1975). Service employment was of only limited importance outside the City of London. Indeed, as Daniels (1977: 261) notes: "The emergence of an office industry with distinctive locational and organizational attributes has been one of the most significant features of postwar economic change in advanced societies."

After 1945, individual entrepreneurs began to buy up potential redevelopment sites, many of which had been affected by war damage, in anticipation that building licences controlling the supply of building materials would no longer be required. These entrepreneurs were well placed to take advantage of the abolition of building licences in 1954, through promoting speculative development designed to meet the growing demand for office and retail floor-space. Development was mainly financed by insurance companies through fixed low-interest mortgages and loans (Dubben & Sayce 1991). In a classic text, Marriot (1967) captures the spirit of the wheeler-dealer property tycoon of the 1950s, listing over 100 ordinary individuals, each of whom became property millionaires in a few years.

By the 1970s, most of the firms founded by such tycoons had matured into investment and development companies, and many had been taken over or had diversified. City Centre Properties, for example, founded by the flamboyant partnership of Charles Clore and Jack Cotton, was acquired by Land Securities in 1966. Trafalgar House, a small development firm founded by Nigel Broakes in the late-1950s, grew substantially and diversified by taking over companies involved in building contracting (Trollope & Colls and Cementation) house building (New Ideal Homes) transportation (Cunard) and even newspapers (at one stage owning the Daily Express) (Ball 1983). The company founder went on to become Sir Nigel Broakes, Chairman of London Docklands Development Corporation, reflecting the eventual acceptance of such property tycoons by the establishment.

By the 1980s, such mature development companies were characterized by caution in their approach to commercial property development. Many financial institutions started to switch investment from property to gilts and equities (see Ch. 2) but others began to undertake direct development. Some commentators believed that room no longer existed for the single property entrepreneur. As the next section explains, the institutional structure of commercial and industrial development changed again in the 1980s, proving such belief mistaken.

Present structure

No strict division exists between developers and investors in commercial property, since development may well be undertaken by financial institutions and investment by mature development companies. Any classification of those involved in development is unlikely to be facilitated by distinctions based purely on external appearances since such rudimentary categories as "property companies" and "investment trusts" are difficult to establish or defend in practice (McNamara 1983). Instead, McNamara contends that it is necessary to classify developers conceptually in terms of their development purpose, revealed by their tactics in buying and selling rights in land throughout the process of development. For example, from research in central Edinburgh, he shows that few property companies own rights in land four years prior to the act of development and that most, but by no means all, have sold such rights four years after the act of development. In contrast, about half the insurance companies examined owned such rights four years prior to development and most, but again not all, retained such rights four years after development.

On this basis, McNamara produces a ninefold classification of land developers, by distinguishing between those who hold rights in land on a short- and long-term basis both before and after development, and by subdividing long-term holders into owner-occupiers and landlords leasing out property. This is shown in Table 6.1.

Table 6.1 Classification of developers by purpose of development.

Before development	After development		
	Short-term	Long-term (leasing out)	Long-term (owning & occupying)
Short-term	Entrepreneurial builder	Land developer–investor	Developer–user
Long-term (leasing out)	Asset clearing, probably investment switch	Property improver/rentier	Expanding developer–user
Long-term (owning & occupying)	Capitalizing assets	Change in returns from property	Owner-occupier/ developer

Source: McNamara (1983)

McNamara (1983) explicitly excludes from his classification those who speculate in land, without undertaking development. However, if rights in land are resold without development, it may not be immediately clear whether they were initially acquired for the purposes of speculation or development, especially if circumstances change in the meantime. Indeed, the distinction between traders and developers is not necessarily sharper than that between developers and investors, particularly since those who start by trading in property may subsequently move into development, and may eventually retain completed developments for investment.

By acknowledging this spectrum of behaviour, but retaining McNamara's (1983) emphasis on tactics on buying and selling land as a basis for classifying developers, it is possible to identify four broad groupings in commercial and industrial development (excluding owner-occupiers) whose conceptual basis is matched by practical experience. These are:

(a) Dealers: those who buy and sell rights in land on a short-term basis, without undertaking development.

(b) Developer/dealers: those who buy and sell rights in land on a short-term basis, with or without undertaking development (known also as trader/developers).

(c) Developer/investors: those who buy rights in land usually on a short-term basis, sometimes selling shortly after development, but usually retaining for long-term investment.

(d) Investor/developers: those who either hold rights in land on a long-term basis prior to development or acquire them shortly before development and who, after development, retain such rights for long-term investments.

Each of these four groups will now be examined in more detail.

Dealers Dealing in property often precedes expansion into development of property. Dealers continuously buy and sell property on a short-term basis, without undertaking development. Dealers profit by adding value between purchase and sale, for example, by restructuring a lease, improving a planning consent, or assembling a development site. Some dealers trade not only in individual properties but also in companies whose stock-market listing undervalues their property assets. Such dealers are pure asset strippers, acquiring a company, breaking up its portfolio, and selling it on to third parties. To dealers, property is thus merely a commodity, to be bought cheaply and sold more expensively.

Mountleigh provides a telling example of the rise and fall of a property dealer. Mountleigh was formed out of two struggling textile companies, Mountain Mills and Leigh Mills, based in Stanningley, Leeds. When textile manufacture finally ceased in 1981, the company's main asset was its industrial landholdings, which past directors had instinctively hoarded. The company's energetic chairman, Tony Clegg, had grand ambitions for Mountleigh, and led it out of textiles into property dealing. Within four years, Clegg had built Mountleigh up into one of the top 25 property companies in the UK, principally by trading. Pre-tax profits rose from £2.5 million in 1985, to £9.2 million in 1986, £33 million in 1987 and reached £71 million in 1988 on a turnover of £530m, of which all but £20 million was attributable to property trading.

Mountleigh's approach and philosophy was quite clear As Clegg stated "We specialize in making money and we will move into any sector of property where we think we can make money. We see ourselves as traders in property, people who can see an angle. We look very hard to find the things that maybe other people have missed . . . We're working on at least six buildings where we are restructuring the leases, either to get them to fall in together, or to get vacant possession to prepare the sites for redevelopment or refurbishment" (quoted in Roberts 1987). According to Foster (1986), under Clegg, Mountleigh became "one of the largest, most innovative, international property and trading groups". In 1987, Mountleigh surprisingly bought a chain of Spanish department stores, as a result of which its employees increased from 77 to 9,500. In the long term, Clegg intended to switch Mountleigh from a trading into a development company, but he never realized his ambition.

In 1989, after a serious illness, Clegg sold his 22.5 per cent stake in Mountleigh for £70.4 million to two American financiers, Peter May and Nelson Peltz, and retired from the company. By this time, much higher interest rates meant that the golden days of property trading were over. Despite ambitious plans to expand into European property, pre-tax profits at Mountleigh declined to £29.1 million in 1989, with pre-tax losses subsequently recorded of £47 million in 1990 and £96 million in 1991. Mountleigh found itself the victim of a sharp decline in UK property values, as a result of which its properties could be sold on only at prices below the original cost of acquisition.

According to *Chartered Surveyor Weekly*, Mountleigh was in an appalling mess by late 1991, with the share price having fallen from 160p to 15p since the departure of Clegg. As a result, May and Peltz both resigned, and Sir Ian McGregor, the 79 year old former head of British Steel and British Coal took over as chairman. However, by then, even Sir Ian's immense business experience could do little to save Mountleigh. In 1992, uncertainty surrounding whether the Merry Hill Centre in Dudley (which Mountleigh had acquired in the late-1980s) would be placed on the proposed statutory register of contaminated land halted its sale for £125 million and prevented Mountleigh from repaying debts of £75.6 million then due to Swiss bond holders. The receivers were called in and Mountleigh collapsed, owing an estimated £550 million.

Developer/dealers Dealers who begin to undertake development evolve into developer/dealers, moving on from one scheme to the next without retaining any rights in land in the long-term. A developer/dealer spots the development potential of a site, acquires the rights in land, commissions the design, seeks planning consent, lets the building contract, provides project management and, on completion, sells or lets the development. If the completed development is let to tenants, the developer/dealer sells out as landlord to an investor. Although developer/dealers are not simply one-man bands, relatively few staff are directly employed since most work is contracted out to builders or professional consultants. No specialists in property management need be hired, since developments are not retained in the long-term. In good times, high rates of development profit can be achieved: in the City of London, typically between 30 per cent and 50 per cent of discounted capital value on office developments (Barras 1984). Such profits are normally reinvested by developer/dealers for rapid expansion.

By the early-1980s the demise of the developer/dealers was widely predicted. Most of the ambitious developer/dealers who originated in the 1950s and the early-1960s, including Nigel Broakes, had matured into developer/investors and had not been replaced. However, such predictions proved inaccurate. A new breed of developer/dealers emerged in the 1980s, energetic, often controversial and particularly skilled at tapping into innovative sources of development finance. This breed came to be known as the merchant developers.

These new entrepreneurs included John and Peter Beckwith, two brothers who had been educated at Harrow and had first trained respectively as an accountant and solicitor. They cleverly sold their company, London and Edinburgh Trust for £491 million at the height of the boom to a Swedish financial institution. At the time, each brother's personal holding was estimated to be worth £40 million (Goobey 1992). Trevor Osborne, who trained as a chartered surveyor in local government, built up Speyhawk, a highly regarded company with a development programme estimated to have an end-value of £500 million in the late-1980s. However, by 1992, when the property boom had collapsed, Speyhawk had slipped into financial trouble, owing 46 banks a total of £300 million. In 1993, it went into receivership. In the provinces, successful developer/dealers included John Hall, who built the Metrocentre in Gateshead, and Eddie Healey who constructed the Meadowhall shopping centre in Sheffield.

Merchant developers thrived in the mid- to late-1980s, as banks competed with one another to make development finance available on ever more advantageous terms and novel arrangements (see Ch. 3). However, the success of merchant developers in funding so many projects at once, primarily through loans repayable to banks rather than through capital raised from shareholders, left them highly vulnerable to the subsequent recession, when the demand for property dropped and the interest payments on outstanding loans rose substantially. As developer/dealers, such companies held little or no investment property, on which to fall back in hard times. Several merchant developers quickly ran into financial difficulties with Sibec, Citygrove and Broadwell Land amongst those who went into administrative receivership in 1990. However, the most spectacular collapse involved the best known merchant developer of all, Rosehaugh.

Rosehaugh, originally a small tea-shipping company, was acquired in the 1978 by a London accountant, Godfrey Bradman. He sold off the tea business and transformed Rosehaugh into a property developer that rapidly achieved national prominence through projects of a scale, or in a location, considered too risky by older established companies. Bradman was no ordinary entrepreneur but a man of far wider interests, becoming a leading campaigner for lead-free petrol and one-time chairman of Friends of the Earth. Rosehaugh prospered through a complex web of subsidiary companies and through forming powerful development alliances, most notably with Stuart Lipton's Stanhope Developments. Rosehaugh Stanhope Developments, the joint company, was responsible for the award-winning 325,000 m² Broadgate Centre in the City of London. Subsequently, Bradman and Lipton established the London Regeneration Consortium, to promote a massive £3 billion development on 54 hectares immediately north of Kings Cross and St Pancras stations.

At the height of its success, Rosehaugh was described as "the most active developer in British business history. This is the company that more than any other is building the London of the late-20th century" (Kynoch 1988). However, Rosehaugh never saw itself as merely a London developer, but also established provincial subsidiaries or development alliances to promote major regeneration projects in Birmingham, Newcastle, Sheffield and Manchester. Although it was never built, Rosehaugh Trafford, the company formed jointly with Trafford Park Estates planned a £500 million development, including 170,000 m² of speculative offices at Wharfside, opposite Salford Quays in Greater Manchester.

Throughout its life, Rosehaugh concentrated on building up its asset base which quickly increased from £18 million in 1984 to £331 million in 1988. Pre-tax profits, which were never substantial, rose to a maximum of £36 million in 1989. By that time, Rosehaugh, was already in financial difficulties owing to such rapid expansion. Bradman was forced to sell one asset after another, in a declining market, in order to repay debts due. Pre-tax losses of £165 million in 1990 and £227 million in 1991 were recorded. In December 1991, Bradman accompanied Her Majesty the Queen at the royal opening of his crowning glory, the Broadgate Centre. The following day, he succumbed to overwhelming pressure from his bankers and resigned as chairman. Rosehaugh was technically insolvent.

Figure 6.2 The fall of Rosehaugh
(*Source: The Guardian*, 1 December 1992).

A new management team struggled for almost a year to keep Rosehaugh afloat by selling almost all the company's remaining assets or transferring them into Rosehaugh Stanhope Developments. In late 1992, Rosehaugh Stanhope Developments' own bankers agreed to refinance its debts over a five-year period. A few days later, Rosehaugh was put into receivership by its main creditor, Barclays Bank, with liabilities estimated at £800 million (see Fig. 6.2). The company's remaining assets amounted to no more than £100m, of which the largest was the vacant Brindleyplace site in the centre of Birmingham. As Kane (1992: 13) commented "The great boom of the Thatcher years is ending, not with a bang, but in a whimper of receiverships. The sub-sector that is feeling the pain is the merchant developer.

These presided over the ambitious schemes of the 1980s – the shopping malls, financial services centres and leisure complexes. Their success was paper thin. Vast edifices were built on flimsy creditworthiness. When the economic climate changed, they were the most vulnerable."

Developer/investors The most influential and well established commercial development companies are those which have matured into developer/ investors. This sector is dominated by the top 16 publicly quoted property companies, almost all internationally active and each having a market capitalization in late-1993 of £100 million or over. The top three companies are Land Securities (£3,675 million), MEPC (£2,037 million) and British Land (£1,269 million). Such companies have grown and diversified over many years, often by taking over smaller firms in the process. Developer/investors typically hold and manage completed developments, retaining the full equity as a long-term investment. Management surveyors are therefore required to negotiate rents and look after buildings on a continuous basis. Developer/investors therefore tend to employ far more people than developer/dealers and can become highly bureaucratic organizations.

To benefit from rental and capital growth, developer/investors concentrate on prime property built to high-quality designs and specifications, with subsequent occupancy restricted to tenants considered unlikely to default on rent payments. In this respect, the most reliable letting is to the British Government, which rents substantial property from developer/ investors in central London. As Peter Hunt, chairman of Land Securities once stated, "our profit and loss account is basically underwritten by the Government and a host of blue chip companies; without us they could not operate" (quoted in Byland 1989). The strength and reliability of investment income, protected even in a recession by long-term leases, shields developer/investors from the full force of a development downturn, to which developer/dealers, who have no investment portfolio of their own, are exposed.

MEPC in the second largest developer/investor in the UK, with a worldwide property portfolio in 1992 of £2.9 billion. Originally known as the Metropolitan Estates and Property Corporation, MEPC expanded gradually but continuously, often by taking over competitors such as English Property Corporation in 1982 and Oldham Estates in 1987. MEPC's takeover of Oldham Estates proved a hard-fought battle and was fiercely resisted by Harry Hyams, Oldham's chairman and one of the original property tycoons identified by Marriot (1967). Since MEPC aims to ensure capital growth by continuously upgrading its investment portfolio, it then dispensed with those properties previously owned by Oldham that it considered incapable of long-term improvement. This provoked the fury of Hyams who, having become a major shareholder of MEPC, turned up at the annual meeting to articulate his criticism of the board.

Although MEPC has substantial overseas interest in Europe, Australia and the United States, in 1992, the UK accounted for 78 per cent of its property portfolio by value. Table 6.2 shows the distribution of MEPC's UK property sectorally and geographically. This reveals the narrow concentration of the MEPC portfolio, geographically in London and the South East, and sectorally on office and retail property. As Figures 6.3 and 6.4 show, in 1987, MEPC owned 39 properties in the City and West End alone, each with a capital value of over £2.5 million. In contrast, Figure 6.5 reveals the company's limited interest in property outside London and the South East.

Table 6.2 MEPC's property portfolio by value in 1992.

	Offices £m	Shops £m	Industrial £m	Residential £m	Total £m	%
London: West End	581.6	92.5	7.8	4.1	686.0	30%
City of London	510.6	3.8	–	–	514.4	23%
South & South East excluding London	215.9	264.4	232.3	0.3	712.9	31%
South West & Midlands	68.7	79.4	9.2	–	157.3	7%
North West & North East	84.5	104.3	6.8	0.3	195.9	9%
Total UK	1461.3	544.4	256.1	4.7	2266.5	
Proportion by sector	65%	24%	11%	–	–	100%

Source: MEPC (1992)

In 1992, MEPC's rental income reached a record £320 million, but its pre-tax profits fell from £143.3 million to £109.6 million. The fall in profits was attributable to a reduction of 12.6 per cent in the value of the company's investment portfolio, which external valuers considered necessary to reflect the national fall in property values. The relative stability of MEPC in the face of such a significant write-down in value indicates that developer/investors are better placed to withstand economic downturn than developer/dealers. For in the mid-1980s, MEPC had also embarked on an ambitious development programme, estimated in 1989 as likely to cost £1.4 billion and to add 370,000 m² to the company's portfolio.

Almost 70 per cent of that programme was concentrated on sites already owned by MEPC and involved either extensive refurbishment of existing property or demolition and redevelopment. The best known example was Alban Gate, a 37,000 m² office block costing £175 million developed at

Figure 6.3 (opposite, top) Properties owned by MEPC in the City of London in 1988 (*Source:* MEPC 1988).

Figure 6.4 (opposite, foot) Properties owned by MEPC in the West End of London in 1988 (*Source:* MEPC 1988).

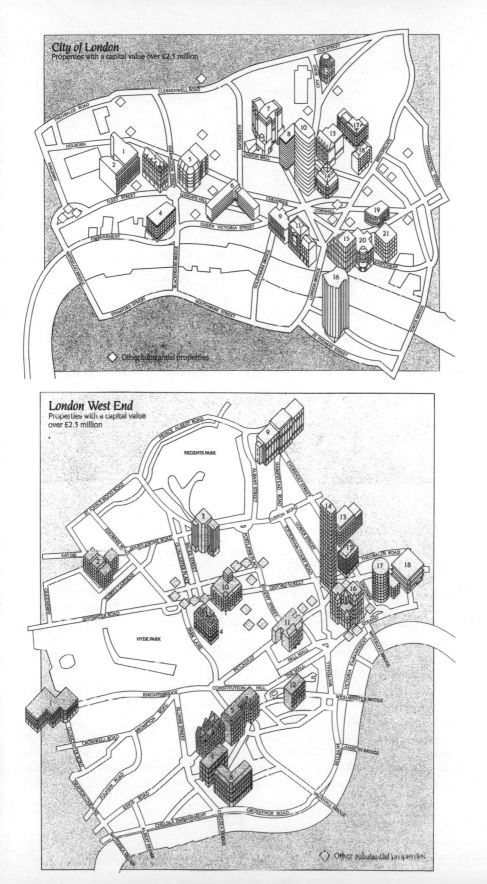

City of London
Properties with a capital value over £2.5 million

◇ Other substantial properties

London West End
Properties with a capital value over £2.5 million

◇ Other substantial properties

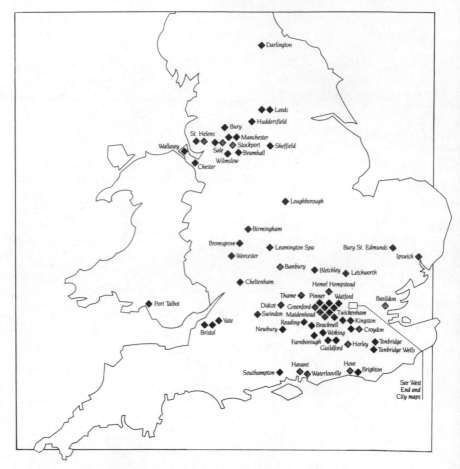

Figure 6.5 Properties owned or interests held in development by MEPC outside London in 1988. (*Source:* MEPC 1988)

London Wall on the site of Lee House, an unpopular 1960s office block owned but demolished by MEPC. Unfortunately, on its completion, Alban Gate was considered by analysts to be worth only £76 million (Whitmore 1992). MEPC responded to such losses by both severely trimming its development programme (so that only £38 million of work remained outstanding by late 1992) and selling poor performing assets with limited potential to improve cash-flow and reduce debts. Subsequently, MEPC chose to switch some of its assets overseas, buying, for example, two American shopping malls for £115 million in 1993.

Although the recession of the early 1990s thus dented MEPC's financial performance and brought its activity as a developer temporarily to an end, its never seriously threatened the viability of the company as a whole. Indeed the scale of MEPC's investment portfolio ensures that the company will remain a highly significant player in the UK property market, whether or not it undertakes further development.

Investor/developers The most important investors in commercial property in the UK have traditionally been insurance companies and pension funds (see Ch 2). Although property diminished in importance in most institutional portfolios during the 1980s, a few very large institutions contradicted national trends by investing heavily in direct development. For example, between 1981 and 1987, Guardian Royal Exchange (GRE) spent approximately £55 million a year on building a total of 16 new developments, of which 12 were office schemes. Direct development offers financial institutions specific advantages, defined by GRE as the opportunity to "maximize capital profit, produce the complete investment with higher yields, control the quality of the buildings and aim for long-term performance" (Westwell & Johnston 1987: 1198). Direct development expropriates the profits of the developer/dealer whose services as a middleman are eliminated. However, it requires institutions to employ in-house development expertise and carry much greater risks themselves. Most smaller insurance companies and pension funds and many larger ones have therefore regarded direct development as an unattractive proposition.

During the 1980s, Norwich Union was one of the leading investor/developers in the UK. Indeed, with a direct development programme of over 140,000 m² of retail floor-space, it became one of the country's most important developers of shopping centres. By 1993, it had a property portfolio of over £2.1 billion, of which 56 per cent was in office property, 40 per cent in retail property and only 4 per cent in industrial property. Developments undertaken by Norwich Union in the late-1980s included The Galleries, a 28,000 m² fashion-led development in Bristol, The Exchange in Ilford, another 28,000 m² development built in partnership with the Prudential, and the Broadwalk Centre, a 18,500 m² development in Edgware. However, pride of place in the development programme was accorded to the Bentall Centre, a 55,000 m² development in Kingston-upon-Thames that included a new 24,000 m² department store for Bentalls itself with a further 100 individual shop units. By 1989, Norwich Union was spending about £500 million a year on direct development in the UK (Branson 1989). Overseas, Norwich Union in France invested funds in the development of smaller shopping centres in Grenoble, Nimes, Bordeaux and Le Mans, and in substantially extending a further centre on the outskirts of Paris.

Norwich Union's development programme was co-ordinated by its own in-house team of surveyors and project managers, with on-site management provided at each centre after opening. Overall, Norwich Union owns and manages 18 shopping centres, some acquired as investments, some built by developers with funding from Norwich Union, but the most recent directly developed. During the 1980s, direct development was regarded by Norwich

Union as the best way to extend its property portfolio. By controlling development production from the outset, Norwich Union believed it could create better investments which would justify the development risk by providing higher returns. However, in the early 1990s, Norwich Union wound down its development programme, since the commercial market was overwhelmed by surplus new accommodation, which could be readily bought for immediate investment at good prices.

Commercial development and urban planning and regeneration
Local planning authorities depend on the commercial development sector to provide new shops and offices. These are usually considered by authorities to boost local trade, offer local employment, and in the case of city-centre development, reinforce established planning policies. In turn, the commercial sector expects planning authorities to protect the asset value of its earlier investments, by restricting opportunities for competing developments elsewhere. Occasionally such shared interests may be articulated explicitly. For example in Greater Manchester, MEPC helped establish a formal alliance between several local planning authorities, including Manchester City Council, and developer/investors such as itself, in order to lobby the Secretary of State for the Environment against a proposed regional shopping centre alongside the M63 at Dumplington, on the outskirts of the conurbation. When this failed, the case was taken to the Court of Appeal. This shows how traditional planning policies, which aim to reinforce the importance of existing town and city centres as prime shopping locations, underpin the investment value of retail property owned by MEPC and others in such centres by restricting the development of competing retail property elsewhere, most notably in out-of-town locations.

Many urban plans implicitly incorporate the interests of the commercial sector by identifying prime development opportunities and by proposing subsequent modifications to transport and other infrastructural networks. Conflict between authorities and the commercial development sector is much less endemic than between authorities and the residential sector. Indeed, challenges to established planning policies from the commercial sector tend to be restricted to companies that specialize in decentralized development, such as out-of-town shopping centres, and have previously been made mainly by planning appeals rather than through the local planning process (Adams & May 1992).

However, where plans have threatened its interests, the commercial sector has not been reticent to challenge local planning authorities. For example, in 1984, a new draft local plan was prepared for the City of London which favoured the protection and conservation of its historic urban environment over and above any proposal for development or redevelopment. Although the draft plan was well supported by most of the amenity/environmental groups and local residents who commented, it was strongly opposed by a powerful coalition of 9 city firms, 12 great livery companies and 17 commercial development interests. The final group was headed by Land Securities, MEPC, Hammersons, Trafalgar House and the Commercial Union.

This property consortium, which was well represented professionally, successfully argued that, by restricting development opportunities, the draft local plan could eventually threaten the City's predominance in world financial markets. The Corporation of London, as planning authority, gave way to these representations and radically altered the plan before it was deposited. A more positive attitude towards development was taken in the deposit version. This allowed for more demolition of older buildings and for new development at a much greater intensity than previously permitted. At the subsequent local plan inquiry, the Corporation of London and the various commercial development interests joined forces to repel the severe criticism of the amenity and environment groups and ensure that the plan, as revised, progressed smoothly to adoption.

More generally, urban regeneration through private-sector property development was promoted as a significant focus of central government policy in the 1980s. Central government sought to persuade the development industry to abandon its traditional disdain for inner urban areas, through two particular forms of intervention. The first attempted to render brownfield sites in inner urban locations as attractive as greenfield sites on the urban periphery, by unblocking supply-side constraints to development, such as dereliction or municipal ownership. The second accorded special publicity to the qualities and opportunities of previously neglected inner urban sites and locations, in the belief that developers and investors had failed to notice such opportunities or had been put off by past experiences or misconceptions (Healey 1991b).

Although some success was achieved in attracting developers and investors to inner urban areas during the development boom of the late-1980s (Healey et al. 1992a), the strategy concentrated on selective supply-side constraints and ignored others, such as private tenure patterns, which research suggested were equally detrimental. Moreover, urban renewal was often the first activity to be sacrificed by the private sector when recession came. This suggests that the risky and volatile nature of commercial property development makes the sector an unreliable partner for the delivery of urban regeneration, irrespective of whether such policy is justified socially or economically. However, the policy was promoted for political as much as economic reasons. As Healey (1991b: 108) contends: "Urban regeneration through property development has the tactical advantage that it produces powerful political imagery. Reconstituting the urban landscape can symbolize the restructured and prosperous economy. The strategy is thus about political publicity as well as real economic effects in localities."

The development professions

Successful development demands a combination of professional skills, traditionally organized into distinct occupational groups. According to Cadman & Austin-Crowe (1983), the architect, planner, quantity surveyor and the valuer/estate agent play leading rôles in the development team, with the structural engineer, electrical engineer, air-conditioning consultant, landscape architect, interior designer, accountant and solicitor all less important. Of course, not all the skills are needed in every case. Although some skills may be retained in-house (particularly in the public sector), it is more common in the private sector to commission a separate team of consultants for each development.

Development professionals facilitate the development process, often depending on its health for their livelihood. The development slump in the early-1990s caused many architects and surveyors to be made redundant, and heightened tension between development professions. The Royal Institution of Chartered Surveyors (RICS), for example, supported the abolition of the Architects' Registration Council (ARC), a statutory body distinct and separate from the Royal Institute of British Architects (RIBA), which restricts the use of the term architect to those with appropriate professional qualifications. The RICS contended that much small-scale design work is actually undertaken by surveyors or architectural technicians and that statutory regulation of architects restricts competition. Nevertheless, the Department of the Environment eventually decided to support the RIBA who lobbied to retain statutory registration for architects.

Throughout the development professions, traditional barriers broke down in the 1980s as competition for work increased and as professional monopolies attracted severe public criticism. For example, solicitors in England began to sell houses, work previously undertaken almost exclusively by surveyors and estate agents. The leading national firms of chartered surveyors began to establish links with the financial services sector, although only one formal integration between a chartered surveying partnership and an investment bank took place (Leyshon et al. 1990).

More importantly, a new breed of multi-functional development agents emerged, with skills in surveying, design, site finding and estate agency (McNamara 1986). Some of these specialized wholly as development consultants, guiding newly established or less experienced developers through every stage of the development process. These agents and consultants originated from a variety of bases, including chartered surveying, architecture, estate agency and increasingly planning consultancy. Indeed, the number of chartered town planners in the private sector more than doubled between 1984 and 1988 (Coombes 1991). Moreover, as Coombes (1991: 23) notes "More developers are employing consultants as they have found that the right planning advice can save time and money. Other companies, such as estate agents, retailers and house-builders, have set up their own in-house planning sections, both to support their own work and to act as independent consultants."

Healey et al. (1982), in their study of the implementation of development plans in High Wycombe and Wokingham in the 1970s, suggested that development agents acting on behalf of the larger and more sophisticated development interests played a key rôle in establishing the principle of land release on particular sites, and subsequently in negotiating the detailed requirements for successful development. As they indicate, at different stages of the development process, development agents may identify opportunity sites for development, persuade landowners to release them, negotiate with the local planning authority, and find appropriate developers and house purchasers. Local development agents usually have considerable knowledge of local planning policy and may well employ staff who have previously worked for the local planning authority.

Planners in private practice have indeed diversified far beyond their original rôle of submitting applications and appeals and are increasingly involved in site finding, feasibility studies and in reviewing particular clients' long-term land needs. Although the planning profession is still dominated by the public sector, with almost two-thirds of its members working in local government (Nadin & Jones 1990), local authorities them selves are making increasing use of planning consultants. Maitland et al. (1991) found that 72 per cent of respondent local authorities employed consultants to undertake some planning work, although few spent more than £10,000 per annum on this purpose. However, in East Cambridgeshire the district's entire local plan was prepared by consultants, while in Berkshire, almost the whole of the county planning department has been "externalized". This could be seen as the forerunner of compulsory competitive tendering for local authority planning work and of the eventual privatization of the planning profession.

At a local level, development professions do not act in isolation but within a well defined and closely knit network in which long-established relationships bind, for example, architects, estate agents and solicitors both to each other and to local building societies, property companies and other development interests, on a formal and an informal basis. This is illustrated for Tyne and Wear in Figure 6.6. Such close links between developers, investors and professional advisers in any locality are essential to the smooth operation of the development process.

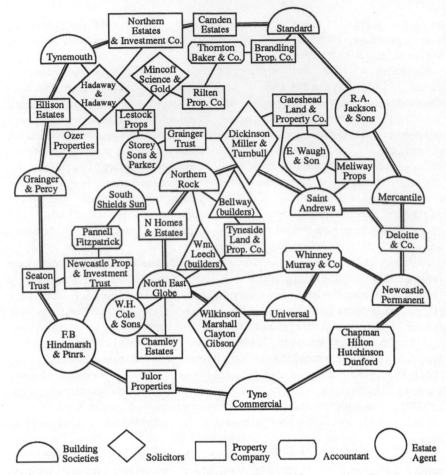

Figure 6.6 The Tyne–Wear connection (*Source:* Community Development Project 1976).

Conclusion

At the Town and Country Planning Summer School held at Exeter in 1980, Tom Baron (then chairman and managing director of Christian Salvesen Properties) described the house-building industry as the biggest and least satisfied customer of the planning system. At first glance, it may appear that the interests of the developers, investors, and their professional advisers conflict with those of local planning authorities, but in reality they share much in common. Local authorities look to the private sector to help implement urban plans, while the planning system offers developers and investors that element of certainty which could never be provided by the free market alone.

As Healey & Barrett (1990: 96–7) contend: "By limiting the possibilities for speculation, and concentrating development opportunities, the state has in effect fostered the centralized and oligopolistic form which has character-ized the development industry in Britain." Indeed, in the residential sector, the restrictive nature of the planning system prevents overproduction and ensures the marketability, at least in the long term, of any dwellings that are produced. In the commercial sector, the planning system helps protect the value of town and city-centre development by restricting the opportun-ities for competing development to be built elsewhere. Both sectors benefit from the efficient provision of infrastructure and its co-ordination through the planning system. Action taken by local authorities to enhance environ-mental quality is usually warmly received by developers and investors, and may even be backed financially, if it helps raise property values.

According to Healey et al. (1988) knowledgeable property developers (particularly those well connected to local authorities or central government) are thus one of the powerful interested parties, in whose favour the contemporary planning system is currently biased. Such bias is quite deliberate for, in a market economy, local planning authorities must work with, rather than over-ride, the private development sector. Developers, investors, and their professional advisers, aware that planning authorities now seek to take account of market criteria, have learnt to use the planning process to their own advantage in order to place their own interests higher up the policy agenda than those of competing groups such as the amenity and environmental lobby. Statutory planning offers the development sector strategic market management of land-use change in which its own interests are incorporated into clear strategic policies that still leave considerable flexibility for detailed interpretation (Healey 1992b). As subsequent chapters suggest, it is likely that both commercial and residential developers will make increasing use of the opportunities that statutory planning provides to influence the planning policies in their own favour.

Notes

1. White land is that which has no notation on the development plan. It is intended to remain undeveloped, at least until the plan is reviewed, but may then be released for development.
2. The names of these two developers have been changed to protect the confidentiality of certain information given in interviews.

CHAPTER SEVEN

Perspectives from the public sector

Although development activity is now dominated by the private sector, it takes place within a framework set to a considerable extent by the public sector, in which development plans and control form an important component. In more recent years, development promotion or *entrepreneurial planning* as it is often described, has become equally significant in many urban areas. This chapter therefore explores how the public sector seeks to encourage, and even initiate private-sector development through such an approach.

The chapter is not primarily concerned with development undertaken solely by the public sector, as the state no longer plays a significant rôle as a direct developer on its own. Nevertheless, it should be remembered that, although much reduced in importance, central government still constructs schemes such as courts, hospitals and offices for its own use, and local authorities still build, for instance, schools, libraries and sports centres. The chapter first highlights the variety of organizations in the public sector who help set the development framework. It then examines the type of activities involved in entrepreneurial planning, investigates various forms of public–private development partnership, and finally considers how some of these have evolved into *growth coalitions*.

The scope of the public sector

It is essential to appreciate the diversity of the public sector to understand how it affects the development process. The public sector is certainly not a monolithic organization that speaks with a single voice or acts in a co-ordinated way. In Chester, for example, in the late-1980s, both the city and county councils wanted to release two strategic sites of 57 ha from green belt to be developed as business parks on the edge of the city. This proposal caused considerable controversy, and the Secretary of State for the Environment eventually intervened to prevent it (Adams et al. 1994).

Different levels of government may therefore find themselves in conflict, and different statutory agencies may pursue competing interests. Privatization of many statutory undertakers in the 1980s merely compounded such divisions. The public sector can thus be likened to an ancient army composed of many different tribes. Although the tribes may be thrown together by necessity in times of crisis, the extent of hostility or fraternity that is often well established between particular tribes, better explains the effectiveness or ineffectiveness of the army as a whole. Successful owners and developers in the private sector have become highly skilled in playing one part of the public sector off against another.

Within the public sector, the strategies, interests and actions of three main groupings of "tribes" set an important context for the development process. These groupings are central government and local government, each split into various departments pursuing specific responsibilities, and other statutory agencies. The impact of each of these groupings on urban planning and the development process will now be highlighted, together with that of statutory undertakers privatized in the 1980s.

Central government

There are four particular ways (apart from the planning system) in which central government helps set the framework for the development process. In the first place, the level of development activity is directly influenced by government economic policy. For example, the relaxation of monetary restrictions in the mid-1980s stimulated an economic boom which itself collapsed when monetary control was tightened in the late-1980s. Moreover, central government has tended to regard the construction sector as an economic regulator, from time to time using it to stimulate or dampen down the economy as a whole.

Secondly, the balance between public- and private-sector development reflects the severity of any restrictions imposed on capital expenditure in the public sector. For example, as central government increasingly tightened the controls on local authority capital expenditure from the early-1980s, council house-building fell substantially. During the same decade, central government introduced target rates of return for nationalized industries requiring capital expenditure for the provision of new infrastructure to be justified on market rather than social grounds. Thirdly, through taxation incentives, central government can enhance the comparative attraction of property as a form of investment or of particular locations or types of property. For instance, the Business Expansion Scheme created a short-lived boom in private-rented development, by encouraging investors to put money into private-rented housing in preference to other forms of investment.

Finally, in particular parts of the country, the urban and regional development policies pursued by central government can help stimulate development in the private sector (as subsequently discussed) or involve development in the public sector. From time to time, for example, central government has sought to decentralize civil service jobs out of London, partly to contribute to regional policy. For instance, in the late-1980s, the Departments of Health and Social Security decided to transfer 2,000 jobs northwards from the capital, and commissioned a 32,500 m² new office development in Leeds city centre, specifically for the purpose. Nevertheless, the regional balance of development activity may be more significantly influenced by the geographical distribution of central government contracts, particularly in defence procurement, even if this effect is entirely unintended. As Breheny & McQuaid (1985) argue, the many defence-related contracts traditionally awarded to companies in the crescent westwards from Hertfordshire around London and then along the M4 corridor to Bristol, has been one of the main reasons for the rapid growth of high-technology industry in that area.

Local government
The rôle of local authorities in the development process extends well beyond their planning responsibilities. Many local authorities are involved in the provision of essential infrastructure such as roads and sewers, either as highway authorities or under agency agreements with water companies. Some local authorities are important landowners in their own right (see Ch. 5). As subsequently discussed, this puts them in a powerful position to initiate public–private development partnerships. Most local authorities are also involved in some form of local economic development (Sellgren 1991). Entrepreneurial styles of planning, explained later in the chapter, are often driven by the more active approaches to local economic development.

In the 1980s, local enterprise boards were established by the Greater London Council and other local authorities, including most metropolitan county councils (Fisher 1986). Although many did not survive the decade, Lancashire Enterprises proved an exception, and by the early-1990s, had been transformed into an international development and investment company. As an limited company no longer fully controlled by the county council, Lancashire Enterprises demonstrates how difficult it can now be to define the boundary in economic development between the public and private sectors.

Statutory agencies
Statutory agencies with specific development responsibilities have tended to be established by central government to help implement urban or regional policies. Some have concentrated on particular types of development, such as English Estates which dates back to 1936, when government factory-building started in the North East. In the residential field, the Housing Corporation, first established by central government in 1964, has channelled increasing public money to voluntary housing associations and societies, which have become the main developers of social housing to rent.

Other statutory agencies, such as the Scottish and Welsh Development

134

Agencies, both established in 1975, have been confined to particular geographical areas. The Scottish Development Agency achieved great success in attracting inward investment to Scotland, particularly from the United States and the Far East. It was also involved in a variety of environmental and urban renewal projects throughout Scotland on which it was spending £58 million a year by 1990. In 1991 it was merged with the Training Agency in Scotland to form Scottish Enterprise (Hayton 1992). The Welsh Development Agency remains in existence having been particularly successful in attracting Japanese investment. It is extensively involved in urban renewal and land reclamation (Pavitt 1990), having restored over 650 derelict sites since its formation. The Land Authority for Wales has a much narrower focus and concentrates on making suitable development land available to the private sector. English Partnerships, the urban regeneration agency for England (which has subsumed English Estates) was established in 1993.

Almost all the new town development corporations established between 1946 and 1970 have now been wound down, and their assets transferred to the Commission for New Towns, prior to eventual disposal. Urban development corporations were first established in London Docklands and Merseyside in 1981. Five more were set up in 1986, four in 1988, one in 1992, and another in 1993. London Docklands Development Corporation, in particular, has generated considerable controversy. The record of the urban development corporations is examined in an extensive literature to which the reader is referred (for instance Brownill 1990, Oakley 1989, Potter 1990, Stoker 1989, Tanner & Tiesdell 1991, Thornley 1991, Bintley 1993).

Private infrastructure companies

In the 1980s, nationalized monopolies responsible for the provision of gas, electricity, telecommunications and water were privatized under complex arrangements intended to regulate their activities and promote competition. From a development perspective, privatization has had two significant implications. Firstly, newly-privatized companies are no longer restricted by public-sector borrowing, but can directly access capital markets to fund infrastructure. Investment in infrastructure is also likely to be more closely linked to specific deals between individual developers (or groups of developers) and the privatized companies, rather than to the planning process. However, as Synnott (1986) found, this tendency began to occur in the water industry some years before privatization.

Secondly, and perhaps of greater importance, privatization has transformed nationalized monopolies into not only private infrastructure companies but also property dealers and developers. Yorkshire Water, for example, closed down a sewage treatment works on the edge of Leeds and entered into partnership with an experienced development company which then obtained planning permission for a 60,000 m² regional shopping centre with leisure facilities, then estimated to be cost £100 million. In 1992, British Gas completed a 10,500 m² office development specifically built for and let to the British Council on three hectares of redundant gas works, immediately to the south of Manchester City Centre. The total cost of the development, known as Grand Island, amounted to over £21 million. British Gas secured approximately £5.5 million of government grant through the Central Manchester Development Corporation, to overcome contamination and dereliction prior to commencing development.

In Greenwich, where British Gas owns approximately 120 ha of redundant gas works at a strategic location on the bend of the River Thames, it is seeking to establish an entirely new district of 4,200 homes, 4,200 m² of retailing, a marina, hotel, conference centre, riverside walks, and light industry. It is estimated that the development will take 10 to 15 years to complete and will cost over £1,000 million. British Gas established a separate development subsidiary, Port Greenwich Developments Ltd, specifically to promote this development in partnership with other interested development companies. These examples illustrate how new development opportunities can be opened up by the privatization of nationalized monopolies. Such developments are likely to become increasingly common as infrastructure companies begin to exploit the full potential of their extensive land holdings.

Entrepreneurial planning

Entrepreneurial planning aims to create opportunities, stimulate investment and promote development. Entrepreneurial planning is quite different from the traditional planning activities of development plan-making and development control. It is action orientated or implementation centred rather than process orientated, requiring planners to work with speed, creativity, flexibility and informality (Lock 1988). Entrepreneurial planners seek to work alongside market operators, understanding their priorities, imitating their behaviour and influencing their decisions. It is a style that Brindley et al. (1989) call leverage planning, since it aims to lever private-sector investment into a weak market through applying public-sector finance. Despite political rhetoric placing faith in the market, entrepreneurial planning is a highly interventionist approach that requires the public sector to play a very active rôle in development promotion (Stoker & Young 1993).

Although the public sector has been involved in clearing sites and providing physical infrastructure to support private-sector development throughout the postwar period (effectively subsidizing development that might not otherwise have gone ahead) leverage planning has been particularly prominent since 1979 (Brindley et al. 1989). It was pioneered in the early 1980s in locations such as Bradford (Falk 1987), Swansea (Howell 1983) and Salford (Robson 1987, Hindle 1993, Law & Grime 1993). It was then widely adopted in the late-1980s in specific market areas that had been weakened by economic decline, and especially by de-industrialization. In particular, entrepreneurial or leverage planning has been especially important in inner cities where its use has been encouraged by central government to help achieve urban regeneration through private-sector property development (Healey 1991b).

However, leverage planning is not merely a central government policy but has been widely accepted and enthusiastically practised by local government, primarily as a result of increasing interest in local economic development (Sellgren 1991). This is because, in contrast to development plan-making or development control, entrepreneurial planning enables local authorities to take positive action to tackle detrimental local circumstances. Yet, although it undoubtedly transforms the physical condition of specific urban sites, the contribution of entrepreneurial planning to economic and social regeneration across entire urban areas is a matter of fierce debate. As Stoker & Young (1993: 59) make clear "This whole 'who benefits?' question is the central dilemma facing those trying to regenerate declining cities in Britain, America and other western industrialized countries. It can be summed up as follows. Do you plan on the basis of what the private sector can be induced to deliver, letting it largely determine patterns of land-use? Or do you analyze local social conditions and plan on the basis of tackling local needs, like access to low-cost housing?".

Stoker & Young (1993) identify a five-stage process in entrepreneurial planning, although they acknowledge that, in reality, the various stages tend to get mixed up with each other. The local authority or lead public-sector organization starts the process by securing access to a redevelopment site through acquiring ownership outright or by reaching agreement with the site owner. Land renewal takes place next in order to tackle dereliction and provide roads, services, electronic cabling and other essential infrastructure. This is followed by public-sector investment in demonstration projects (such as a museum or leisure centre) to inject confidence and convince the private sector that an apparently run-down area has a positive and prosperous future. In the fourth stage, development packages are then marketed (with subsidies, if necessary), to tempt private investors. As these are taken up, entrepreneurial planning moves into its final stage: that of implementing private-sector schemes. Stoker & Young (1993) contend that successful entrepreneurial planning depends on choosing the right site, developing a strategy, exploiting available subsidies, spotlighting or publicising successful schemes, and assembling a team of people with all the relevant skills.

Entrepreneurial planning has been promoted most successfully in specific pockets of severe urban decline. Department of the Environment (1988) contains 14 detailed and interesting case studies. A further 15 are available in Price Waterhouse et al. (1989). Another valuable and continuously updated series is the Urban Development Information Service published in loose-leaf form by the Planning Exchange. Three types of development promotion evident in entrepreneurial planning, namely promoting and marketing an area, making land available and packaging development grants, will now each be explained.

Promoting and marketing an area

Development promotion aims to persuade the private sector to invest in areas that it would normally consider unattractive. This makes a radical transformation in the image of such areas essential. There are several ways to do this. Glossy publicity, with advertising on TV and in the national press is a common approach. This was pioneered by new town development corporations in the 1970s, originally to attract industrial development. It was copied by regional development agencies, and by many local authorities in areas of economic decline. Simple visual images presented every such area as well located at the centre of Britain's motorway network, benefiting from a skilled and reliable workforce, having newly built but cheap premises, and within easy reach of the most scenic countryside in the UK. The rapid multiplication of such superficial marketing images reduced competitive industrial promotion to "a zero-sum game" in which the value of each area's campaign was cancelled out by that of others.

Much more sophisticated place-marketing, embracing techniques and strategies derived from product-marketing, took over in the 1980s. Marketing consultants, appointed to repackage and sell an urban image, undertook a comprehensive audit of a city's strengths, weaknesses, opportunities and competitors. To help focus city-based campaigns, they devised slogans such as "Glasgow's Miles Better" and "Bradford Bounces Back" (Wilkinson 1992). Wilkinson provides a thorough and fascinating analysis of attempts to reposition Newcastle upon Tyne in the competitive urban marketplace. However, Wilkinson (1992) argues that, unless such image-marketing is more successfully related to urban regeneration, it may prove incapable of substantiation in the long term.

Marketing images can be reinforced through flagship projects. These have been defined as "significant, high-profile and prestigious land and property developments which play an influential and catalytic rôle in urban regeneration" (Bianchini et al. 1992: 245). Examples include Albert Dock in Liverpool, the International Convention Centre in Birmingham and, on an area basis, Salford Quays in Greater Manchester. According to Bianchini et al. (1992: 255): "Flagship projects can have a significant rôle in breaking the spiral of urban economic decline by helping cities to improve their internal and external images, to find niches in the new international division of labour, and to pursue consumption revenues of various kinds through tourism, retailing and other consumer service industries." Bianchini et al.

contend that flagship projects provide powerful political statements, beyond any contribution that they make to urban economic regeneration. However, they warn that such projects should not be used as an alternative to stimulating long-term indigenous economic growth through investment in education, training, enterprise development, communications, research and technology.

Urban events or spectacles provide another way to substantiate marketing images. Annual events may be organized, such as the Castlefield Carnival in Manchester. Opportunities may also exist to take advantage of high-profile international spectacles such as the Tall Ships Race 1992, or even to create them, as the London Docklands Development Corporation did in 1988, when it commissioned Jean Michelle Jarre's Destination Docklands Concert. This sight and sound extravaganza at the vacant Royal Docks, was intended to celebrate the development that would launch it into the information technology stage.

Development strategies or frameworks are an essential part of development promotion and are quite different in nature from statutory development plans. They tend to be short, informal and generalized documents setting out the broad philosophy, but leaving plenty of scope for flexibility at a site specific level. Strategic infrastructure provision would normally be identified together with the broad mix of development proposals. The publication of development strategies is often intended to help build the momentum for change and regeneration. Most are professionally designed with colour graphics and eye-catching photographs. Their preparation often owes more to image-making than to effective strategic planning.

Making land available

There is a marked difference between the allocation of land in urban plans and its actual availability for development. Land can be considered ready and immediately available for development only when it is held in active ownership and when planning permission has been obtained, physical problems overcome and infrastructure provided. Planning, physical and infrastructural, ownership and price constraints can all impede development. Planning constraints are more prevalent at the urban periphery, often preventing the development of attractive greenfield land, but urban regeneration is more likely to be impeded by a critical combination of physical, infrastructural, ownership and price constraints on brownfield land (Adams et al 1988).

Development promotion seeks to tackle these constraints in order to make land genuinely available for development. For example, land reclamation may be required to overcome physical constraints such as ground contamination or extensive dereliction. This may be followed by strategic landscaping to enhance environmental quality. Investment in new infrastructure may also be essential. For instance, vehicular access within a site and to the wider highway network may need to be improved. Alternatively, development may not be possible without improved connections to gas, electricity, telecommunications, water and sewerage systems.

Ownership constraints arise where passive owners refuse to sell development land, or are willing to do so only on terms and conditions considered unattractive to prospective purchasers. Owners who are willing to sell, but only at prices substantially in excess of those recorded in recent open-market transactions, may cause price constraints. Ownership and price constraints are particularly characteristic of inner urban land markets, where they constrain the market availability of development land and prolong land vacancy (Adams et al. 1985). In theory, ownership and price constraints might be overcome by compulsory purchase, but as subsequently explained, this has severe practical difficulties. In the past, widespread passive ownership in the public sector was alleged to constrain the availability of land, especially in inner cities. Since 1980, central government has been able to force the sale of vacant public land, by issuing compulsory disposal notices. This power was used on 82 separate occasions between 1984 and 1990. However, most local authorities have always been prepared to sell land to employment-generating uses, regarding such sales as both an active form of development promotion and a useful source of capital receipts.

Development grants

Development grants and subsidies are an essential component of entrepreneurial planning since they can be used to promote development that would not otherwise be commercially viable. At any one time, a complex list of grants and subsidies may be obtainable from a variety of public, private and voluntary sources. Development promotion requires an up to date knowledge of the particular grants available in specific locations and of the individual rules of eligibility that need to be satisfied before applying for each grant. Some grants are restricted geographically while others are targeted towards particular forms of development. In 1989, over 80 separate forms of financial assistance for development were available from the public sector alone (Butler & Moore 1989). The most important sources were central government, and in particular Departments of the Environment and Trade & Industry (responsible respectively for urban and regional development assistance) and the then European Community. For certain developments, statutory agencies concerned with tourism, countryside, listed buildings or rural development, for example, can make an important contribution towards funding.

In the private sector, well known companies often devote a share of their profits to corporate social responsibility, much of which goes towards the sponsorship of sports and arts events (Stoker & Young 1993). However, some is directed to supporting urban regeneration, for example, by helping to clear up and landscape vacant inner-city land. A useful contribution to funding development can also come from the voluntary sector. Any charitable grants obtained towards development costs may well be matched pound for pound by the central government. More importantly, "third-force organizations" such as development trusts, are able to fund restoration and construction work that would not be commercially viable, by combining the expertise and enthusiasm of their own members with innovative use of limited resources. They to raise finance from a variety of sources, such as central and local government, private companies and charities, but are themselves entirely independent. These organizations represent a third force in development beyond the public and private sectors since: " . . . instead of trying simply to influence policy making, they get involved in carrying out projects on the ground" (Young 1993: 27).

Successful development promotion demands skills and expertise in tapping into what might initially appear to be a confusing array of potential funding sources. This activity has generated a new vocabulary which includes such words as additionality and leverage. Entrepreneurial planning seeks to identify, and make available from public funds, the minimal additional sum necessary to turn unprofitable developments into profitable ones. As a result, the amount of private investment levered into a particular area for a given level of public subsidy can be calculated.

Development promotion involves both packaging and programming finance (Department of the Environment 1988). Financial packaging refers to the skills and expertise necessary to put together a combination or package of different grants from a variety of sources in order to make a single development viable. Each funding source has its own priorities and rules of eligibility, and time must be spent not only in formulating grant applications but also in carefully targeting them towards particular objectives of that funding agency. However, success in attracting funds from one agency increases the likelihood of gaining further resources from others, thus enabling a financial package to be constructed. A good example of this is provided in Table 7.1 which illustrates how the restoration and development of Wigan Pier, successfully promoted by the borough council, depended on a package derived from no less than eight separate sources.

Development that is not commercially viable may have to take place slowly over several financial years. Finance must therefore be programmed to ensure that particular grants are made available in the financial year when the work they support is intended to take place. For substantial and complex projects, finance may need to be programmed up to five years in advance (Department of the Environment 1988). Lengthy timetables and bureaucratic procedures in the public sector, designed to ensure that applications for funding are fully assessed to achieve best value for public money, make advance programming of finance essential in development promotion.

Table 7.1 Financial package for restoration and development at Wigan Pier.

	£
Wigan Metropolitan Borough Council (main programme)	1,530,000
Urban programme	1,000,000
European regional development fund	410,000
Private sector/sponsorship	300,000
Greater Manchester Council	250,000
Urban development grant	240,000
Countryside Commission	160,000
English Tourist Board	140,000
Derelict land grant	100,000
Total	4,130,000

Source: Department of the Environment (1988)

Skills needed in development promotion

As Stoker & Young (1993) therefore contend, those in local government seeking to promote development require new skills including accountancy, finance, valuation and management alongside traditional knowledge of surveying, law, engineering and design. In many ways, development promotion is a form of trouble-shooting requiring the services of what has been described as a "project champion" (Department of the Environment 1988: 16). Indeed, the success of particular developments may well depend on the presence of a "driving force" defined as an individual or team with the ability to carry the vision of the development through to a successful conclusion (Department of the Environment 1988).

Compulsory purchase[1]

As a broad principle, local authorities are empowered by the legislation that sets out their responsibilities for education, highways, housing, etc. to acquire land for such functions by agreement, or, with the specific consent of the Secretary of State, by compulsory purchase. Furthermore, councils are authorized more generally under the local government acts to acquire land for any permitted function. However, local authorities may wish to acquire land not in pursuit of their own functions, but rather to promote better planning. For example, development considered desirable in planning terms may be impeded by passive owners who refuse to sell, or by multiple ownership of what would best be developed as a single site. If local authorities can acquire such land by agreement, they may do so under Section 120 of the Local Government Act 1972, which enables them to buy land for the benefit, development or improvement of their area.

If a local authority wishes to acquire land for planning purposes, but the owner refuses to sell, the authority may issue a compulsory purchase order under Section 226 of the Town and Country Planning Act 1990. This takes effect on confirmation by the Secretary of State for the Environment. Section 226 applies to land that the local authority, supported by the Secretary of State, considers desirable to acquire in order to secure development, redevelopment, or improvement or to achieve proper planning of the area in which it is situated. Land can be compulsorily acquired under this section only if the particular purpose would be unlikely to be achieved without the exercise of compulsory powers. Land that meets these requirements may also be acquired by agreement under Section 227.

Local authorities who acquire land for planning reasons by compulsory purchase are entitled, under Section 233 of the Town and Country Planning Act 1990, to sell to the private sector in order to secure its best use or to achieve the proper planning of the area. In normal circumstances, disposal requires the consent of the Secretary of State for the Environment only if the local authority intends to sell for less than the best price reasonably obtainable, taking account of the terms and conditions of sale. Urban development corporations are not covered by these sections, but have their own powers of compulsory purchase for planning purposes under Section 142 of the Local Government, Planning and Land Act 1980.

In theory, where development considered desirable is impeded by multiple ownership or by passive owners, local planning authorities are well empowered to purchase land by compulsory purchase, and then to sell to whichever developer willing to implement planning policies makes the highest offer. However, in practice, few local authorities exercise these powers regularly and most regard compulsory purchase as a last resort. There are three reasons for this. The first is administrative and legal. Compulsory purchase is a lengthy and cumbersome procedure with no certain outcome. Substantial opposition may be generated by a compulsory purchase order. For example, in the early-1990s, 200 objections were received in Birmingham to the city council's compulsory acquisition of land required for the redevelopment of the Bull Ring Centre. Many of these came from traders then operating within the centre. If objections are received, local authorities must make a strong case at public inquiry to show that the particular planning purpose cannot be achieved without compulsory acquisition. The Secretary of State certainly does not confirm every order submitted.

The second reason is political and ideological. Many local authorities, by no means all of a right-wing persuasion, regard compulsory purchase as an undue interference in private land markets. They consider it not to be a legitimate rôle of local government to support certain private interests above others, whether such action enables planning policies to be implemented or not.

The third, and perhaps the most important reason, is financial. Compulsory purchase is simply a very expensive business. Disposed owners are entitled to claim compensation not merely to cover the loss of land and property but also to meet the legitimate costs of disturbance, together with any reasonable bills that they incur in instructing surveyors, solicitors or other professional advisers to handle their case. It is therefore not surprising that financially constrained local authorities are highly reluctant to incur such costs. Indeed, most authorities are prepared to undertake compulsory purchase for planning reasons only when persuaded to do so by a particular developer who agrees in advance both to purchase the land from the authority as soon as compulsory acquisition is complete and to reimburse the authority in full for any expenses incurred.

Public–private development partnerships

Development partnerships represent an extension of entrepreneurial planning in which the public sector moves beyond the general promotion of development and enters into specific contractual arrangements with one or more private-sector partners, agreeing to share the risks and rewards of development. A joint-venture partnership is thus established, in which the financial returns to each partner depend on the profitability of the development as a whole. Such a partnership is not created simply by the public sector providing development grants and subsidies to the private sector nor even by the public sector buying land, putting in roads and sewers and then inviting bids from private developers. At the core of a development partnership is the concept of two or more partners pooling resources (not necessarily on an equal basis), and subsequently sharing the risks and rewards of development.

The public sector can make several attractive contributions to such a partnership. Many partnerships benefit from the initial provision of land owned by the public sector. A greater range of government grants and subsidies (for instance, from the European Union) can be accessed by the private sector if it operates in partnership with the public sector. The private sector may also benefit from the exercise of state powers such as compulsory purchase. Moreover, partnership with the public sector, especially in urban regeneration, is highly attractive to private developers since it reduces uncertainty and makes projects more viable. For instance, there is much less likelihood that planning permission will be refused, if the application is submitted by a public–private development partnership. Access to sources of information normally held by the public sector, such as enquiries from potential inward investors, may also be facilitated. Finally, local authorities, in particular, are able to contribute their own local knowledge and expertise to any partnership. Early commitment and involvement by senior officers in an authority can often save a developer substantial time and money at a later stage.

However, the public sector also gains substantial benefits by participating in partnerships. It is able to draw on private-sector expertise and, if the development is successful, to reap financial rewards. Nevertheless, local authorities are usually quite careful not to take a majority share in such a partnership, since, under the Local Government and Housing Act 1989, the capital expenditure of the partnership would then be treated by central government as that of the local authority itself, and would be subject to stringent financial control. Local authorities may also regard partnerships as a mechanism to encourage the private sector to take more of the stake in local communities, and eventually to support community ventures financially. More significantly, development partnerships enable the public sector not simply to encourage development but to initiate it and see it through to completion. Traditionally, development partnerships have been an important means to promote city centre redevelopment. More recently, more varied forms of partnership have blossomed as local authorities have sought innovative ways to encourage local economic development. The main types of development partnership will now be explained.

Single-project partnership

A single-project partnership involves a specific development at a specific time. For example, a local authority owning a prime site may advertise for a development partner. If more than one developer responds, the winner is normally chosen by open competition on the basis of a financial offer, supported by illustrative drawings of the intended development. The winning developer then enters the site (normally under a building licence), constructs the development and on its completion, is granted a ground lease (in most cases of 99 or 125 years).

The income from the development is then divided up between the partners according to whatever formula is specified in the partnership agreement. It may be that the local authority will wish to take a substantial initial payment or premium when the lease is signed, even if the ground rent paid at first by the developer is then reduced. The local authority may choose to take the premium in kind, for instance, by requiring the developer to provide a public library on site. Alternatively, the local authority may decide not to take a premium at all, but to receive a share of the rack rents paid by tenants. This share would normally be calculated on the basis of original site value as a percentage of total development costs. In any event, as the rack rents increase over time, the local authority's income from the development, either in the form of ground rent or as a percentage of the rack rents, also increases. Both parties therefore share rental and capital growth in the development, with the local authority retaining a perpetual interest in the land, enabling it to control future development and redevelopment at the end of the 99 or 125 years. Furthermore, closer design control can be exercised by the local authority as landlord than as planning authority.

A good example of a single-project partnership was provided by the development of 247 flats and 20 shops by Kantel Developments (Edinburgh) Ltd at Ingram Square, Glasgow between 1985 and 1988. This involved the conversion of an old warehouse together with adjoining infill development. Kantel had originally wanted to develop only part of the site on its own, but found that it was not be financially viable to do so. It therefore approached Glasgow District Council and the Scottish Development Agency. The council was able to put some of its own land into the project, enabling the whole block to be developed. It also made approximately £1 million available in housing improvement grants. The Scottish Development Agency provided a £1 million interest-free loan.

Since the public sector was involved in the development as a full partner, Kantel was able to borrow the remaining £6 million needed to fund development from its own bank at a preferential rate of interest. In this case, the completed development was sold rather than let, with the flats marketed at between £22,000 and £50,000. The profits were split between the three parties as previously agreed with Kantel taking 50 per cent, and the Scottish Development Agency and Glasgow District Council 25 per cent each. The partnership thus enabled a successful development to be undertaken that none of the parties would have been able to accomplish on their own.

Multi-project partnerships

Multi-project partnerships are an increasingly popular way for those local authorities convinced of the benefits of working closely with the private sector, to establish a continuous relationship with a particular partner or group of partners over a period of time. A multi-project partnership is normally established to undertake a number of projects in a development programme. In most cases, a development company is specifically set up for this purpose. These companies represent an evolving trend in public–private partnership (Whitney & Haughton 1990). They take various forms, but fall into three main types which the following examples illustrate:

(a) *Companies jointly established between a local authority and a single private-sector developer.* This category is well illustrated by Kirklees Henry Boot Partnership Ltd, established in 1989 as a joint development company between Kirklees Metropolitan Borough Council and Henry Boot Inner City Ltd. The company was set up to undertake a rolling programme of approximately 80 separate urban regeneration projects in Kirklees over a minimum 10 year period. As a developer, it was expected to assemble land from both local authority and private sources, secure finance, undertake development, market completed property, and sell to end users. As far as possible, local labour, services and contractors were to be employed. Henry Boot and Kirklees subscribed equally to the initial capitalization of the company, holding shares accordingly, and appointing half the board of directors. By 1992, each partner had contributed £2.5 million of capital to the joint company. In the long term, a percentage of the company's profits is expected to be paid into a trust to subsidize community projects in the borough.

Kirklees Henry Boot Partnership soon became active in a variety of commercial, industrial, retail and residential developments in the borough. Two fine Victorian buildings in the centre of Huddersfield were refurbished by the company for council offices, with local trainees extensively employed in the work. By 1993, four residential developments were on site, with an end value in excess of £11 million, and at least six more were in preparation. However, the single most important scheme proposed was the new Kingsgate centre, a 23,000 m² retail development with a value of £75 million planned in Huddersfield town centre. The site was acquired for the company under a compulsory purchase order made by the local authority. The order was confirmed by the Secretary of State early in 1994, almost a year after a public inquiry into the 34 objections that had been received. At that time, the development was expected to start later in 1994 and take three years to complete.

(b)   *Companies jointly established between a local authority and several private-sector developers.* Birmingham Heartlands Ltd provides a good example of this category. This company was established in 1987 by Birmingham City Council and five private development companies (Bryant, Douglas, Galliford, Tarmac and Wimpey), and was supported by the local chamber of industry and commerce. It was intended that company would lead the physical, economic and social regeneration of an area of approximately 800 ha in inner Birmingham, to the east of the city centre. The company began work by adopting development frameworks for two sub-areas, Bordesley Village and Waterlinks. At Bordesley Village, proposals included affordable housing for sale and rent, a village centre, improvements to existing council houses, and major environmental enhancement centred on the Grand Union Canal. Here, Bryant, Tarmac and Wimpey began construction of 118 houses, part financed by a £1.4 million city grant. At Waterlinks, a separate development company, Waterlinks plc was established by four of the five private-sector partners to undertake a £28 million development, part financed by a £6.2 million city grant. The development included modern business and industrial accommodation, new leisure facilities and quality housing, together with the improvement of the adjoining canal. Birmingham Heartlands Ltd proved an effective forerunner to the urban development corporation that was established for the area in 1992 on the basis of continuing co-operation between the council and its private-sector partners.

(c)   *Companies established as wholly owned subsidiaries of a single local authority which then enter into separate partnership arrangements for different developments with different developers.* A helpful example of this category is Leeds City Development Company, established as a wholly owned subsidiary of Leeds City Council in 1987. Five prominent Leeds businessmen (including the chairman of Leeds United) were appointed to the board alongside six city councillors. It was intended that the company would buy land from the council, prepare development proposals, enter into separate partnership arrangements with different developers for each project, and then split any profits between the council and the particular developer. Approximately 65 projects with an estimated value of £350 million were planned when the company was formed. To begin with, the company agreed what were intended to be permanent partnership arrangements with Mountleigh and P&O Developments Ltd. However, both of these main partners proved less committed than originally hoped, and a much wider range of developers were drawn in (Whitney & Haughton 1990). According to Whitney & Haughton (1990: 263), Leeds City Development Company could best be described as "a jointly controlled vehicle for involving the private sector in developing local authority land holdings."

Growth coalitions

Harding (1991 & 1992) contends that where multi-project partnerships are established on an almost permanent basis between public and private sectors, they begin to take on the characteristics of local growth coalitions. This term originated in the United States and became increasingly important in the UK in the 1980s. A growth coalition can be considered as a formal alliance between public- and private-sector interests built around a common agenda of promoting local economic growth. According to Harding (1991 & 1992), property owners and developers tend to be key players in local growth coalitions. Other supporting interests may be utility companies or the local media, particularly if they expect to benefit from increased local economic activity or greater intensity of property use. Auxiliary contributors may include universities, cultural institutions, professional sports clubs, labour unions, the self-employed and small retailers.

Some growth coalitions are brought into being by local authorities. These would include the already-mentioned examples of Birmingham Heartlands Ltd and Leeds City Development Company. Elsewhere, other organizations have taken the lead. For example, the Confederation of British Industry (CBI) promoted "The Newcastle Initiative" and "The Wearside Opportunity", while Business in the Community (BiC) set up partnerships in Calderdale and Blackburn. In Scotland, "Aberdeen Beyond 2000" and "Glasgow Action" were both initiated by the local business community supported by the Scottish Development Agency (Lloyd 1992).

Although individual members of growth coalitions may be heavily involved in particular property developments, a coalition itself has a wider rôle in promoting the image of its city as a successful business location. Coalitions also provide a means of corporate decision-making in which local authorities consult with, and obtain the support of, powerful business interests in both formulating development policy and lobbying externally for status and finance. For as Harding (1992: 231) contends: "A unified city voice is increasingly important in lobbying higher levels of government (National and European), thus favouring localities in which public–private coalitions are active."

Conclusion

This chapter has shown that the public sector plays a critical rôle in encouraging and even initiating private-sector development, especially in the context of urban regeneration. Significant activities in entrepreneurial planning include promotion and marketing, making land available, and packaging government grants. Development partnerships are increasingly common and have begun to evolve into local growth coalitions. However, in many places, such activities have been initiated by organizations other than local planning authorities and carried forward by professionals not trained as chartered town planners.

This is not due simply to the growth of unelected development agencies and corporations in the 1970s and 1980s. Indeed, during the same period, an increasing number of local authorities created specialized economic development units to undertake the type of work described in this chapter. Although some planners moved into these new organizations, developing new skills and new ways of thinking, many local authorities preferred to appoint administrators, accountants, surveyors and even former business managers to push ahead with entrepreneurial planning. As subsequent chapters contend, this highlights the extent to which the traditional separation of plan-making from implementation has significantly weakened the effectiveness of development planning as a form of intervention in the development process, especially at the local level.

Notes

1. This section refers to legislation in England and Wales. Scottish legislation for compulsory purchase by local authorities in such circumstances is broadly similar.

PART 3

LOCAL DEVELOPMENT PLANNING

CHAPTER EIGHT

The practice of local development planning

Development planning has broad appeal in a democratic society, apparently enabling control of future land-use and environmental change to be taken away from private landowners and developers and placed firmly within the arena of public debate and decision. Once that debate is resolved and a plan is adopted, local authorities can exercise their administrative discretion on individual planning applications with greater consistency. However, unless plan-making is closely linked to implementation, such plans may fail to guide or encourage development in the private sector. Development planning may therefore create a facade of democratic control when in reality, it may hinder but never initiate development proposals.

Democratic belief in plan-making requires statutory procedures that are thorough, precise and evenhanded. Such procedures are almost inevitably resource-intensive, particularly in time and expertise, making central and local government regularly question whether statutory plan-making is worth the resources it consumes. Although statutory development plans thus fell from grace in the early to mid-1980s, no satisfactory replacement was discovered. In the early 1990s they regained popularity, since, as subsequently explained, the status of development plans in general, and of statutory local plans in particular, was enhanced by the Planning and Compensation Act 1991. Nevertheless, central government sought firmly to restrict the form and content of statutory plans to land-use and development matters.

This chapter explains how such plans are prepared, what form they take and how they are used in practice. Case studies of Cambridge, Greenwich and Surrey Heath illustrate different purposes in plan-making. The chapter concentrates on England and Wales, but significant differences in the Scottish system are identified. Development planning is also considered from a European context. Although the chapter summarises the statutory framework for plan-making and identifies significant ways in which it relates to the development process, it does not seek to provide a comprehensive account of current legislation or guidance. For this, readers should examine the relevant legislation and guidance directly (especially Department of the Environment 1992c & d) and consult a specialist law text such as Moore (1992).

The chapter contends that development plans are products not merely of technical evaluation but rather of conflict and compromise between those interests most directly concerned with land-use and environmental change. This conflict is at its most intense at the local level where, for example, the allocation of land for new housing development in a local plan may have an immediate impact on those living in the vicinity. The chapter therefore concentrates on statutory local plan preparation, identifying opportunities for interested parties such as amenity societies, landowners, developers and other interests to make representations seeking to influence plan content in their favour.

Statutory development plans

A statutory development plan is one prepared fully in accordance with town and country planning legislation. This means that statutory procedures must be followed precisely in its preparation and that its content must take full account of central government guidance. In England and Wales, the relevant legislation is the Town and Country Planning Act 1990 (Part II) as amended by the Planning and Compensation Act 1991 together with the Town and Country Planning (Development Plan) Regulations 1991 (SI No. 2794). The transitional arrangements necessitated by the Planning and Compensation Act 1991 are explained in a circular issued jointly by the Department of the Environment (1991) and Welsh Office (numbered respectively 18/91 and 71/91). Planning Policy Guidance 1: General Policy and Principles (Department of the Environment 1992b) sets out the purpose of development plans within the planning system, while more specific guidance on statutory plan preparation and content is provided in Planning Policy Guidance 12: Development Plans and Regional Planning Guidance (Department of the Environment 1992c). A good practice guide has also been published by the Department of the Environment (1992d).

In Scotland, the relevant legislation is the Town and Country Planning (Scotland) Act 1972 as amended (particularly by the Planning and Compensation Act 1991) together with the Town and Country Planning (Structure and Local Plans) (Scotland) Regulations 1983 (SI No. 1590). More specific guidance is provided by circulars and National Planning Policy Guidelines issued by the Scottish Office Environment Department.

A statutory development plan should be distinguished from an informal or "bottom-drawer" plan not prepared in accordance with statutory procedures, but previously regarded by many local planning authorities as a quick way to produce informal and flexible planning policy. Such bottom-drawer plans are deemed unsatisfactory by the Secretary of State, and are certainly incompatible with current legislative requirements. In contrast, statutory development plans carry the force of law and enjoy a privileged position in the planning system. For example, Section 70(2) of the Town and Country Planning Act 1990 requires that, when a planning application is determined, local planning authorities should have regard to the development plan, whenever material to the application, alongside other material considerations. Furthermore, the Planning and Compensation Act 1991 appeared significantly to enhance the status of statutory development plans by introducing the new Section 18A into the Town and Country Planning (Scotland) Act 1972 and Section 54A into the Town and Country Planning Act 1990. This states that "Where, in making any determination under the planning Acts, regard is to be had to the development plan, the determination shall be in accordance with the plan unless material considerations indicate otherwise".

According to the Department of the Environment (1992b: para. 25) "In effect, (the Planning and Compensation Act 1991) introduces a presumption in favour of development proposals which are in accordance with the development plan. An applicant who proposes a development which is clearly in conflict with the development plan would need to produce convincing reasons to demonstrate why the plan should not prevail". However, it remains uncertain how this statement is meant to be reconciled with the declaration in the same document that "applications for development should be allowed, having regard to the development plan and all material considerations, unless the proposed development would cause demonstrable harm to interests of acknowledged importance" (Department of the Environment 1992b: para. 5). Such uncertainty remains to be resolved by judicial and policy interpretation (Gatenby & Williams 1992, Blaney 1993, Millichap 1993).

Development plans vary in type between metropolitan and non-metropolitan areas. Once changes to the development plan system envisaged by the Planning and Compensation Act 1991 are fully operational, all non-metropolitan areas in England and Wales will be covered by a structure plan providing the strategic planning framework and by local plans, waste local plans and minerals local plans, setting out detailed proposals for land-use and development. In metropolitan areas (Greater London and the six main English conurbations) each district planning authority is required to prepare its own unitary development plan, of which Part I will be broadly similar to a structure plan and part II to a local plan. In the meantime, plans prepared under earlier legislation may continue to be operational until replaced. In Scotland, the preparation of local plans, as well as structure plans, has been mandatory since 1973. The development plan for any area is therefore rarely a single document, and in the long term, will be so only in English metropolitan areas. The various types of development plan are now considered.

Structure plans

Structure plans are intended to set the strategic planning framework for at least 15 years ahead, resolving the balance between development and conservation and making sure that realistic provision for development is made in line with national and regional policy. The plan should help secure consistency between the local plans for neighbouring districts. A structure plan comprises a written statement illustrated by a key diagram which is *not* on a map base. The written statement is accompanied by an explanatory memorandum in which policies and proposals of the plan are justified, and other relevant background material is contained. Structure plans in England and Wales are prepared by county planning authorities. In the past, some county councils have prepared separate structure plans for different parts of their county, but in future the whole of a county will be covered by a single structure plan. In Scotland, structure plans can continue to be prepared either for the whole or part of a region. Since all three countries already have full structure plan coverage, structure planning is now concerned with alteration, review or replacement of previously approved plans. Structure plan preparation usually provides some opportunity for public comment and consultation. However, experience shows that interested organizations are more likely to be involved in structure planning than individuals. Indeed, members of the public normally find it harder to relate to strategic matters than to controversial local issues that appear to have a more immediate impact.

Local plans

Local plans contain detailed policies and specific proposals for the development and use of land. They allocate land for particular purposes such as housing or employment, and set out policies to guide development control on a day-to-day basis. They may designate action areas in which comprehensive development, redevelopment or improvement is envisaged within 10 years. Local plans are expected to be in general conformity with the structure plan. A local plan consists of a written statement and a proposals map on an ordnance survey base. The map is intended to illustrate the detailed policies and proposals in the written statement, identifying sites for particular developments or land-uses and areas where specific development control policies will apply. A reasoned justification of the policies and proposals in the plan should be contained within the written statement. Local plans normally look 10 years ahead, although for conservation and other similar policies, a longer or even indefinite timescale may be appropriate. The preparation of local plans provides opportunities for participation by local communities and other interested parties in plan-making.

Local plans are normally prepared by district planning authorities. By 1993, approximately 80 per cent of Scotland was covered by an adopted local plan. In contrast, only 20 per cent of England and Wales had been covered by adopted local plans in 1988, and local plan preparation remained discretionary until 1991. However, the Planning and Compensation 1991 requires all non-metropolitan district planning authorities in England and Wales to prepare district-wide local plans dealing with all relevant topics except minerals and waste disposal. Furthermore, the Planning and Compensation 1991 requires non-metropolitan county planning authorities in England and Wales to prepare specific local plans dealing with waste disposal and mineral workings. Each authority may choose whether to tackle these matters in one local plan or in two. In national parks, waste and minerals planning is the responsibility of the national park authority who may either prepare separate local plan(s) for waste and minerals or include both matters in its park-wide local plan.

The Government expects nationwide plan coverage in England to be virtually complete by the end of 1996 but other commentators suggest that a 75 per cent coverage by that date is more realistic (McClenaghan & Blatchford 1993). The introduction of mandatory local plans in England and Wales has certainly led to a rapid upsurge in local plan-making activity. In July 1992, the planning inspectorate anticipated that it would hold 240 development plan inquiries in the following 12 months.

Unitary development plans

Unitary development plans combine the functions of structure and local plans in Greater London and the other metropolitan areas of England. Part I sets out general policies for the development and use of land in the district and is similar to a structure plan except that it does not contain a key diagram. Part II takes these general policies forward in a written statement making specific development and land-use proposals. These are shown on a proposals map with an ordnance survey base. Action areas may be designated in Part II. Part II also contains a reasoned justification both of the general policies in Part I and of the specific proposals in Part II. The Department of the Environment recognize Part II as analogous to a local plan in non-metropolitan areas. *The term "statutory local plan" is henceforth used to include Part II of unitary development plans.*

Supplementary planning guidance

Supplementary planning guidance includes documents such as design guides or development briefs that do not form part of the development plan but may elaborate policies and proposals for specific areas or types of development. They may be taken into account as material considerations in deciding planning applications, but they do not have the special status of development plans. Supplementary planning guidance must not be used to define policies and proposals that should properly be included in a development plan. Local authorities who attempt to do so deprive the public of the right to debate contentious policies or proposals at local plan inquiry, thus opening up the possibility that such policies or proposals will be challenged in and quashed by the High Court (Moore 1992).

Central government guidance

Central government provides national and regional policy guidance to co-ordinate and ensure consistency in development plan preparation. In England, for example, three types of guidance are particularly important. Regional Planning Guidance Notes (RPGs) provide a regional context for structure plan preparation in non-metropolitan areas and for unitary development plan preparation in metropolitan areas. Planning Policy Guidance Notes (PPGs) mainly deal with specific topics such as green belts or land for housing development. Minerals Policy Guidance Notes (MPGs) aim to create consistency in minerals planning. In Scotland, National Planning Policy Guidelines (NPPGs) are issued by the Scottish Office Environment Department. Through such guidance, central government attempts to introduce its own agenda into local planning policy. Central government guidance is a material consideration in deciding planning applications and local planning authorities must therefore take it fully into account in statutory plan preparation.

The form and content of statutory development plans

Statutory development plans are essentially concerned with the management of land-use and environmental change (Healey et al. 1988). They may take account of social and economic considerations, but they are certainly not social or economic plans. They may have resource implications, but in no sense are they expenditure-based plans. Indeed, statutory development plans are required by current legislation to concentrate almost exclusively on the use and development of land. As the Minister responsible stated "Policies and proposals should stick to land-use matters" (Young 1992: 4). Furthermore "The Secretary of State wishes to emphasise that plans must make realistic provision for the development needs of the area" (Department of the Environment 1992c: para. 5.1). Although these matters can prove highly contentious, the Department of the Environment believes that "Such plans, which should be consistent with national and regional planning policy, provide the primary means of reconciling conflicts between the need for development, including the provision of infrastructure, and the need to protect the built and natural environment" (1992b: para. 17).

All statutory development plans in England and Wales are required to include policies on the conservation of natural beauty and amenity, the improvement of the physical environment and the management of traffic. Furthermore, although not social or economic plans, development plans are expected to take full account of social and economic, as well as environmental considerations. Relevant social considerations may include the impact of planning policies on particular groups in society, such as ethnic

157

minorities, religious groups, elderly and disabled people, single parent families, students, and disadvantaged and deprived people in inner urban areas. Relevant economic considerations may include structural change in the local economy and socioeconomic factors such as car ownership levels, unemployment and income levels. Relevant environmental considerations extend from the global warming aspects of development patterns to more local concerns such as landscape quality, wildlife conservation and environmental health. Other relevant matters include the provision of transport and utilities infrastructure, and the availability of resources, taking into account national economic policies and the resources available to implementing agencies.

Nevertheless, statutory development plans make no attempt to marshal land, labour and capital resources into a phased development programme. Indeed, they are not intended to be planning documents in this sense, even within their narrow focus on land-use and development. Rather, the statutory planning process provides a democratic mechanism to determine whether, and on what basis, claims on land made by certain interest groups, such as house-builders, should be preferred to those of other interests, such as amenity societies. As "a prime means of resolving competing claims over the development and use of land" (Department of the Environment 1992d: para 2.41), statutory development plans allocate land for development but do not directly address the processes by which development takes place. The plans therefore depend heavily on market mechanisms to implement development allocations, becoming not merely responsive to the market but often subservient to it. According to the Minister "The market is unpredictable and innovative. Plans must be sufficiently flexible to adapt to new development proposals" (Young 1992: 4).

The Department of the Environment (1992c) places great emphasis on clarity and precision in plan presentation. Plans should be worded to leave no room for ambiguity, avoiding jargon, and expressing intentions in a way that can easily be understood by all potential readers. Good practice requires a user friendly style of presentation both in the main text and in supporting illustrations (Department of the Environment 1992d). Over elaborate argument in plans incurs the displeasure of the Secretary of State. A brief and clearly presented explanation of planning policies is commended to local planning authorities as more likely to carry conviction with residents, developers and others concerned with development issues.

Although the Department of the Environment identifies relevant structure plan topics such as housing, the economy and strategic transport, the precise content of statutory local plans is left to the discretion of local planning authorities. However, most statutory local plans address a wide range of planning matters, usually arranged either on a topic or area basis. A topic-based approach, for example with separate chapters on housing, environment, employment and transport etc., is normally considered appropriate where strong challenges are expected to particular policies and proposals. An area-based approach provides a helpful way for the members of the public to find out exactly what is planned in their own neighbourhoods. Occasionally, the two approaches may be skilfully combined without undue repetition, as happened with the Birmingham UDP (Department of the Environment 1992d). Area and topic-based approaches may be appropriate in plans where the control of development is the prime aim and basis of implementation. However, they appear inappropriate where more active intervention is required to stimulate development (see Ch. 12). Although central government guidance may need to be interpreted flexibly to encourage more active approaches, guidance that is too restrictive produces plans that lack vision and are merely development control documents (Armstrong et al. 1993).

The preparation of statutory local plans

The Planning and Compensation Act 1991 initiated rapid expansion in local plan-making activity as district planning authorities throughout England and Wales sought to meet the statutory requirement for district-wide local plan coverage. Thereafter, local planning authorities can decide at any time to bring forward proposals to alter an existing plan or replace it with a new one. However, the Secretary of State expects plans to be reviewed regularly, and suggests that this should normally take place at least once every five years. Although statutory local plans are therefore periodically to be reviewed, authorities are required continuously to gather survey information and monitor plan implementation. In particular, three types of information have to be kept under regular review. These are the principal physical and economic characteristics of the area, the size, composition and distribution of its population, and its communications, transport system and traffic. The collection of survey data is thus regarded not as a discrete event at the start of plan preparation, but rather as a continuous activity. Figure 8.1 shows plan preparation procedure in England and Wales. This official diagram (Department of the Environment 1992c) is intended to apply to all types of statutory plan including structure plans. The diagram rightly suggests that plan preparation is lengthy and complicated.

Nevertheless, three main stages in the preparation of statutory local plans (consultation, deposit and post-inquiry) can be readily identified. These are shown in Figure 8.2 (derived from Fig. 8.1) in which references to structure plan preparation are eliminated. The first stage involves preliminary work, publicity and consultation with the plan usually published in draft form. In the second stage, the plan is finalized and placed on deposit, enabling formal objections to be submitted, and subsequently to be debated at local plan inquiry. The third stage involves consideration of the inquiry report, the possibility of modifications and final adoption. Significant difference in the Scottish local plan system will again be identified as the three stages are explained.

The three stages provide a series of opportunities for those interested to seek to influence plan content. At the consultation stage, opportunities are by nature informal, but as preparation progresses, they become increasingly formal. At the deposit and post-inquiry stages, representations must be submitted formally in the approved manner. Once the plan is adopted, it can be challenged only through the courts for a short period on strictly limited grounds. No special statutory provision is made in plan preparation to involve those who own or wish to develop land. Instead, such interests typically make full use of the normal opportunities to influence plan content. Indeed, these opportunities both enable members of the public to make representations about the future of their local environment and encourage those landowners and developers who would most benefit financially from extra development, to attempt to influence decisions to their own advantage. Conflict between such interests is at its most intense in local plan-making, particularly as local plans have now become more important in determining planning applications. In explaining the three stages, particular attention is therefore given to the various ways in which interested parties can make representations.

The consultation stage

Prior to the Planning and Compensation Act 1991, all local planning authorities were required to give adequate publicity to matters proposed to be included in a statutory local plan, making persons interested aware of the opportunity to submit representations. Authorities were required to consider any representations that were received during a six-week period prescribed for such publicity and participation. The Department of the Environment encouraged the publication of a draft plan as the most effective focus for publicity and participation. A prescribed period for publicity and participation has so far been retained in Scotland, where it remains four rather than six weeks.

However, local planning authorities in England and Wales are now required merely to consult with other local planning authorities and parish or community councils in the area, neighbouring planning authorities and a prescribed list of government departments, statutory agencies and infrastructure companies. Under the regulations, the extent and nature of any wider publicity and consultation is to be determined by the local authority. However, the Secretary of State is keen to ensure that adequate publicity is given to plan proposals and that local people and other interests such as amenity and conservation groups and business, development and infrastructure interests are encouraged to become involved in plan preparation. In practice, it is therefore likely that local planning authorities will continue

PLAN PREPARATION PROCEDURE

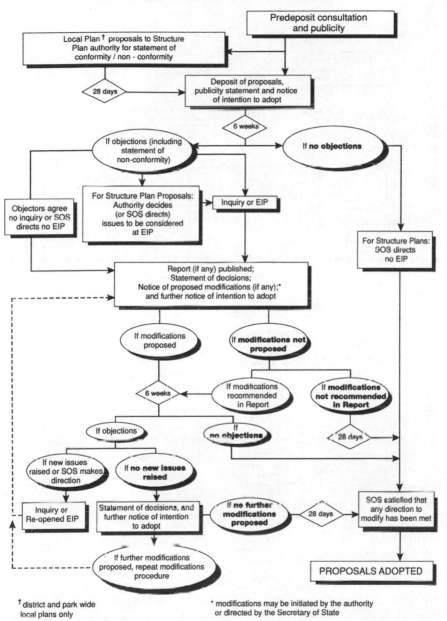

Figure 8.1 Statutory plan preparation procedure in England & Wales, 1992 (*Source:* Department of Environment 1992).

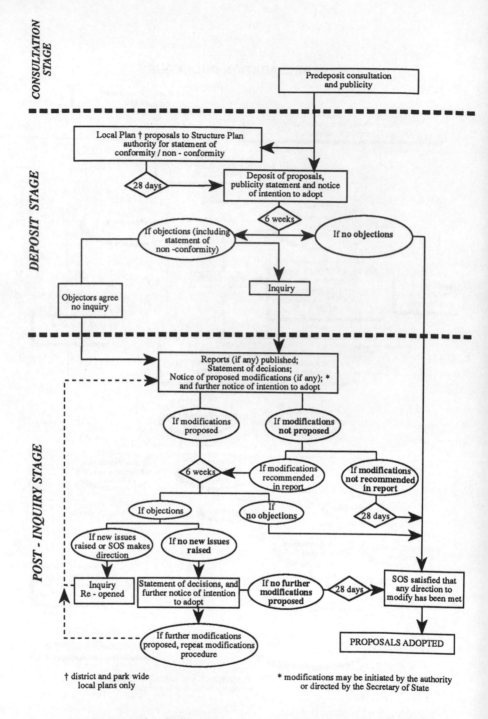

CONSULTATION STAGE

Predeposit consultation and publicity

DEPOSIT STAGE

Local Plan † proposals to Structure Plan authority for statement of conformity / non - conformity

28 days

Deposit of proposals, publicity statement and notice of intention to adopt

6 weeks

If objections (including statement of non -conformity)

If no objections

Objectors agree no inquiry

Inquiry

POST - INQUIRY STAGE

Reports (if any) published; Statement of decisions; Notice of proposed modifications (if any); * and further notice of intention to adopt

If modifications proposed

If modifications not proposed

6 weeks

If modifications recommended in report

If modifications not recommended in report

If objections

If no objections

28 days

If new issues raised or SOS makes direction

If no new issues raised

Inquiry Re - opened

Statement of decisions, and further notice of intention to adopt

If no further modifications proposed

28 days

SOS satisfied that any direction to modify has been met

If further modifications proposed, repeat modifications procedure

PROPOSALS ADOPTED

† district and park wide local plans only

* modifications may be initiated by the authority or directed by the Secretary of State

Figure 8.2 Statutory local plan preparation procedure in England & Wales, 1992 (*Source:* Adapted from Department of Environment 1992).

to publish draft local plans and encourage representations to be made informally at the consultation stage. Indeed, the Department of the Environment (1992d) commends a wide range of consultation techniques such as publicity in the local media, targeted market research, household leaflets, area-based newsletters and videos. The extent of public participation in local plan-making and its influence on local politics is considered in detail in the next chapter.

Although landowners and developers are not included by central government on the prescribed list of consultees, Stratford upon Avon District Council invited such interests at the consultation stage, to register sites that they wished to see allocated for development in the South Warwickshire Local Plan. The Department of the Environment (1992d) comments that, although this approach may help identify development pressure in advance, it could unduly raise expectations among landowners and developers. Indeed, local planning authorities are usually reluctant to accept suggestions for further development at the consultation stage, particularly if they are under pressure from amenity and conservation interests to reduce development allocations. All representations received during the consultation stage are evaluated by the local planning authority at the start of the deposit stage.

The deposit stage

A local planning authority may decide to revise a draft plan in the light of representations received during consultation. Since a statutory local plan is expected to conform generally to the structure plan, a copy of the finalized plan is sent to the structure plan authority immediately before deposit, requesting a statement of general conformity. The structure plan authority must respond within 28 days stating whether the local plan is, or is not, in general conformity with the structure plan. Every effort should normally be made to resolve any differences between the authorities prior to the formal request, but if the structure plan authority issues a statement of nonconformity, it counts as a formal objection to the deposit local plan. The local plan is then placed on deposit by official notice, and a six-week period allowed for objections and supporting representations. Copies of the plan and a statement explaining earlier publicity and consultation are made available for public inspection, and are sent to the Secretary of State. Notice is given that if no objections are received, the plan will be adopted at the end of the deposit period.

Objections may be submitted by any person or organization. Objections may be made not merely to what is contained in the plan but also to what is omitted. Alternative development sites to those chosen by the local planning authority may therefore be put forward. This is a common tactic among landowners and developers owning sites with development potential not allocated for development in the plan. Objections that are duly made (submitted in writing to the correct address within the prescribed six-week period) entitle the objector to appear at a local plan inquiry before an independent inspector (known in Scotland as a reporter) appointed by the Secretary of State. Representations in support may be submitted in a similar way to objections but do not carry any right to appear at an inquiry. However, in the event of an inquiry, the inspector will fully consider supporting representations, and has discretion to hear them in person.

All objections and representations that are duly made are first examined by the local planning authority. Local planning authorities may offer to meet objectors to try informally to resolve objections where misunderstandings exist, or where areas of common ground suggest that mutually agreeable changes to the plan might be made. Such informal discussions are encouraged by the Department of the Environment. If any objections that are duly made are neither resolved nor withdrawn and the objector wishes to appear before an inspector, arrangements will need to be made for an inquiry. However, if no objector chooses to appear in person, but all are prepared to submit written representations, no inquiry is needed and no inspector is appointed. In this case, the local planning authority considers all the written representations, and then publishes a statement of decisions which explains the reason for the decision made on each objection.

When an inquiry is necessary, at least six weeks notice must be published and given to objectors. A preliminary meeting for all parties is normally arranged by the inspector well in advance of the inquiry to resolve procedural matters such as programme and timetable. The inspector is required to conduct the inquiry in accordance with well established principles of impartiality, openness and fairness. Although participants may choose how to put their case, the inspector will maintain customary standards of order and discourage repetition. The inspector has the discretion to hear late objections (submitted outside the six-week deposit period), but will not do so if they repeat ground covered in duly made objections.

The purpose of the inquiry is to identify relevant facts and arguments, enabling the inspector to report to the local planning authority on their merits, and to recommend possible modifications to the plan. The inspector therefore hears the evidence, and allows an opportunity for those presenting it to be questioned. Matters of a general nature may be heard before more detailed objections, possibly by means of a round-table discussion chaired by the inspector. However, in most instances, the objector's submission is heard first, followed by the local planning authority's response. Representations in support of the local planning authority may also be heard. Witnesses may be called by each party and cross-examination will take place. Questions may also be put directly by the inspector. In exceptional cases, inspectors can exercise the right to summon witnesses to present specific evidence. At the end of each case, the objector is normally given the right to reply.

The inspector will also give thorough and detailed consideration to written representations from objectors who chose not to appear in person at the inquiry. Objectors who appear at the inquiry must meet their own costs and are not entitled to any expenses or legal aid. Although the Department of the Environment (1992c) contends that written representations carry the same weight as those made in person at the inquiry, evidence is presented in Chapter 10 to suggest that pro-development objectors who actually appear in person enjoy higher rates of success than those who merely opt for written representations. The Department of the Environment (1992c) further believes that it is not necessary for objectors at local plan inquiries to be represented professionally or to feel that the lack of professional representation puts them at a disadvantage. In practice, most land and property interests such as development companies are professionally represented, for example by barristers and planning consultants, while most residents' groups and amenity societies are not. Evidence again presented in Chapter 10 suggests that professional representation further enhances the success rates of pro-development objectors.

The post-inquiry stage

After the inquiry, there is normally a lengthy delay during which the inspector prepares a detailed report for the local planning authority. The third stage of statutory local plan preparation, which is initiated by the submission of the inspector's report, covers possible modifications to the plan and formal adoption. In the report, the inspector reaches conclusions on the evidence presented at the inquiry, and makes recommendations to the local planning authority. Although authorities tend to adopt the vast majority of recommendations made by inspectors, they retain the discretion not to do so, providing that they explain their reasoning in full. However, Grant (1982: 127) states that: ". . . it would be simplistic to suggest that the planning authority retain a broad discretion in the matter. The wording of an inspector's report may be such that rejection of his recommendations will be hazardous, certainly politically and possibly also legally." The local planning authority is obliged to prepare a statement of decisions on all the inspector's recommendations which explains the reasons for each decision. The inspector's report, the statement of decisions, and any modifications that the local planning authority proposes to make to the plan are then made available for public inspection.

If the local planning authority proposes no modifications that it considers materially affect the plan, it may adopt the plan after 28 days notice, provided that the authority has accepted all recommendations made by the inspector. If any recommendations have been ignored, the authority must allow six weeks for objections to the absence of such modifications, before adopting the plan. Of course, if the local planning authority proposes formally to modify the plan, the modifications must be advertised, and a six-week period be allowed for objections and supporting representations.

By this stage, objections cannot relate to the contents of the original plan, but only to proposed modifications or to the absence of modifications recommended by the inspector. If no objections are received, the authority may proceed to adopt the plan. However, if objections are submitted to either modifications proposed by the local planning authority or the absence of modifications recommended by the inspector, they must be fully considered by the authority, and a statement of decisions published which explains the reasons for each decision. The authority may decide to make further modifications in response to objections, in which case the modification procedure must be repeated. Alternatively, a further inquiry may be necessary in exceptional cases, for example, where objections raise new issues not previously considered. A second inquiry may also be required if the local planning authority decide to withdraw or significantly alter a modification that had originally been put forward to meet an earlier objection at the deposit stage. However, second inquiries are extremely rare. In normal circumstances, if the local planning authority, after having considered all objections and supporting representations on the modifications, does not propose to make further modifications, it may adopt the plan after 28 days notice.

Once the plan is adopted, any person aggrieved may challenge its validity by application made to the High Court within six weeks of the first published notice of adoption. However, the grounds for legal challenge are strictly limited. In order to succeed, a person must show that the plan itself is beyond the powers conferred by the legislation or that the legislative requirements for plan preparation and adoption have not been correctly followed. In each case, the only remedies available are the quashing of the plan in whole or in part, or an interim order to suspend its operation, again in whole or in part. The plan is safe from such legal challenge once a period of six weeks from notice of adoption has elapsed.

A statutory local plan thereafter remains in force until altered, repealed or replaced through similar procedures. However, local planning authorities are required by legislation to keep under review matters expected to affect the planning or development of their area. The Department of the Environment comment that "Monitoring and evaluation should be seen as a linked process by which information collected is used to assess the success and effectiveness of plan policies" (1992d: para. 5.3). The Department considers that this process, if successful, can provide a clear framework for measuring progress in implementing plans and for reviewing them when necessary.

Intervention by the Secretary of State

Although local planning authorities are principally responsible for the preparation of statutory local plans, four main opportunities exist for the Secretary of State to intervene. First, the Secretary of State is a prescribed consultee at the consultation stage, and may comment informally on the draft plan. Secondly, at the deposit stage, the Secretary of State has the right to object, and has used this opportunity with greater regularity. As Sir George Young (1992: 4), the minister responsible stated: "The number of objections made by the Department has increased sharply. Over the last few months, objections of the order of 18 per plan have not been uncommon. These have been made to a whole range of policies, including non-land-use policies, excessively inflexible policies and those which stray into the territory of other control regimes, such as building regulations."

Thirdly, at the post-inquiry stage, the Secretary of State may direct the local planning authority to modify the plan at any time before it is adopted. This is likely to happen particularly if the plan is at odds with national, regional or structure planning policies. Finally, the Secretary of State has reserve powers to call in all, or part of, the plan at any time before its adoption. These powers are exercised only in limited circumstances where intervention by central government is clearly justified, for example, where the plan raises issues of national or regional importance or where it gives rise to substantial controversy extending beyond the area of the plan-making authority. It should also be noted that the Secretary of State is required to call in the plan if the Minister of Agriculture, Fisheries and Food maintains an objection at the post-inquiry stage.

Decision-making in statutory local plan preparation

Statutory local plans are produced through various policy processes (Healey et al. 1988) operating at different stages of plan preparation. During early formulation of a draft plan, decision-making may well conform to a techno-rational process dominated by the expertise of professional town planners who appear to set out options with scientific reasoning. Of course, any attempt to express matters of judgement (such as environmental quality) in quantitative form through techno-rational analysis needs to be regarded with scepticism. However, plan-making soon moves forward into consultative processes involving negotiation and debate with concerned and affected interests. Decisions that may appear technically correct can be quickly swept aside through corporatist negotiation, bargaining, pluralist politics or open democratic debate. At the inquiry, decisions will be reached through a semi-judicial process with the inspector evaluating the competing merits of conflicting arguments as they are tested through cross-examination and investigative debate. Once the inspector's report is received, the plan proceeds to adoption primarily through a politico-rational process, in which final decisions are reached by politicians in the arena of representative democracy. However, every step in statutory plan preparation is overshadowed by a bureaucratic-legal process, since all decision-making must comply with relevant formal procedure and legal rules.

Each policy process is constituted by its own access criteria (governing who get involved in decision-making) discourse criteria (governing the style and procedure by which matters are debated) and decision criteria (governing the basis for an acceptable decision). Healey et al. (1988) contend that particular criteria may advantage particular interests. For example, the style and procedure of debate at a local plan inquiry (expressed by discourse criteria in the semi-judicial policy process) may favour those interests who can afford to instruct barristers to present their case. However, such interests may be disadvantaged in the post-inquiry stage by discourse criteria in the politico-rational process, which may well be expressed by the cut-and-thrust of party politics. This may accord little respect to those who can afford costly legal representation.

This theoretical excursion has crucial practical significance since it emphasizes that statutory local plans are the product not merely of technical evaluation but of processes such as negotiation, cross-examination and critically, party politics. Statutory plan preparation encourages conflicting interests to make use of whatever policy process is most likely to influence plan content in their favour. Statutory local planning should therefore be regarded not as a technical exercise to discover the "best" planning solution (even if one exists), but as an arena in which conflicts of interests are articulated and subsequently resolved.

Conflict resolution or mediation through statutory local planning is certainly expensive and time-consuming. According to Nadin & Daniels (1992), English shire districts intended to spend over £50 million on planning policy in 1990–91, an average of £993 per 1,000 population. However, the Department of the Environment (1992c) contends that local authorities who fail to keep plans up-to-date, encourage speculative applications and appeals, and incur the higher costs of uncertainty. As Nadin & Daniels (1992) suggest, local authorities may try to control costs, achieve better value for money and speed up plan preparation, by using planning consultants more often.

Early local plan preparation took over four years on average from start to finish (Bruton et al. 1982). Throughout the 1980s, central government both exhorted local authorities to accelerate plan preparation and streamlined statutory procedures, especially on public participation, to help achieve this. Yet, by 1992, it still took an average of two years from completing the consultation stage to commencing the inquiry (McClenaghan & Blatchford 1993). Furthermore, the average length of local plan inquiries increased from just over one week in 1989 to eight weeks in 1992 (Department of the Environment 1993). The enhanced status of statutory plans is likely to exacerbate this trend. Lock (1991) argues that local plan inquiries are becoming effect a string of planning appeals, and suggests that radical changes are needed to reverse this tendency. The Department of the Environment (1993) contends that no substantial reduction in the cost or length of local plan inquiries is feasible, without substantive reform of their nature and purpose.

Since inspectors normally take three times the length of an inquiry to produce their report, when allowance is made for the remaining period through to adoption, it is unlikely that any significant acceleration has taken place in plan preparation since the early 1980s. Whether statutory local planning is worth the time and resources it consumes can be answered only in terms of the usefulness of the plans themselves. The next section therefore investigates three different statutory local plans to identify how they have been used in practice.

Statutory local planning in practice

Statutory planning provides a common way to address specific issues of importance in different localities. This is helpfully illustrated by the three plans prepared in the 1980s, examined in this section. These are the Cambridge Green Belt Local Plan prepared by Cambridgeshire County Council to restrain development (adopted in 1992), the People's Plan for Greenwich prepared by the London Borough of Greenwich to promote urban regeneration (adopted in 1989), and the Surrey Heath Local Plan prepared by Surrey Heath Borough Council to manage growth (adopted in 1985).

Cambridge Green Belt Local Plan

Since the 1950s, planning policies for the historic city of Cambridge have emphasized urban containment. A green belt was initially approved in 1954, subsequently enlarged and then confirmed, for three to five miles from the city edge, by the Cambridgeshire Structure Plan in 1980. The Cambridge Green Belt Local Plan (CGBLP) was intended to review and finalize precise boundaries. At the time, such a single-issue or subject local plan was allowed by the Department of the Environment.

Manufacturing activity had traditionally been small in scale in Cambridge, with the local economy highly dependent on the university. However, by the early 1980s, pressure for extra housing and high-technology development was intense (Brindley et al. 1989). This was related to the "Cambridge phenomenon": the term applied to the rapid growth of small and technologically innovative firms that had often originated within the university. The CGBLP sought to balance the unique character of Cambridge, expressed in its historic townscape, tight urban form and its physical separation from most surrounding villages, against immediate and long-term development pressure, considered of national significance by politicians and the media (Crang & Martin 1991). The Structure Plan Review, approved in 1989, aimed to divert some of this pressure to two new settlements beyond the green belt, one to the north of Cambridge and the other either to the east or west.

The CGBLP aimed to finalize green belt boundaries, encourage recreation

169

and tourism, enhance landscape quality, and provide clear policies to control development within the green belt. Although a draft plan was published in 1983, it took nine more years before the final version (shown in Fig. 8.3) was adopted. This was due to continuous controversy of a highly political nature (reported in detail in Ch. 9) which was generated primarily by the exclusion from the green belt of several significant sites adjoining the existing built-up area and the inclusion of others. At the height of this controversy, in the mid- to late–1980s, agricultural land in the Cambridge area was worth about £5,200 per ha. In contrast, development land on the edge of Cambridge was worth, £735,000 for residential use, £1.5 million for high-technology use and £2 million for retail use.

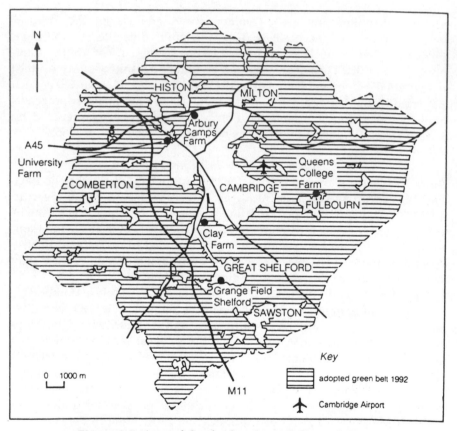

Figure 8.3 Area of Cambridge Green Belt Local Plan.

In such circumstances, plans like the CGBLP that aim to restrict development do not merely allocate uses to land but also distribute financial benefits to owners and potential developers, by denying value to land within the green belt, but substantially enhancing the value of land outside it (see

Ch. 11). Throughout the preparation of the CGBLP, landowners and developers were therefore keen to secure the exclusion of potentially valuable sites from the green belt, while amenity and conservation societies, supported by local residents, worked hard to ensure that the same sites were actually included. However, once adopted, such restraint-orientated policies are relatively simple to implement, since they provide a clear and consistent basis to control development (and if necessary, to win planning appeals) while not necessitating positive action to initiate or co-ordinate development.

People's Plan for Greenwich

Although the National Maritime Museum, Royal Naval College and Cutty Sark make the historic centre of Greenwich an international tourist attraction, some of the worst social, economic and environmental conditions in inner London exist a short distance away. Despite widespread poverty, development pressure from London Docklands began to spill over to riverside locations such as Greenwich Reach (see Ch. 3) during the 1980s. The People's Plan accorded highest priority to new jobs and housing for local people and thus aimed to protect existing low-value housing and industrial uses from high-value luxury development. The plan represented an explicit attempt by a left-wing Labour council to deploy statutory plan-making to the particular benefit of disadvantaged groups and areas.

The plan itself is organized into topics such as jobs, housing and shopping, but is prefaced by an analysis of the needs of 14 disadvantaged groups (such as ethnic minorities and the unemployed) and 12 areas of stress (evident in Fig. 8.4). Specific policies addressed, for example, the need for advice services and community law centres, especially in areas of stress, and the importance of existing bus and rail services. The Department of the Environment (1985) found it hard to reconcile such community-based planning with the official view that statutory local plans should be restricted to land-use and development matters, commenting that the draft local plan contained: "a substantial number of corporate policies on largely non-land-use matters . . . which should not be included as policies or proposals in a local plan. This level of detail tends to detract from the primary rôle of a local plan of providing clear and precise guidance to owners and developers of land".

Since public-sector resources for community-based development were severely constrained, the plan sought to extract as much community benefit as possible from the private sector. For example, it aimed to make at least half the new dwellings on housing sites over two hectares available for rent to persons in housing need, by means of planning agreements with private developers. Similarly, childcare facilities were sought in shopping or leisure developments over 2,000 m². By this approach, the plan tried to harness the development process to meet community aspirations. In practice, such policies proved a valuable baseline in subsequent negotiations with individual

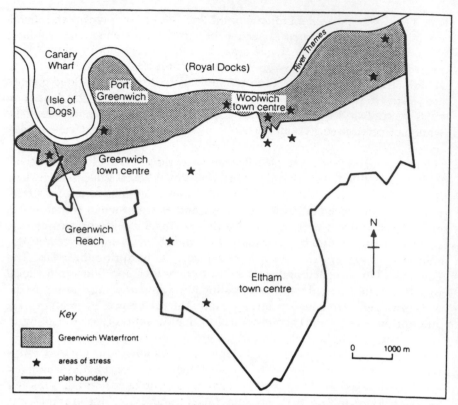

Figure 8.4 Area of People's Plan for Greenwich.

developers. Between 1989 and 1992, five significant housing developments, each with 25 per cent affordable homes due to be built by housing associations, received planning permission. At Port Greenwich, over 1,000 affordable homes were proposed in the biggest such development (see Ch. 7).

The People's Plan thus charted a fresh direction in Greenwich and achieved some success in securing community benefits from private developers. In the Unitary Development Plan, prepared in the early 1990s, this direction was carried forward, although less ambitiously. Political change in Greenwich after the adoption of the People's Plan, produced a new Labour leadership, keen to work in partnership with the private sector. In 1991, the council established the Greenwich Waterfront Development Partnership, a not-for-profit company involving business representatives working alongside those of the council and local community. The partnership was intended to lead the regeneration of over 200 ha of derelict industrial land along Greenwich's seven-mile river frontage (Rifkin & Williams 1991). It is indeed significant that, in an inner urban area where needs are great but resources are few, a development partnership (see Ch. 7) was considered a more effective mechanism than a statutory development plan as currently defined, to challenge urban decline through initiating and co-ordinating action on the ground.

Surrey Heath Local Plan

Surrey Heath is a highly popular residential area, located on the borders of Berkshire Hampshire and Surrey. The M3 passes through and the M4 is easily accessible. Heathrow Airport is 25 minutes away by car. The district is an important military centre and was traditionally known for nurseries and market gardening. Some light industrial estates and newer high technology buildings are found in Camberley and Frimley. Other towns and villages within the district include Bagshot, Windlesham, Lightwater, Bisley, West End and Mychett. Rapid urbanization between 1961 and 1980 saw the stock of dwellings in Surrey Heath increase by almost 90 per cent to 26,600 as a growing influx of population was attracted by the area's environmental quality and easy commuting distance to London Waterloo. By the 1980s, house prices were among the highest outside London, producing a mismatch in the local labour market, rapidly increasing land prices and growing pressure on the local planning authority to allow more and more residential development.

In 1971, the Strategic Plan for the South East (SPSE) included the western two-thirds of Surrey Heath within Planning Area 8. This became perhaps the most notorious of the five regional growth areas in the South East. The outer boundary of the Metropolitan Green Belt runs midway through Surrey Heath, with the eastern half designated as green belt. Between 1976–80, the district experienced its fastest rate of population growth at 7 per cent per annum. Nevertheless, despite combined opposition from county and district councils, the Secretary of State, in approving the Surrey Structure Plan in 1980, increased the housing land target of 37,600 dwellings proposed by the county council by an additional 12,000–13,000. At the same time, he commented that "there is capacity in the Area 8 part of Surrey Heath to support a significant proportion of further development proposed for Surrey as a whole".

After intense negotiations between the county and district councils, it was agreed that the Surrey Heath Local Plan would provide for 6,200 new dwellings between 1978 to 1991 (a further increase of 24 per cent above the 1978 level). As an exercise in comprehensive growth management, the plan addressed a full range of topics, including shopping, employment, public utilities, recreation and open space. It aimed to generate 3,400 additional jobs during the plan period, including 2,000 in services and 1,400 in manufacturing. However, the single most contentious issue proved to be the allocation of sufficient land to meet the 6,200 housing land target, with local residents, landowners and developers such as Charles Church (see Ch. 6) all making extensive representatives on various alternative development sites.

By the time the plan was approved in 1985, approximately 2,100 houses

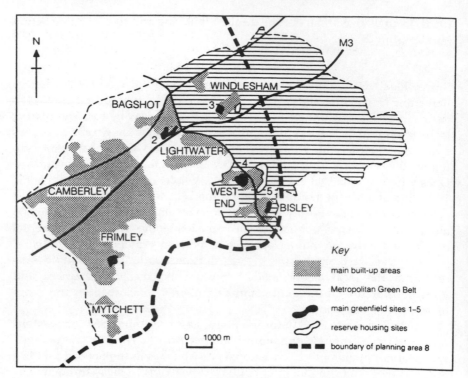

Figure 8.5 Area of Surrey Heath Local Plan.

had been built since 1978 and a further 1,785 had been granted planning permission. Maximum allowance was then made for more intensive use of the existing built-up area to preserve attractive environments elsewhere. Surrey Heath Borough Council calculated that almost 900 dwellings could be built on small and infill sites within existing settlements. Five major greenfield sites of 69 ha in total were then identified to accommodate the remaining 1,430 dwellings (see Fig. 8.5). Development briefs were subsequently prepared by the local authority to coordinate the provision of infrastructure and the phasing of development on most of these sites. Nevertheless, allocated housing land throughout Surrey Heath was developed faster than the local authority anticipated or could control. Indeed, in 1987, only two years after the plan was adopted, the council could no longer demonstrate an effective five year supply of housing land, and began to lose significant planning appeals. This weakness was not rectified until the early 1990s, when a local plan review reduced the rate of new residential development proposed for the decade ahead, below that which had occurred in the 1980s.

Surrey Heath illustrates strategic market management of residential growth through a statutory local plan. The planning process provided a democratic mechanism, involving local people and politicians, enabling development pressure to be directed to selected sites, and preventing urban sprawl in an attractive environment. As long as enough building land remained available, the plan could contain development. Yet, once that was taken up, pressure broke out again, necessitating planning by appeal until the local plan review.

Development planning in the European Union

Throughout the European Union, town and country planning evolved gradually during the 20th century in response to urban growth and development. The particular planning system in each country reflects its own history and politics, embodied in its constitutional structure. Nevertheless, development planning in the UK is distinctly different from that in the rest of the European Union, for whereas the British development plan is a "servant" capable of flexible interpretation in development control, elsewhere it is the "master" acting as a legally binding document that specifies precisely what is, or is not, to be permitted (Davies 1992a). The most thorough analysis of Western European planning systems involved comparative studies of England (Davies 1988a), Denmark (Edwards 1988), France (Punter 1988), Germany (Hooper 1988) and the Netherlands (Davies 1988b) jointly commissioned and published by the Department of the Environment (1989).

Planning systems in all four of these European countries are characterized by rigidity and legal certainty and are essentially plan-led (Department of the Environment 1989). Administrative control of development is therefore a procedural activity, in which applications are tested against legally binding town plans and building regulations to determine whether or not they qualify for a permit. Although each of overseas systems incorporates some flexibility for negotiation on particular development proposals, in most cases where these conflict with the plan, the plan itself must be altered. Furthermore, each country has created a more formalized plan hierarchy than exists in the UK, with higher-level plans administratively binding lower-level ones. The actual process of plan preparation is broadly similar in all five countries, with the main variation concerning opportunities for public participation and objection. For example, all countries provide some system of formal hearing to consider objections, except Denmark where reliance is placed on informal participation.

Although more discretion has subsequently been introduced in certain European systems, for example with the Dutch adopting flexible but still legally binding *globaal plans*, the British have moved noticeably in a European direction by enhancing the importance of development plans in development control decisions (Davies 1992b). Yet, despite explicit reference in the Maastricht Treaty to "town and country planning" and "land-use" as matters on which the European Commission may initiate legislation, Williams (1993) argues that this is most unlikely in the immediate future, since such legislation would almost certainly be vetoed in the Council of Ministers. Indeed, the President of the European Commission has confirmed that town and country planning is considered within the competence of member states and particularly their regional and local governments (Martin 1992). This accords with the European principle of subsidiarity which states that action should be taken at the European level only if its objectives cannot be sufficiently or satisfactorily achieved by member states acting individually.

Davies (1992b) contends that there is no immediate prospect of European legislation to harmonize development planning across the Community. Instead, he considers that pressure will continue to be exerted throughout Europe to enhance the efficiency of planning systems, to extend environmental legislation (for example, by requiring environmental assessments of development plans) and to strengthen citizens' rights in planning (for example, by providing third parties in the UK with rights to object to any planning permission granted in conflict with a development plan). According to Williams (1993), national planning systems may well be scrutinized in relation to the Single European Market, which was completed in 1992 to ensure free movement of goods, services, people and capital throughout the Community by removing all internal tariff and non-tariff barriers. For example, he suggests that any excessive variation in planning systems between member states that permit the establishment of pollution havens in certain countries from which firms can undercut competitors in other countries, could constitute a non-tariff barrier breaching the Single European Market.

Although member states remain responsible for statutory development planning, Williams (1993) explores the increasing importance of spatial planning and spatial development within the Community. Spatial policies can be traced back to 1973, when the European Regional Development Fund was established to help implement the Community's newly formulated regional policy. At the same time, the Community's first Action Programme on the Environment was devised. In the mid-1980s, the Environmental Assessment Directive was introduced. Williams (1993: 9) considers this: "one of the most important land-use planning instruments to be formulated within the framework of EC environmental policy."

Subsequently, in its fifth Action Programme on the Environment in 1991, the European Commission proposed that sustainability should underpin all land-use and economic development planning at local, regional, national and transnational levels. Other spatial issues under consideration by the Commission include cross-border planning studies, and the completion of missing links in European transport and communications networks. As Williams (1993: 4) comments: "Spatial policy is now increasingly recognized as having a rôle to play in the achievement of the EC's fundamental objectives

. . . It is now explicitly on the agenda of the EC Commission. It is not simply a question of international comparisons of planning systems or internationalization of planning concepts." As a result, local planning practice may need to take increasing note of European spatial policy, whether or not local planning procedures remain the responsibility of individual member states.

Conclusion

Although statutory local plans open up or restrict development opportunities, they are not designed to promote active or co-ordinated intervention in the local development process. Indeed, as this chapter has explained, statutory local planning in the British context is narrowly conceived as a well organized procedure to identify and resolve conflicts between interests such as residents, amenity groups, landowners, and developers over the use and development of land. Each of these interests can be expected to participate enthusiastically in plan-making, where necessary to achieve their own ends. Yet, the local planning process is no level playing field, allowing all participants an equal chance of success. Rather, it is a highly political activity controlled by various policy processes, each of which may suit particular interests better than others. The next chapter therefore examines the politics of local development planning, while the following chapter confirms that certain interests are more successful in influencing plan content than others. On this basis, the effectiveness of local development planning is evaluated in Chapter 11.

CHAPTER NINE

The politics of local development planning

Urban planning is an inherently political activity in that it seeks to distribute scarce environmental resources through the decision-making processes of the state. Indeed, statutory development planning would have no legitimate basis without the existence of state power. In local planning, this is exercised primarily to resolve conflicts of interest over the use and development of land. Development plans that appear to favour particular interests (such as house-builders) above others (such as environmental groups) provoke intense controversy. Indeed, environmental interests often expect politicians to protect them from development. In turn, local politicians may nurture and encourage such expectations by failing openly to acknowledge the limited power of the state to intervene effectively in the development process. Development planning can thus become highly politicized, with alliances and divisions between politicians not always explained by traditional party politics.

This chapter examines the extent to which statutory local plans are shaped by political pressures. In particular, it explores how community views on development are brought to political attention and discusses how they are evaluated by politicians. The chapter centres around a notable example of political controversy in plan-making, highlighting the 11-year battle to define the Cambridge green belt through the statutory local plan introduced in the last chapter. This case study suggests that the greater the extent of environmental costs and benefits to be distributed through a statutory plan, the more politicized the plan-making process is likely to become. As a result, although the introduction of participation in plan-making was officially intended to produce greater understanding, co-operation and consensus between all parties, in practice, it has provided a framework for the articulation and resolution of conflicts of interest (Bruton & Nicholson 1987).

The way in which politicians relate to planning matters, and indeed, to political issues generally, is fundamentally determined by their view of the nature of democratic decision-making. Three contrasting models of democracy, which provide legitimacy to the planning process in different ways, are identified by McConnell (1981). In representative democracy, decisions are taken by elected representatives who may fail to achieve 50 per cent of the popular vote, but who may nevertheless chose to ignore minority interests. In pluralist democracy, a broader coalition of interests is constructed to make decisions, often reflecting some form of proportional representation. In popularist democracy, politicians seek directly to involve the public in decision-making through referenda and public participation. The success of popularist democracy is highly dependent on the extent to which those elected are willing to devolve power to the unelected. The distribution of power between elected politicians and members of the public in plan-making will therefore reflect the particular model of democracy in operation at the time.

In the late-1960s, the publication of the Skeffington Report by the Ministry of Housing and Local Government (1969) officially introduced the concept of public participation into statutory planning in the UK. However: "There is a critical difference between going through the empty ritual of participation and having the real power needed to affect the outcome of the process" (Arnstein 1969: 216). This led Arnstein, from own her experience of federal social programmes in the United States, to produce her celebrated ladder of citizen participation, showing successive levels of power over decision-making ceded by the state to ordinary citizens (see Fig. 9.1). These range from forms of non-participation at the foot of the ladder, contrived by some to substitute for genuine participation, to citizen power at the top of the ladder.

The further up the ladder, the more power is ceded by the state, not only to determine means but also to control ends. This suggests that below a certain threshold, attempts by the state to involve members of the public in decision-making are likely to prove unsuccessful and, where tokenism breeds disillusion, counter-productive. A helpful and detailed exploration of the relevance of Arnstein's approach in the present British context is provided by Gyford (1991). Indeed, since the 1960s, the scope and significance of environmental politics in the UK has broadened far beyond invited involvement in statutory plan-making (Young 1993). As widespread environmental concern became central to national and international political debate in the 1980s and 1990s, new development at the local level was often seen as an immediate and visible focus for such concern. The chapter therefore begins by comparing the ways in which local perceptions of development become known.

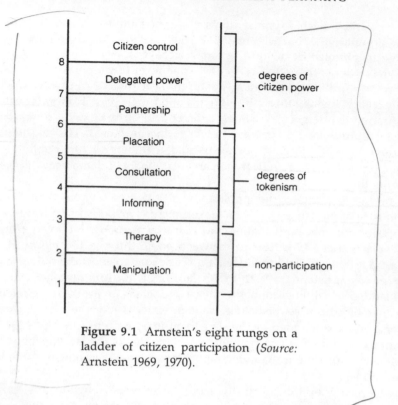

Figure 9.1 Arnstein's eight rungs on a ladder of citizen participation (*Source:* Arnstein 1969, 1970).

The articulation of community views

There are four main ways in which local communities articulate their views on planning and development matters. Arnstein (1969) is concerned primarily with the first, public participation, in which the state takes the initiative to invite involvement from communities, who then chose whether or not to respond. This makes it quite unlike the other three – direct protest, environmental groups, and community architecture – in which the state primarily reacts to initiatives taken by communities. Activities not classified on Arnstein's ladder, such as direct protest, may well be fostered if opportunities for participation are considered too restrictive. This has often happened in the case of new road construction. In statutory local planning, participation has been narrowly interpreted by most local authorities and corresponds in practice to the degrees of tokenism (placation, consultation or informing) on Arnstein's ladder. From now on, it will therefore be described not as participation but as consultation. Each of the four ways will now be explored.

Public consultation

At least two periods for publicity and consultation in statutory plan-making had originally been required in the late-1960s. However, since consultation is resource-intensive, delaying plan-making without necessarily producing consensus, central government enthusiasm dwindled over time. Although one statutory period is still retained in Scotland, opportunities for consultation in England and Wales are now left more to the discretion of individual local authorities (see Ch. 8). In public consultation, local authorities seek to gather comment through public meetings, exhibitions, and questionnaires etc., but they remain highly reluctant to cede power for planning decisions to those communities most affected. "Planning for Real" exercises can offer a notable exception to this. These provide local people with resources such as materials or technical expertise, in order to prepare plans of their own. In Swindon, for example, participants were encouraged to move proposals around a model of the town (Wates & Knevitt 1985).

In 1983, a People's Plan for London's Royal Docks was produced by Newham Docklands Forum with the support of the then Greater London Council (Brownhill 1990). At the time, the London Docklands Development Corporation (LDDC) wished to see substantial commercial development at the Royal Docks, and all but dismissed the People's Plan. Yet, ten years later, after the collapse of the development boom, a *Planning for Real* weekend at the Royal Docks, which involved local residents, community architects and potential developers and was attended by the Prince of Wales, was part sponsored by the LDDC . When the outcome of such popular planning is taken up by state authorities, mere tokenism in Arnstein's ladder is replaced by citizen power.

However, once invited to participate in plan-making, members of the public who wish to prevent development of particular types within existing urban areas (such as high-value commercial offices), or of any type at the urban fringe, may well expect the local planning authority to keep speculative developers at bay. Of course, the same developers are likely to regard statutory plan consultation as an excellent opportunity to influence plan content to their particular advantage. Politicians must therefore determine whether the results of consultation accurately reflect community aspirations as a whole, or whether they merely represent the entrenched opinions of articulate or powerful groups.

Some authorities, concerned that such exercises tend to be dominated by articulate middle-class residents keen to protect their own environment, have made great efforts to reach out to those most disadvantaged by market forces. In Sheffield, for example, the city council established 12 special advisory groups to consider the draft local plan for the city centre. Each group was intended to draw into plan-making particular interests that would otherwise be unlikely to participate, such as the low paid and specific ethnic minorities (Alty & Darke 1991). Such approaches need to be flexible, sensitive and informal to overcome any reluctance to participate owing to cultural, educational or financial factors, or any suspicions of authority held by disadvantaged groups.

Direct protest

Developments that threaten much valued local environments often give rise to spontaneous protest, capable of capturing the political agenda without the need for public consultation to be initiated by the local planning authority. This type of protest may be co-ordinated by informal pressure groups or networks either already in existence or specially formed for the purpose. According to Ambrose (1986: 76), these groups: "seek to influence the behaviour of the development system either by exerting pressure on the national or local state or by direct negotiation with property developing institutions or possibly, as a final consciousness-raising gesture by direct action on a building site." Such groups aim to lobby politicians directly, having mobilized popular support through protest meetings, petitions and effective use of the local media. However, as Ambrose (1986: 76) further notes, many citizens' groups: "lack permanence, often coming together . . . in response to a specific threat to what they regard as important and then often dissolving when the issue is resolved against them or more rarely partly in their favour." Occasionally, such protest can spill over to election time, if action groups put up candidates against councillors who they contend have collaborated with developers rather than protected local interests.

In some cases, developers may seek to pre-empt such protests through direct debate with local communities during early stages of project formulation. For example, well before any planning application was submitted, the London Regeneration Consortium (LRC) appointed community liaison officers and mounted a full public exhibition to explain its £3.5 billion proposed redevelopment at Kings' Cross London. However, the reluctance of LRC to make significant changes to its proposals in response to representations suggests that such direct debate initiated by developers may be intended merely to provide early warning of the nature and extent of the local community protest.

Environmental groups

Environmental groups have become increasingly active and successful in promoting and conserving the environment from threatened development. According to Lowe (1988), such interests should no longer be regarded as isolated pressure groups or representatives of passing fashion, but reflect the changing nature of contemporary society evident in new daily patterns of employment, recreation, residence and consumption. At a national level, the Council for the Protection of Rural England (CPRE) is closely associated with the anti-growth lobby, while the Town and Country Planning Association (TCPA) is more detached, having promoted the concept of planned decentralization from existing cities (Herington 1984). The Civic Trust, which has a broader concern with urban environmental quality, has campaigned vigorously against urban wasteland.

Environmental groups at the local level are often linked to regional networks or to national organizations. For example, most local civic societies relate nationally to the Civic Trust. Such local groups benefit not only from the skill and expertise of their own members (who, if retired, may be prepared to devote substantial time and effort to planning cases) but also from access to national resources made available by parent organizations. Indeed, well established environmental groups are highly experienced in deploying resources and exploiting political networks. They make formidable opponents whom developers ignore at their peril.

Community architecture planning and development

The fourth way in which communities can articulate dissatisfaction with conventional development products achieved national prominence in the 1980s. "The movement is called 'community architecture'. It is an umbrella term which also embraces 'community planning', 'community design', 'community development' and other forms of 'community technical aid'. It emerged from a growing realization that mismanagement of the built environment is a major contributor to the nation's social and economic ills and that there are better ways of going about planning and design" (Wates & Knevitt 1987: 17). Community architecture extends well beyond *Planning for real*, since it seeks to equip local people to carry out their own projects. It often involves the type of third-force organizations considered in Chapter 7.

Community architecture represents a fundamental challenge to the traditional division between developer, investor and user in much conventional development since it "is based on the simple principle that the environment works better if the people who live, work and play in it are actively involved in its creation and management instead of being treated as passive consumers" (Wates & Knevitt 1987: 13). Moreover, community architecture threatens the apparent control of the built environment that many officials and politicians believe they exert. It has therefore been viewed with distinct suspicion in some quarters. However, the significance of community architecture is measured by the intense debate it has provoked, and the extensive literature it has generated. Wates & Knevitt (1987), for example, provide an excellent overview. McDonald (1986) recounts detailed experience in Liverpool, while Hall (1989b) outlines community-based projects initiated by the Town and Country Planning Association. A detailed case study of successful community-based planning and development at Coin Street in London is described by Brindley et al. (1989).

Politics and planning around Cambridge

In 1981, Cambridgeshire County Council began work on the Cambridge Green Belt Local Plan (CGBLP) which, as Chapter 8 explained, was intended to review and finalize the city's green belt boundaries, encourage recreation and tourism, enhance landscape quality, and provide clear policies to control development. The plan was not adopted until 1992. This section is not primarily concerned with the content of the plan, but with the political controversy that surrounded its preparation and adoption. Although substantial development pressure in, and around Cambridge, was bound to produce intense conflicts of interest in defining the green belt, the decision-making process was rendered more complex by political uncertainty at the county council. Indeed, Cambridge provides a classic case of political influence on plan-making, with open conflict evident between county and district councils and between central and local government, and with temporary political coalitions, highly vulnerable to local opinion, trying their best to reach planning decisions. The key events in the preparation of the CGBLP are shown in Table 9.1.

The early days

The CGBLP started life in a stable political climate in the early-1980s, with the Conservatives firmly in control of the county council. The green belt area takes in land within three administrative districts: the City of Cambridge, South Cambridgeshire and a small part of East Cambridgeshire. Although the rural authorities of South and East Cambridgeshire were then dominated by independent councillors, in the City of Cambridge party politics are much more important. Although Labour was the largest party in the city council throughout the 1980s, it achieved overall control only for a short period in 1986 and 1987. Despite reservations expressed by the district councils, the county council decided to take responsibility itself for the CGBLP to ensure a consistent approach throughout the plan area. It soon moved to publish a consultation plan in September 1983, which, although supervised by elected members, fully reflected the technical approach of professional planning officers. Following publication, 10 weeks were allowed for public consultation. This involved a travelling exhibition to encourage public comment, five public meetings and eight seminars with parish councils.

Representations on the consultation plan were received from 13 statutory consultees (government departments, statutory undertakers etc.), 16 parish councils, 22 local societies and environmental groups, 16 land or estate agencies representing 40 separate clients, and 78 members of the public. Shortly after the end of the consultation period, the county council received 218 separate but identical postcards signed by a total of 463 residents living in the vicinity of University Farm in West Cambridge, protesting at the

184

Table 9.1 Key events in the preparation of the Cambridge Green Belt Local Plan.

Event	Date	Status of Clay Farm	Status of Arbury Camps Farm
Cambridgeshire Structure Plan approved which required CGBLP to be prepared	Aug 1980		
Consultation plan	Sept 1983	Excluded from green belt	Green belt
Deposit plan	May 1984	Excluded from green belt	Green belt
Local plan inquiry	Jan & Feb 1985		
County council elections	May 1985		
Inspector's report	Aug 1985	Excluded from green belt	Excluded from green belt
Planning sub-committee considers inspector's report	Oct 1985		
Round one modifications published	Nov 1985	Excluded from green belt	Green belt
Deposit of round one modifications opportunity for objections	Dec 1985 & Jan 1986		
Planning subcommittee considers objections to round one modifications	Sept 1986		
Round two modifications published	Oct 1986	Green belt	Excluded from green belt
Deposit of round two modifications opportunity· for objections	Nov & Dec 1986		
Planning subcommittee meets with Policy committee to consider all objections to both sets of modifications	Feb 1987	Green belt	Green belt
Decision by full county council	Mar 1987	Green belt	Green belt
Secretary of State intervenes	June 1987		
Structure Plan Review examination-in-public	Oct 1987		
Cambridgeshire Replacement Structure Plan approved	Mar 1989	Green belt	Excluded from green belt
County council elections	May 1989		
New settlements inquiry	Nov 1989–Aug 1990		
Secretary of State announces final decision on new settlements	Mar 1992		
Round three modifications published	May 1992	Green belt	Excluded from green belt
Deposit of round three modifications opportunity for objections	May & June 1992		
Decision by full county council	June 1992	Green belt	Excluded from green belt
Cambridge Green Belt Local Plan adopted	Aug 1992	Green belt	Excluded from green belt

site's exclusion from the green belt. This episode provided early warning of the storm of protest that erupted later in plan preparation. Although the county council made a number of minor changes to the plan in response to consultation, when the deposit version was published in May 1984, it was not markedly different from the consultative draft. During the six-week deposit period, 465 separate objections were received. A local plan inquiry was therefore held in January and February 1985.

Those appearing at the inquiry highlighted the significant conflict between interests seeking to roll back the inner boundary of the green belt to allow more development on the edge of Cambridge, and those wishing to tighten the inner boundary in order to restrict development even further. Pro-development objectors included the University and several of its colleges which owned valuable sites capable of development, the House-Builders Federation (HBF), and many private landowners and developers, mostly represented by lawyers, planners, surveyors or other development consultants. Anti-development objectors included the CPRE, the Cambridge Preservation Society, certain parish councils and numerous local residents.

In August 1985, six months after the inquiry, the inspector submitted his report. Although generally in support of the county council, he recommended 53 separate modifications, 12 to the written text, and 41 to the proposed boundary of the green belt. The publication of the inspector's report was eagerly awaited by those living around two strategic sites on the edge of Cambridge, each with high development potential. Residents in the vicinity of Clay Farm, an area of 32 ha on the southern fringes of the city (see Fig. 9.2[1]), where the city council hoped to see 900 affordable houses built, were disappointed to find that the inspector had upheld the deposit plan, recommending that the site should be kept out of the green belt. Furthermore, at Arbury Camps Farm, an area of 34 ha adjoining the A45 by-pass to the north of Cambridge (see Figs 9.3, 9.4), which the deposit plan had included in the green belt, the inspector took issue with the county council, and recommended a modification to remove this site from the green belt. Both groups of residents vowed to defend these sites from development by mounting vigorous campaigns to have the respective recommendations made by the inspector overturned by the county council.

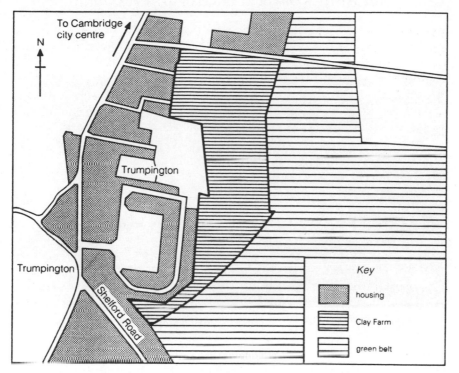

Figure 9.2 Clay Farm, Trumpington, Cambridge.

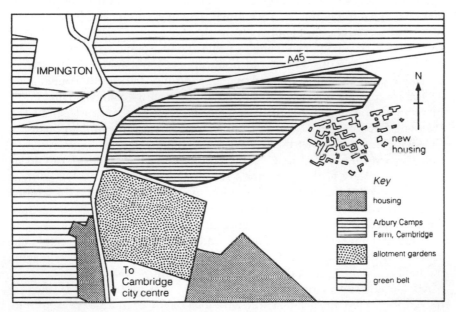

Figure 9.3 Arbury Camps Farm, Cambridge.

Figure 9.4 The A45 bypass and Arbury Camps Farm, Cambridge

Political circumstances change

In normal circumstances, the CGBLP might then have been adopted in under 12 months from the receipt of the inspector's report, with the minimum of debate. However, in the local elections held in May 1985, the Conservatives lost overall control of the county council. The new county council consisted of 29 Conservatives, 26 members from the Alliance of Liberals and Social Democrats, 21 Labour members and one independent. For the next four years, during the critical period of political decision-making on the CGBLP, no single party therefore enjoyed overall control of the county council.

Despite such significant political change, the county council's Director of Planning and Research (DPR), in placing the inspector's report before the Planning Subcommittee (PSC) in October 1985 sought to maintain business as usual, contending that the inspector's recommendations be accepted in full. However, he added that: "if the county council's proposed modifications are contrary to the inspector's recommendations or relate to matters not considered at the public local inquiry, then it is essential that the county council should identify material planning considerations for the actions they wish to take. Whereas the county council is only obliged to take his recommendations into account, members are advised that it would be extremely difficult to defend an aspect of the plan where the inspector has recommended a change" (Cambridgeshire County Council 1985: para 2.3).

After briefly considering the overall tone of the inspector's report, the PSC moved to discuss 10 specific sites, with local ward councillors present and contributing to the debate in most of these cases. Almost without exception, local councillors sought to have sites added to the green belt against the inspector's recommendations. Nevertheless, the PSC, still influenced at this stage by the technical report of the DPR, accepted all but three of the inspector's 53 recommendations. In these three cases (one of which was Arbury Camps Farm) the PSC refused to take land out of the green belt, thus breaking ranks with the inspector. Furthermore, the PSC decided to add another site to the green belt contrary both to the deposit plan and the inspector's recommendations, and took the opportunity to make three minor drafting corrections to the plan. Cambridgeshire County Council therefore published 54 proposed modifications to the CGBLP in November 1985 (subsequently referred to as the Round One modifications). These were placed on deposit between December 1985 and January 1986.

The storm breaks

No objections were received to 32 of these 54 proposed modifications, but the remaining 22 generated 274 representations of which 72 per cent were concentrated on the eight most controversial sites. Most objections were fairly predictable. Landowners and developers generally sought to have more land removed from the green belt, while conservation groups and local residents contended that more land should be added. More importantly, residents and conservation groups in certain villages surrounding Cambridge, hoping to overturn recommendations made by the inspector to exclude land from the green belt, gained the support of both South Cambridgeshire District Council (SCDC) and, in most cases, the local county councillor as well. In the most controversial of these eight sites, a petition signed by almost 1,200 people was submitted against the modification proposed by the county council in line with the inspector's recommendations to exclude 16 ha of farmland at Queens College Farm, Fulbourn.[2]

By the time the PSC met again in September 1986, extensive local opposition had thus been mobilized to certain modifications proposed in accordance with the inspector's report. The PSC received a report from the DPR, summarizing all the objections made to the modifications proposed earlier. The report warned against making any further concessions to the various objectors and bluntly concluded: "It has been my advice that it would be extremely difficult to defend green belt boundaries where the county council has decided to oppose the inspector's recommendations and I would consider that, on appeal the inspector's recommendations would be treated as a material consideration." (Cambridgeshire County Council 1986: para 4.1).

Nevertheless, responding to substantial local feeling and the pressure which this placed on local councillors (most of whom were again at the meeting, either as committee members or to put their own local case) the Labour, Liberal and Social Democratic members of the PSC combined to outvote the Conservatives and retain more sites within the green belt. Five of the earlier modifications made in accordance with the inspector's recommendations to take land out of the green belt (including that at Fulbourn) were thus withdrawn in response to local opposition, while a sixth modification again recommended by the inspector, which had put land with potential for high-technology development into the green belt, was withdrawn following representations by the landowner.

However, four major new modifications (known as the Round Two modifications) were also made at this meeting. Two of these, responding to representations from landowners and developers, implemented recommendations made by the inspector, but originally ignored by the county council, to remove Arbury Camps Farm and land at Cambridge Airport from the green belt. The other two put yet more land into the green belt that the inspector (and indeed the county council in the deposit plan), thought should have been excluded. One of these sites was Clay Farm, where a petition signed by 1,300 people and supported by the local ward councillor had been received. Although only 60 objections had been received contending that the other site, University Farm, should be placed in the green belt, these reminded some councillors present of the 218 separate but identical postcards that the site had generated at the earlier consultation stage.

When the second round of modifications was placed on deposit, a further 61 objections were received. Opposition to the removal of Arbury Camps Farm from the green belt was led by SCDC and six local parish councils seeking to prevent the expansion of Cambridge in their direction, while support was expressed by the HBF, Cambridge City Council and the landowner. Cambridge City Council also led a coalition of interests that opposed the inclusion of Clay Farm in the green belt. This coalition included the owner of a major part of Clay Farm, the HBF, and a national house-builder. More surprisingly, these interests were supported by several outlying parish councils, who believed that the development of Clay Farm on the edge of the city would take pressure off their own villages.

The county council decides

By early 1987, no consistent basis therefore existed to defend the various modifications made by the county council, apart from political necessity and intrigue. The Conservatives who had controlled the council when the CGBLP was originally prepared, and who at that time had sought to contain the growth of Cambridge, now appeared to vote for any modifications necessary to allow the expansion of existing industry. Labour members of the county council also wished to see more employment land provided on the edge of Cambridge, but shared the desire of the Labour majority on the city council to make land available for affordable housing. The Alliance of Liberal and Social Democrats, most of whom had achieved electoral success through community-style campaigning, was highly conscious of the electoral possibilities created by public dissatisfaction with the CGBLP.

Indeed, the Alliance appeared to thrive in the heady atmosphere of continuous debate and unpredictable meetings, whereas the Conservative and Labour groups, based on solid and well understood political values expressed through group meetings and party discipline, found it much harder to adjust to the political realities of a "balanced" council with no single party in control. In the end, the county council had to reach decisions on the CGBLP through a process of political bargaining on individual sites, which might have been construed as a form of traditional "horse-trading" between councillors representing different wards.

In February 1987, a joint meeting was held between the PSC and the county council's Policy Committee at which it was decided to press ahead with all the first round modifications, apart from five of the six previously withdrawn, and with three of the four second round modifications. The sixth modification from the first round previously withdrawn was reinstated, once more removing land at Grange Field, Shelford from the green belt. The fourth modification from the second round, Arbury Camps Farm, was also withdrawn in response to local opposition, so placing the land back in the green belt.

A month later, a meeting of the full county council considered the whole plan for the first time. The political pact sealed at the joint meeting the previous month, remained virtually intact. However, on this occasion, a majority was found once again to withdraw the first round modification affecting Grange Field, Shelford, thus returning the site to the green belt for the second time. Furthermore, a motion to block another of the second round modifications (Cambridge Airport) was also approved, so extending the green belt even further into Cambridge against the inspector's original recommendations. The county council then published the necessary statutory notice to enable the CGBLP to be adopted within six weeks.

The Secretary of State intervenes

However, in June 1987, only a matter of days before the expiry of the statutory notice and the intended adoption of the plan, Nicholas Ridley, Secretary of State for the Environment in the Conservative Government, intervened by issuing a formal direction to prevent the county council from adopting the CGBLP without his express permission. The Secretary of State acted in response to submissions from Cambridge City Council, SCDC and private sector landowners and developers that the political bargain struck in the county council had served to extend the green belt boundary too far into Cambridge, leaving insufficient room to meet the city's development needs in the long term. The Secretary of State decided that the matter should be resolved through the Examination in Public (EIP) into the submitted Structure Plan Review (SPR).

When the EIP was held in October 1987, Cambridge City Council attacked what it called the "hokey-cokey" CGBLP, and pressed for the release of Clay

Farm for housing development and Arbury Camps Farm for employment use. SCDC now presented the views expressed earlier by certain outlying parish councils that Clay Farm should be developed in order to divert pressure away from their villages. Indeed, SCDC suggested that other potential housing sites on the edge of Cambridge should also be released for this purpose.

The HBF was keen to see Clay Farm developed for housing, while the Confederation of British Industry (CBI) thought that both Clay Farm and Arbury Camps Farm should be removed from the green belt. A highly respected national firm of planning consultants appeared at the EIP on behalf of the owners of Arbury Camps Farm to seek its release. In contrast, the CPRE, the Cambridge Preservation Society and the Trumpington Environmental Action Group all pressed the case for a tight green belt around Cambridge. They were supported by the existing Member of Parliament for South West Cambridgeshire (whose constituency included Clay Farm) and two of his predecessors. The Secretary of State, in responding to the discussion at the EIP and to the report of the appointed panel, struck the inevitable compromise, modifying and approving the SPR in a way which effectively retained Clay Farm within the green belt, but removed Arbury Camps Farm from it.

Towards adoption

Following the approval of the SPR in March 1989, the Secretary of State directed Cambridgeshire County Council in June 1989 to consider modifying the CGBLP in accordance with his decision on the structure plan. A month earlier, the Conservatives, had regained control of the county council, taking 45 seats at the local election, in comparison with 21 seats gained by Labour and 9 by the Liberal Democrats. However, by that time, a lengthy public inquiry was expected into a series of separate proposals for new settlements in the Cambridge area. This further delayed progress on the CGBLP.

In 1991, when the Secretary of State announced the outcome of this inquiry, it was clear that none of the settlements likely to be approved would affect the outer boundary of the green belt. The county council, now in Conservative control, decided to make the minimum changes necessary to allow the CGBLP to be adopted. In May 1992, it therefore published two further modifications (known as the Round Three modifications), finally taking Arbury Camps Farm and adjoining land out of the green belt. Although the Conservatives had regained the power to reverse their earlier defeats inflicted by the Labour, Liberal and Social Democratic councillors between 1985 and 1989, they chose not to do so, preferring instead to demonstrate their ability to manage statutory procedures smoothly, without further debate or controversy. By this time, public interest had diminished, and only eight objections were received to the third round of modifications.

The CGBLP, thus modified to comply with the compromise brokered by the Secretary of State, was finally adopted on 28 August 1992.

However, when one political controversy ends, another begins. In June 1992, Cambridge City Council had placed a new local plan for the whole of the city on deposit. This proposed three locally important changes to the green belt and one of strategic significance: the removal of Clay Farm to allow for the 900 affordable homes that the city council had always wanted to see built. Although the county council first announced that the Cambridge Local Plan was not in general conformity with the SPR, the Conservatives lost control of the county council once more in the May 1993 elections. The new administration, controlled by Labour and the Liberal Democrats, then accepted the release of Clay Farm in the next review of the structure plan, which was placed on deposit in November 1993. Since the Conservatives in the county council expressed vehement opposition to this, in due course the Secretary of State will no doubt be asked to intervene again.

The political evaluation of community views

Cambridge is certainly not typical of the relationship between planning and politics in the country as a whole, but it does bring together in an exaggerated form, many of the factors that influence political decision-making in planning issues. This section draws on experience from Cambridge and elsewhere to highlight how elected representatives evaluate community views on planning and development matters.

Technical advice

An extensive literature explores the relationship between professional officers and elected members in planning decisions. Blowers (1980) contends that county councillors in Bedfordshire sought to correct the failure of the county planning officer to place local concerns above national needs in minerals planning. Since planning distributes costs and benefits among individuals and social groups and increasingly affects the quality of urban life, he attacks the notion that it can be treated separately from politics. Although planning officers traditionally claim political neutrality, they need political support and initiative to get things done. However, Blowers (1980) maintains that officers tend to mistake politics as a mechanism for decision-making, rather than its motivation. Reade (1987) criticises professional planning officers for straying beyond technical analysis into policy formulation, which he considers the legitimate rôle of politicians. Indeed, according to Reade (1987), planning officers are caught in a "rôle muddle" created by their failure to clarify the distinction between their own activity and that of politicians. As Blowers (1980) argues, an increasingly sophisticated electorate is no longer prepared to accept planning decisions that may appear technically correct, but which may impose high resource costs on local communities. As the Cambridge case study shows, the more controversial an issue becomes, the less elected representatives are likely to accept technical advice from officers.

Wider implications

Experienced politicians can soon calculate whether they will gain or lose through close association with strongly articulated community feeling. Many local ward councillors, particularly with small majorities, are keen to be photographed with local protestors on threatened development sites, believing that this enhances their prospects of re-election. In Cambridge, ward councillors certainly kept a keen eye on the next local election. Council leaders may take a different view, particularly if wider concerns are at stake. For example, if land owned by the local authority can be sold for development, council revenues will be boosted. Indeed, the council may already have entered into partnership with the prospective developer. Any form of redevelopment within existing urban areas may be welcomed if it removes dereliction and boosts the tax base of an authority. In city centres, redevelopment is often considered by political leaders to create a powerful visual image, enhancing a city's position in the urban marketplace. The extent to which council leaders give way to community protests in planning decisions may thus depend on whether anything material is at stake for the authority as a whole.

The broader political agenda

Politicians are often keen to plug local planning decisions into the broader political agenda. This is constantly changing. In the 1980s, much higher levels of unemployment in the UK caused many local authorities to take a keen interest in economic development. In Cheshire, for example, employment land policies were reformulated to maximize the prospects for economic growth. As a result, it became much more difficult for community groups to prevent factory-building on open fields (Adams et al. 1994). By the late-1980s, the enterprise culture started to give way nationally to a new environmental culture (see Ch. 4). Many local authorities decided to prepare environmental audits and strategies (Steeley 1990). Community protests that take advantage of such an agenda are harder for politicians to ignore.

One way in which this broader political agenda may feed through into decision-making is through political manifestos. Planning and development issues have rarely occupied a significant place in political manifestos, either at the national or local level. However, from time to time, urban planning achieves the political prominence that many consider it deserves. For example, in 1982, the new Labour Council elected in Camden was committed by its manifesto to: "retaining existing housing and essential shops . . .

194

totally oppose speculative office development . . . keep land and buildings at present used for industry available . . . to press for changes in the planning laws, and to decentralize planning as part of an overall area management policy" (quoted in Forsyth 1985). Local manifestos may have important consequences for the relationship between members and officers in local government for, as Forsyth (1985) argues, such firm commitments remove officers from involvement and control over the process and content of policy formulation and action.

Central–local conflict

Local politicians must consider whether by accepting community views, the local authority might find itself in direct conflict with central government over planning policy and if so, whether there is any likelihood that the locally driven perspective would succeed. In Cambridgeshire, it could be argued that local politicians effectively abandoned responsibility for taking unpopular planning decisions in the belief that the Secretary of State would have to intervene, and would thereafter carry the blame for unwanted development.

This strategy has its limitations. In the early-1990s, SERPLAN (the Regional Planning Conference for the South East of England) suggested that Hampshire should allow for the construction of 92,000 new dwellings between 1991 and 2006 as its contribution to regional housing growth (Breheny 1993). This suggestion was firmly resisted by Hampshire County Council who suggested a lower figure of 73,000. Dudley Keep, chairman of Hampshire County Council, declared that Hampshire: "was not going to be kicked about by more development". He added that the proposal to accommodate 92,000 additional dwellings over the 15 year period "would put a strain on the county which it cannot tolerate. We've been mucked about for 30 years. It is time to say enough is enough" (quoted in *Planning* 1992). As Breheny (1993: 11) comments: "Hampshire is now known as the most defensively-minded county in the South East. Politicians feel that the county has done more than its fair share in accommodating growth in the South East."

However, Michael Howard, who belonged to the same political party as Mr Keep, and was at the time Secretary of State for Environment, modified the submitted Hampshire structure plan in March 1993 to increase the housing land allocation from 61,000 to 73,500 new dwellings for the 11 year period from April 1990 to March 2001 alone. This higher figure appears compatible with the SERPLAN target of 92,000 dwellings over the longer 15 year period from 1991 to 2006. Nevertheless, Mr Keep was reported to be delighted at the outcome, suggesting that his original statement may have been intended as a bargaining ploy in a battle between central and local government, rather than a realistic forecast of likely planning policy.

Elections

In the end, the electoral implications of community protests are likely to weigh heavily on the minds of politicians. Where majority parties are well entrenched in political control of a council with little immediate prospect of defeat, difficult decisions may be easier to take. Alternatively, when elections are imminent or where, as in Cambridgeshire between 1985 and 1989, no single party enjoys overall control, much greater attention may need to be paid to community protests.

According to Blowers (1980), although local elections are won or lost primarily on national issues, local politicians still behave according to the law of anticipated reactions, believing that they will receive electoral rewards either for thrift or for improving standards of service. He further contends that the electoral process makes councillors seek a close relationship with their electorate " . . . through public meetings, petitions, the press, surgery, or visits to constituents. Through such contacts, councillors expect to be able to gauge public reaction to certain issues and to articulate the needs and demands of the public they represent" (Blowers 1980: 30–31). Such regular contacts make elected councillors reluctant to accept planning advice that they consider could be to their disadvantage at the next election.

Conclusion

This chapter has contended that urban planning is a highly political process not only because it seeks to distribute environmental resources between groups in society, but also because it exposes politicians at national and local level to widely held local views which are often forcibly articulated through the statutory planning process. Nevertheless, many landowners, developers and investors have great difficulty in coming to grips with the political nature of plan-making. They tend to assume that technical reports tabled by professional planning officers or recommendations made by inspectors will automatically be accepted by elected councillors on planning committees. The Cambridge example demonstrates that this can be far from the truth. Actors in the development process are more likely to influence decisions in the planning process if they fully understand the variety of ways in which community views are articulated, the nature of local decision-making, and the range of factors that politicians take into account when evaluating their views.

However, local communities that gain political support in any campaign to prevent development must remember that the developer is entitled to appeal against refusal of planning permission, and must therefore be prepared to put their case at any subsequent public inquiry into the planning appeal. In contrast, community protests that fail to persuade local planning authorities to refuse applications for new development have no similar right to appeal, but must rely instead on the very limited opportunities to challenge the legality of such decisions in the courts (Hough 1992). Commentators such as Healey (1989) have therefore suggested that the statutory planning process could be improved by providing third parties, such as community groups and aggrieved local residents, with the right to appeal against planning permission granted in conflict with an adopted statutory development plan.

Notes

1. For the location of Clay Farm and other sites mentioned in this chapter, in relation to Cambridge as a whole, see Figure 8.3.
2. Despite its name, this land was no longer owned by Queens College, but by the occupying farmer.

CHAPTER TEN

The power to influence local development planning

Statutory local plans are prepared through a complex procedure intended to identify and resolve conflicts of interest between those who value land in different ways. An essential focal point for such conflict mediation is the local plan inquiry, which offers an opportunity to test formal objections submitted at the deposit stage. As Chapter 8 explained, the inquiry is meant to provide equal access to all who wish to participate and is conducted by an independent inspector (or a reporter in Scotland) appointed by central government. After the inquiry, recommendations made by the inspector are submitted to the local planning authority, which decides whether or not to accept them. Of course, such final decisions may sometimes be made for political rather than technical reasons.

Applying the distinction drawn by Healey et al. (1988), the local plan inquiry is thus a semi-judicial policy process, in which cross-examination is employed to test the merits of opposing arguments. In contrast, the subsequent period, in which the inspector's report is considered by the planning authority, is dominated by a politico-rational policy process, often most evident in the cut and thrust of party politics. Some interests may be better placed to take advantage of such policy processes than others. Indeed, statutory plan-making procedures, at least from the deposit stage onwards, can be likened more to a minefield, over which those involved must tread with great care, than to an even playing field in which conflicts of interest are settled through fair competition.

This chapter investigates the tactics which enable particular interests to benefit most from formal procedures in local plan-making. Such tactics, if carefully followed, convey the power to influence local development plans. The chapter is based on empirical research (reported in detail in Adams & Pawson 1991) into the outcome of 4,850 formal objections to a representative sample of 16 local plans.[1] The research revealed a clear distinction between three broad types of interest: those in favour of further development, those against, and those concerned mainly with planning policy. The chapter contends that, although sheer weight of numbers gives strength to anti-development interests, pro-development interests in particular, rely on

·more subtle means of persuasion, such as professional representation and formal presentation at the local plan inquiry. The chapter seeks to unravel the comparative importance of these factors by examining how success rates in local planning vary between different types of objection.

Success rates

The 4850 objections raised 843 different planning issues, with several objections often registered to the same issue. Indeed, certain controversial issues generated very large numbers of objections. The proposed development of one field, for example, may prompt 200–300 similar objections from nearby residents. The distinction between objections and issues is significant, since the most controversial 10 per cent of issues accounted for 70 per cent of all objections. If, in an extreme case, the only modifications made to the plans had been to satisfy the 70 per cent of objectors who raised these 10 per cent of issues, it could be concluded that, although the vast majority of objectors had been satisfied, the plans remained mainly intact. Separate analysis of objections and the issues that they raised is therefore essential.

Modifications may be proposed to a local plan where objections are upheld by the inspector or the local planning authority, or both. Although planning authorities tend to adopt the vast majority of recommendations made by inspectors, they retain the discretion not to do so, provided a full and clear explanation is given in each case. However, in the plans studied, over 90 per cent of inspectors' recommendations were adopted, a proportion very similar to that previously recorded by Crispin et al. (1985). Almost always, effective influence thus requires acceptance by the local planning authority of a modification recommended by the inspector to meet an objection. A series of alternative outcomes, shown in Table 10.1. may therefore arise. Success rates can be defined as the number of objections upheld divided by the total number received. They are normally expressed in percentage terms. Success in influencing the inspector (outcomes 2 plus 3 in Table 10.1) needs to be calculated separately from that in influencing the local planning authority (outcomes 2 plus 4). On this basis, 55 per cent of objections succeed with the inspector but only 51 per cent with the local planning authority, while 22 per cent of issues raised succeed with the inspector but only 18 per cent with the authority. These mean success rates act as benchmarks against which subsequent performance will be analyzed. Objectors who achieve above-average success rates can be considered to have secured greater access to the critical decision-makers in local planning.

Earlier work suggested that inspectors concentrate on what they consider to be the technical merits of the case, while local planning authorities accord equal consideration to the political aspects of local planning (Adams

Table 10.1 Outcome of 4,850 local plan objections and issues consequently generated.

Outcome	Objections		Issues	
	Number	Proportion	Number	Proportion
1. No modification recommended or proposed to plan	2112	44%	658	78%
2. Modification recommended by inspector, wholly or partly adopted by LPA	2432	50%	150	18%
3. Modification recommended by inspector, not adopted by LPA	224	5%	30	4%
4. Modification not recommended by inspector but adopted by LPA	82	1%	5	–
Totals	4850	100%	843	100%

Source: Adams & Pawson (1991).

& May 1990). This may explain why slightly more objections and issues succeed with the inspector than with the local planning authority. However, as far higher success rates are noticeable for objections than for issues, it is necessary to distinguish between those interests in favour of further development, those against, and those concerned primarily with policy matters (such as local transport). This is shown in Table 10.2, which reveals that the vast majority of the 4850 objections (over 70 per cent) were against further development, but that most issues debated at the local plan inquiry revolved around planning policy or the need for further development. As Table 10.2 further shows, anti-development interests achieved the highest rates of success not only for objections but also for the issues that these objections raised. The next section seeks to explain this.

Table 10.2 Success rate by nature of local plan objection and issue.

	Objections			Issues		
	Number	Success rates		Number	Success rates	
		Inspector	LPA		Inspector	LPA
Anti-development	3526	64%	63%	180	34%	32%
Pro-development	428	22%	13%	237	17%	12%
Policy-orientated	896	33%	28%	426	19%	17%
Means success rates	4850	55%	51%	843	22%	18%

Source: Adams & Pawson (1991).

How anti-development interests succeed

As Marsden et al. (1993: 187) suggest: "Throughout much of the English lowlands, as well as in attractive and accessible upland areas, anti-development and preservationist attitudes dominate much local decision-making and political organization." Anti-development objections were particularly prominent in the local plans for North Leeds, the Nottinghamshire Green Belt, South Westmorland, Totnes and Wells. These coincided, in each case, with an above-average number of multiple objections to the same issue. Table 10.3 demonstrates how success rates more than tripled when over 50 objections were registered to a single issue. This indicates that both inspectors and local planning authorities were influenced by substantial numbers of objections to the same issue. Moreover, the most controversial issues that generated the greatest number of objections were almost invariably those where the objectors sought to prevent further development. Indeed, as Table 10.4 reveals, anti-development issues accounted for only 10 per cent of cases where a single objector was involved, but 90 per cent of cases where 50 or more objectors were involved.

Table 10.3 Success rate by number of objectors per local plan issue.

Objectors per issue	Number of issues	Success rates (%)	
		Inspector	LPA
1	562	17	15
2–9	212	26	22
10	47	33	24
50+	22	68	68
Totals and mean success rates	843	22	18

Source: Adams & Pawson (1991).

Table 10.4 Nature of local plan issue by number of objectors per issue.

Objectors per issue	Nature of issue			
	Anti-development	Pro-development	Policy-orientated	All issues
1	60	178	324	562
2–9	67	52	93	212
10–49	33	7	7	47
50+	20	0	2	22
Totals	180	237	426	843

Source: Adams & Pawson (1991).

Such multiple objectors rarely instructed professional representation in their fight to prevent development, but often appointed one of their own number to act as an unpaid agent. This practice was encouraged by some inspectors, exemplified by the case of multiple objections to the allocation of a site in Kirkby Lonsdale for housing and car parking in the South Westmorland Local Plan. Here, the inspector (Hewitt 1988: 27) noted that "44 individual objections were submitted . . . Whilst I refer later in my report to individual points of objection which were not generally repeated by others, many of the submissions were of a similar nature and in fact most of the local residents objecting chose to be represented by Mr W. Fishwick who presented a co-ordinated case by calling several local people as witnesses. This considerably assisted the organization of the inquiry . . . Where the same or similar points were made by successive parties I have not necessarily repeated them but have reflected the weight of opinion in framing my recommendations." The inspector upheld the objections and recommended that the proposed allocation be deleted from the local plan.

Table 10.5 Success rates for types of local plan objector.

Objector	Number of objections	Success rates (%)	
		Inspector	LPA
Private individuals	3603	62	60
Elected representatives	35	37	40
Amenity & environment groups	237	37	34
Small businesses	110	34	34
Parish & town councils	82	27	29
Resident groups	122	32	27
Government organizations*	33	30	27
Political parties	96	28	27
Local authorities	66	30	26
Property & development companies	239	33	23
Miscellaneous	73	27	23
Non-property limited companies	154	43	21
Total and mean success rates	4850	55	51

* Includes government departments, quangos, statutory undertakers and nationalized industries.
Source: Adams & Pawson (1991)

The classification of interests shown in Table 10.5, confirms the success of private individuals who band together against the same development. Since local planning authorities do not keep sophisticated information on each objector, this classification is based on a much simpler approach than theoretically desirable (see, for instance, Rydin 1986, Healey et al. 1988). However, the interests of certain objectors can be readily defined in relation to the nature of their objection. For example, property & development companies were almost exclusively concerned with planning policy and particularly with promoting development. Approximately 75 per cent of objections from non-property limited companies were concerned with planning policy, while over half those received from small businesses sought to promote development.

In contrast, while 4 per cent of private individuals sought to promote development (presumably on their own land) and 10 per cent made representations on policy matters, 86 per cent objected to development, demonstrating the continued strength and vitality of "nimbyism". For as Lowe (1988) points out, successive waves of middle class newcomers have firmly established themselves in attractive parts of the countryside. He argues that: "these groups have entrenched their interests within the local planning system, building up formal and informal links with planning authorities, influencing development plans and pressing for the imposition of protective designations" (Lowe 1988: 41–2). The impact of such anti-development interests on the formulation of housing land policy in Berkshire, for example, has been well demonstrated by Short et al. (1986).

Private individuals were not merely the most successful interest. Since they were so dominant numerically, they were also unique in achieving above-average success rates with the inspector and the local planning authority. Yet, once multiple objections are discounted and attention is concentrated instead on the 562 issues raised by a single objector, private individuals drop from the top of the success league almost to the bottom. Although sheer weight of numbers helps to explain the success of the anti-development lobby, different factors may be decisive when the pressure of multiple objections is not a consideration. Indeed, as the next section shows, success rates in issues that revolve around policy matters or the need for further development are enhanced by professional representation and by formal appearance at the local plan inquiry.

How pro-development and policy interests succeed

Professional representation

Professional representation was commissioned by only 561 of the 4850 objectors. The total number of professional representatives instructed by these 561 objectors was 882, since in certain cases, two or three professional representatives were instructed to present a single objection. Approximately 55 per cent of all such professional representation was provided by development consultants (chartered surveyors, chartered town planners and other development consultants) with 45 per cent provided by lawyers (barristers and solicitors). As Table 10.6 shows, 50 per cent of the 882 professional representatives were instructed in order to promote development and a further 40 per cent on planning policy. Professional representation for anti-development interests was insignificant. The three most frequent users of professional advice (property & development companies, non-property limited companies and small businesses) accounted for over 70 per cent of all professional representation. As Grant (1989) confirms, developers, for example, are quite prepared to invest in the specialist skills of gifted lawyers, many of whom have been attracted to planning work.

Table 10.6 Type of professional representative by nature of local plan objection.

Nature of objection	Barrister		Solicitor		Surveyor		Planner		Other dev't consultant		Total	
	No.	%	No.	%	No.	%	No.	%	No.	%	No.	%
Anti-development	6	3	26	13	15	6	14	9	27	32	88	10
Pro-development	133	66	53	27	108	46	112	70	31	37	437	50
Policy-orientated	63	31	120	60	115	48	33	21	26	31	357	40
Totals	202	100	199	100	238	100	159	100	84	100	882	100

Source: Adams & Pawson (1991)

Barristers in the research generally represented property & development companies and small businesses, while non-property limited companies preferred to instruct solicitors. Surveyors were twice as likely as planners to be appointed as expert witnesses by property & development companies, who were instructed by such companies no more often than other development consultants, such as highway and drainage engineers. Non-property limited companies relied very largely on surveyors as expert witnesses. In contrast, small businesses made very little use at all of the services of the surveying profession and instead preferred to be represented by planners and other development consultants.

Solicitors achieved overall success rates of 45 per cent with the inspector and 30 per cent with the local planning authority in comparison with respective figures of 35 per cent and 25 per cent for barristers. Among other professional representatives, other development consultants, such as drainage and highway engineers, achieved the highest relative success rates, possibly owing to their technical expertise on infrastructure matters. Yet, as Table 10.7 shows, for objections as a whole, professional representation appears to be associated with reduced success rates. However, this picture is reversed once the power of multiple objections is discounted and attention is concentrated instead on those 562 issues raised by a single objector. As the earlier Table 10.4 revealed, all but 60 of the 562 single-issue objectors in Table 10.7 were concerned with planning policy or with promoting development. Detailed analysis confirmed that when a barrister, solicitor, surveyor, planner or other development consultant was instructed for pro-

Table 10.7 Success rates by type of representation.

	Objections			Single objector issues		
	Number	Success rates		Number	Success rates	
		Inspector	LPA		Inspector	LPA
Not professionally represented	4289	57%	54%	400	13%	12%
Professionally represented	561	36%	26%	162	25%	21%
Totals and mean success rates	4850	55%	51%	562	16%	15%

Source: Adams & Pawson (1991)

development objections, success rates with both the inspector and the local planning authority improved consistently over and above the relevant benchmark means, except for surveyors in relation to the planning authority. Although barristers and other development consultants were able also to improve success rates for policy objections with both the inspector and the local planning authority, solicitors and surveyors could do so only with the inspector, and planning consultants with neither. In contrast, neither barristers, surveyors nor planning consultants were able to enhance the success of anti-development objections above the benchmark means, although solicitors and other development consultants both achieved this with the inspector and the local planning authority.

The power of professional representation to influence local development planning is thus concentrated on pro-development and, to a lesser extent, on policy objections rather than on anti-development ones. This explains why over 70 per cent of professional representatives at local plan inquiries appear on behalf of those in the business sector who normally wish to see more development take place. In such cases, a full professional team rather than a single expert may well be instructed to counterbalance the benefit of multiple objections often enjoyed by the anti-development lobby.

The composition of such a team is usually designed to avoid its members having to stray into matters beyond their own professional competence. Chartered town planners, for instance, should not be expected to present detailed evidence on highway engineering, nor chartered engineers to give an expert opinion on green belt policies. Such weakness would soon be exposed by a good advocate on the other side. Particular care therefore needs to be taken to selecting the most appropriate professional representative or team of representatives for the inquiry. Indeed, those professional representatives who have built up considerable expertise as expert witnesses by concentrating on statutory plan inquiries, are likely to enjoy higher success rates than the mean for their respective professions.

Nevertheless, local planning authorities appear much less impressed than inspectors by professional representation. Although the facts of the case and the merits of the arguments are matters of prime concern to the inspector, political considerations may be equally important to the local planning authority. This helps to explain why success rates are generally lower with the local planning authority than with the inspector. Successful professional representation demands awareness of the political priorities of the local planning authority and the strongly held views of its leading councillors, and thus requires understanding of both the technical and political aspects of local development planning.

The method of presentation

Objectors to a statutory local plan must decide whether to appear formally at the local plan inquiry or to submit written representation to the inspector. Although two-thirds of the 4850 objections were resolved through written representations, 56 per cent of the 843 issues that they raised were discussed at the inquiry. Discussion at the inquiry appeared to improve the chances of success for issues, but not for objections. As Lavers & Webster (1991: 810) suggest: "Although the right to appear includes the right to be represented by counsel, solicitor or any other person, many objectors at inquiries are disadvantaged by representing themselves, being exposed to questioning by professionals and undertaking questioning on their own behalf." This can be quite intimidating for private individuals. Even when they do appear at inquiries, such objectors tend to concentrate on presenting their own case, but rarely question those who put opposing cases (Department of the Environment 1993).

As a result, inquiries appear dominated by the pro-development lobby, while most of an inspector's homework is devoted to the written representations of the anti-development lobby. Indeed, as Table 10.8 shows, three objections in every four against development were resolved through written representations. In contrast, two objections in every three in favour of development were discussed at the inquiry. The three types of objector most likely to instruct professional representation (property & development companies, non-property limited companies and small businesses) were each among the four most likely to appear at the inquiry.

Although the method of presentation appeared immaterial to the success of anti-development and policy-orientated objections, success rates for pro-development objections more than doubled when objectors appeared at the inquiry. However, since fewer than 10 per cent of objectors favoured further

Table 10.8 Method of presentation by nature of local plan objection.

Method of presentation	Anti-development		Pro-development		Policy orientated	
	No.	%	No.	%	No.	%
Written representations only	2635	75%	140	33%	474	53%
Discussion at inquiry	891	25%	288	67%	422	47%
Totals	3526	100%	428	100%	896	100%

Source: Adams & Pawson (1991)

development, this influence was more than outweighed in aggregate success rates by the overwhelming number of anti-development objections. The strength of the anti-development lobby appeared to come primarily from the multiplicity of objections submitted against particular proposals, rather than necessarily to the manner of presentation. Pro-development objectors do not have the advantage of numbers and therefore depend on professional representation and formal appearance at the inquiry to enhance their chances of success.

Conclusion

This chapter has suggested that the power to influence local development planning is achieved in one of two ways. Those many individuals who wish to prevent development are best advised to club together and make multiple objections. Those in the business sector wishing to influence planning policy or promote development must be prepared to commission professional expertise to present a well researched case. This does not imply that the merits of submissions from the anti-development lobby are irrelevant or that no benefit could accrue to the pro-development lobby, if, for example, several property & development companies were to present a combined case at inquiry.

Indeed, the success rates identified in this chapter represent no more than statistical calculations of probability. Although solicitors as a whole achieved higher success rates than barristers, for example, it does not follow that every solicitor was more successful than every barrister, or more significantly, that the presence of a solicitor was the decisive factor in each case. Single causal relationships cannot readily be established in this way, since success may be attributable to several or none of the variables mentioned. For instance, professional representatives may advise clients not to pursue objections that appear to have little chance of success. If these are weeded out at an early stage, success rates for professional advisers will be higher. The findings in this chapter should thus be considered not in isolation but as an extension of earlier case studies, including those reported both in Chapter 5, which explored the ability of landowners to maximize their development opportunities through local planning, and in Chapter 9, which considered the political significance of the anti-development lobby in Cambridge.

These various sources of evidence confirm that the critical decision-makers in local planning are swayed backwards and forwards by the persuasive power of professional representation for development and by the numerical strength of any local opposition to it. Such pressures are likely to increase rather than decrease as a result of the Planning and Compensation Act 1991, which, in attempting to enhance the status of statutory local plans, raised the stakes at local plan inquiries. The inspector and local planning authority thus face not merely the task of conflict mediation but also the temptation of conflict resolution in favour of those interests that appear most powerful.

As a result, pro-development interests who seek to restore or reinforce their power in the market may be equally well served by local development planning as anti-development interests who seek to protect the environmental resources that they value. Indeed, some landowners and developers may specifically seek to restrict their competitors' access to development land and obtain a monopoly share for themselves through participation in the local planning process (Adams 1987, Adams & Kent 1991). Such outcomes indicate that, when local development planning fails explicitly to promote equity and efficiency, it can be readily captured by those with power to exploit it for their own ends. This is unlikely to diminish until planning authorities accord greater priority in urban planning to those who can neither afford professional expertise nor muster great numbers to articulate their need for better access to urban services and facilities.

Notes

1. The 16 local plans were chosen to provide a representative sample of those adopted in five English regions between September 1988 and September 1989. In the North West, where relatively few plans were adopted during this period, the timescale was extended to March 1990. The sixteen local plans were for Armthorpe, Edenthorpe, Kirk Sandall, Barnby Dun and Adjoining Areas in Doncaster, Central Rushcliffe, Chard, Dartmouth, City of London, Epping and Ongar, Mole Valley Rural Areas, Nottinghamshire Green Belt, North Leeds, Royal Borough of Kingston upon Thames, Roydon, Nazing and Watham Abbey, South Rochdale, South Westmorland, Totnes and for Wells.

CHAPTER ELEVEN

The effectiveness of local development planning

Statutory development planning is intended to provide a democratic mechanism for the social management of land-use and environmental change. At the local level, it is designed not to foster comprehensive intervention in the development process (except in specifically designated action areas), but rather to identify and resolve conflicts of interest over the use or development of land. Indeed, statutory local plans are mainly concerned with the allocation of land for particular types of development. This chapter therefore examines the contribution of such plans to good urban planning, which, through shaping market behaviour (as Ch. 4 suggested) endeavours to enhance equity, efficiency and sustainability in the built environment to an extent that improves and is seen to improve upon the outcomes that would otherwise be generated by the market alone.

The chapter first demonstrates that statutory local plans interact dynamically with land & property markets. Although historic patterns of value embedded in land & property markets constrain development plans, plans themselves modify future patterns of market value. As a result, those who can most benefit financially from such modifications, notably landowners and developers, seek to influence statutory local plans in their own favour. The chapter contends that, wherever they succeed, such plans dispense financial and environmental resources to those already advantaged by the market. This exemplifies the inherent bias in statutory planning towards powerful and well resourced interests. Such bias is quite deliberate, for, in a market economy, the implementation of statutory local plans is heavily dependent on landowners, developers, investors, infrastructure companies and other agencies. The chapter explains how statutory local plans are weakened in their ability to influence market behaviour by their narrow scope and poor connection to implementation. This suggests that statutory local planning, as a resource-intensive activity of growing importance, is in urgent need of reform.

Local planning and land & property markets

The power of historic patterns of value

In the late-1960s, Leeds City Council undertook a review of the city development plan. A particular issue in West Leeds concerned the shortage of open space. Technical analysis revealed that the number of playing fields was well below the appropriate provision per 1,000 of population. To the planners at the time, the solution seemed simple: more land in West Leeds needed to be allocated for public open space. The most suitable location appeared to be the relatively flat floor of the Kirkstall Valley. This area was mainly in private ownership and was partly occupied by long-established industrial premises. Despite this, when the Leeds Development Plan Review was approved in 1972, the existing factories were coloured green on the map and allocated for public open space. However, the intended playing fields were never provided. To implement the proposal, the city council would have had to acquire all ownership rights in the land by compulsory purchase. Compensation payable to the owners would have been based on the open-market value of the existing factories in the property market, rather than the nominal value of the factory sites as open space.

As this example shows, local development plans ignore land & property markets at their peril. Until a simple and inexpensive way is devised to write down historic patterns of value established by earlier generations, the scope of local development planning within built-up areas will remain constrained by the open-market value of existing property. The acquisition and demolition of such property, however obsolete, is not a cheap option for local planning authorities. For example, in the 1980s, the London Borough of Camden constructed a small park behind Tottenham Court Road, to meet the desperate need for some play-space for local children. The site was under one hectare but cost well over £1 million to acquire. This was far more than was spent on the play equipment or the high-quality landscaping for the park. Such examples provide sombre lessons for planners who try to rearrange urban land-uses through local development planning. For in such cases, the power of land & property markets normally require low-value uses (such as open space) to be replaced with high-value uses (such as superstores or business parks) and not vice versa.

The modification of future patterns of value

In 1989, a Venezuelan company, Organizacion Diego Cisneros (ODC) paid approximately £240 million for 1.7 ha opposite St Paul's Cathedral in the City of London. The site, known as Paternoster Square, was occupied by a collection of uninspiring office blocks built in the 1960s. ODC intended to replace these outmoded buildings with brand-new development built at a much higher density. When this became public knowledge, the proposed development drew widespread and sustained criticism. The Prince of Wales added his voice to the many organizations and individuals who considered that the ODC design represented gross overdevelopment in a highly sensitive location. An alternative classical design for the redevelopment of Paternoster Square at a much lower density was produced by the architect, John Simpson. This was well received by the Prince and by many interested organizations and ordinary Londoners.

When it became clear that planning permission would be unlikely to be granted for its scheme, the Venezuelan company decided to cut its losses. Only a few months after having paid £240 million for Paternoster Square, ODC sold the site for approximately £150 million to a British and American development partnership. The new partnership announced that its development would be inspired by traditional concepts of urban design, with fine streets, public spaces and materials in harmony with the older buildings that remained in the area. However, if no planning system had existed, once ODC had acquired all ownership rights in the 1.7 ha, it would have been able to press ahead with a highly intensive office development, immune to public criticism. The planning system effectively reduced the open-market value of the site by approximately £90 million.

This demonstrates that, although land & property markets constrain plans through **historic patterns of value**, the planning system itself critically influences land & property markets through modifying **future patterns of value**. Although statutory planning procedures draw an artificial distinction between use, value and ownership (concentrating almost exclusively on the former) every piece of land affected by a local development plan not only has a use but a value and an owner. By allocating uses to land, such plans create opportunities for owners to capture value from the potential for development. As the next section reveals, many owners participate local plan preparation in order to find a golden nest egg that guarantees their financial security for a lifetime.

The capture of development value

Statutory development plans that allocate land for particular uses help determine the specific market sector in which the land is sold. For instance, agricultural land in the green belt is normally traded at the agricultural land prices (with perhaps some additional hope value to represent the possibility of its eventual release for development in the distant future). In contrast, land allocated for residential development will be traded at residential land prices. The difference between these two sectors can be quite staggering. For example, in the South East, the average value of one hectare in 1993 was £626,000 if traded as bulk residential building land, but only at £4,497 if traded as arable agricultural land (Valuation Office 1993).

No intermediate market of any significance exists in the UK between land intended to remain in agricultural use and that likely to receive planning permission for residential development (Goodchild & Munton 1985).

Indeed, from an economist's perspective, local development planning creates rentals gaps between sectors which reinforce sectoral divisions in the land market (Keogh 1985). The reallocation of land in a local plan (or through the unexpected granting of planning permission) from one sector of the market to a more valuable one in which demand for development exists, creates the chance for landowners (or in certain circumstances, for developers or the state) to capture the difference in value between the two sectors. This difference is commonly termed development value. For example, if agricultural land is reallocated for residential development, it will immediately be traded at residential rather than agricultural land prices, provided the demand exists. In contrast, in North America, where planning controls are much weaker, an active intermediate market between agricultural and residential land has been identified (Brown et al. 1981).

Statutory planning encourages owners of low-value land to seek its transfer to higher-value sectors through involvement in the planning process, especially as no lasting method to tax development value has ever been agreed between political parties. Those who can predict, or more likely influence, the reallocation of land stand to make a considerable fortune. For example, if it were possible to buy hectare of land in the South East at £4,497 in the agricultural land market, have it reallocated for residential development and sell it for £626,000 in the residential land market, a gross return of 138 times the original sum invested would be achieved. In reality, it may take many years and great effort before reallocation happens or planning permission is granted. Furthermore, capital gains tax,[1] and attempts by local planning authorities to extract some of the development value through planning gain, may reduce gross returns.

The involvement and influence of landowners in statutory local plan preparation in Cambridge, Greenwich and Surrey Heath was demonstrated by case studies in Chapter 5. The 95 owners investigated were typical of those owning land with the highest development potential and the best connections to existing services (Adams & May 1991 & 1992). It was discovered that 72 per cent of such landowners made at least one representation to the local planning authorities during plan preparation. Of the remaining 28 per cent, some had concluded options or conditional contracts with residential developers who considered that the sites would eventually be released, but who were willing themselves to make representations to hasten the process. The research confirmed that the principal motive for landowner involvement in local planning was to promote the transfer of land from low-value to high-value uses (most commonly from green belt to housing). The highest level of landowner involvement was therefore seen in Cambridge where 92 per cent of owners investigated made at least one representation during plan preparation. The lowest level (57 per cent) was recorded in Greenwich, where the built-up nature of the borough restricted opportunities to enhance land value through development.

Table 11.1 Landowner success rates in Cambridge, Greenwich and Surrey Heath.

Stage	No. of representations	Success rates (%)
1. Consultation	41	16
2. Deposit and inquiry with LPA	47	30
" " " with inspector		49
3a. Post inquiry "new matters"	7	100
3b. Post inquiry on the modifications	18	11
All stages combined	113	25

Source: Adams & May (1992)

As Table 11.1 shows, 25 per cent of all representations submitted by the 95 landowners produced subsequent change in the plans. At the consultation stage, landowner success was limited. This was primarily because of the pressure placed on local planning authorities during consultation to take full account of representations submitted by members of the public, rather than accede to those from landed interests. The bulk of landowner representations and the battle for influence was thus postponed until subsequent stages of the plans. Apart from the few cases that introduced new matters after the inquiry, landowners achieved their highest success rates at the deposit and inquiry stage. During this stage, 30 per cent of landowner representations succeeded with the local planning authority, but a much higher proportion (49 per cent) were supported by the inspector. The difference is explained by the failure of local planning authorities to accept all the inspectors' recommendations. Following the local plan inquiry, only 11 per cent of landowner representations on the plan modifications were accepted, but all of those which introduced new matters proved successful. By coincidence, each of the latter complemented evolving planning policies and the local planning authorities were therefore happy to incorporate these last-minute suggestions into the adopted plans.

It is therefore well worthwhile for those who own or wish to develop land to attempt to promote its transfer from a low-value market sector to a higher one through involvement in local development planning. Indeed, success rates achieved by landowners in Cambridge, Greenwich and Surrey Heath compared favourably with those recorded in Chapter 10 for the broader category of pro-development objectors who submitted representations to the other 16 local plans. The work in Cambridge, Greenwich and Surrey Heath confirmed that experienced professional representation, rather than any ability to take advantage of political conflict or to control the availability of development land, was the main source of landowner influence.

Two examples highlight the importance of experienced professional representation. An individual landowner had previously acquired a site on the edge of Cambridge as an investment. For 20 years previously, the land had been in the green belt. The county council proposed to confirm this designation, since it considered the site still met green belt objectives. The owner objected on the grounds that a green belt designation would prevent her from "securing a proper use for the site", and would instead aggravate its neglect since it was no longer part of a viable agricultural unit. She was surprised to find that these arguments were not particularly relevant to green belt designation. Failure to seek proper professional advice rendered her weak case ineffective and exposed her lack of understanding of the planning system. The inspector recommended that the site be retained in the green belt.

The second example concerns a site then owned by the Property Services Agency (PSA) in Greenwich. This was initially allocated by the local planning authority for light industrial use. Representations carefully submitted by a chartered surveyor, employed in-house by the PSA, convinced the local authority that planning permission for retail warehousing would be likely to be granted on appeal by the Department of the Environment. The authority therefore agreed to modify the plan before the inquiry to allow the possibility of some retail warehousing and housing development as well as light industry. The PSA subsequently sold the site to a property development company who intended to use the retail warehouse allocation in the local plan as a basis to seek planning permission for a superstore.

In a market economy, local development plans do not merely allocate uses to land, but create opportunities for owners to capture development value. Substantial landowner involvement in plan preparation can therefore be expected, particularly as the reallocation of land to higher-value uses is normally lucrative enough to encourage landed interests to obtain the best professional advice. Indeed, those who benefit most financially from local development planning appear able to influence plans in their own favour, precisely because they can afford such advice. As the next section therefore suggests, statutory local planning may serve to reinforce rather than to redistribute, power entrenched in the market.

The distributional impact of local planning

According to Healey et al. (1988), landowners who benefit financially are only one of several powerful interests, in whose favour the contemporary planning system is biased. Others include certain types of industrial firms, knowledgeable property developers, and well organized community and environmental pressure groups. Business leaders, for example, are not reluctant to suggest that planning should give priority to their particular interests. According to Lord Sainsbury (1989), for instance, planners need for a better understanding of commerce, a greater emphasis in their training on the needs of industry, and a stronger obligation to their customers, including his own retail company. The British Property Federation (1986) suggested that all local planning authorities should be required to invite important employers in their area to serve on a Business Advisory Committee that would seek introduce a business perspective into plan preparation and development control. Statutory local planning appears most influenced by professional expertise, usually instructed by landowners, developers or investors, and by the strength of representations from articulate middle-class residents keen to preserve their own environment and protect their property values. As statutory local plans do not explicitly consider the ownership or value of land, they implicitly resolve conflicts in favour of those with most market power.

Blowers (1980) therefore contends that planning reflects the existing pattern of power in society, often benefiting the rich at the expense of the poor. Such unintended distributional consequences take place behind the abstract notion of the public interest, which disguises the differential impact of statutory local planning on different groups in society. Although the Department of the Environment (1992c) encourages local planning authorities to consider social needs and problems in local plan preparation, actual plan content must be limited to social considerations relevant to land-use policies. This advice suggests, for example, that social considerations could be reflected in policies to promote affordable housing, sport & recreation or crime prevention, and in proposals to allocate land for schools and higher education, places of worship or other community facilities.

However, as the People's Plan for Greenwich recognizes, urban economic decline is a prime cause of social stress and deprivation. A variety of economic considerations relevant to statutory development planning, including structural economic change, and unemployment and income levels, are identified by Department of the Environment (1992c). Although some authorities may wish to express their priorities for economic development through a local plan, the main economic contribution of such plans is again officially seen as one of land allocation. Local authorities are thus expected to ensure choice, flexibility and competition in the market by providing a sufficient variety of sites that are capable of early development for employment use.

Since earlier criticism of the narrow concentration of statutory planning on land-use matters, expressed by both Bruton (1983) and the Nuffield Foundation (1986), greater official recognition has certainly been accorded to the relevance of social and economic factors in plan preparation. However, statutory local plans remain rooted in land-use allocation and are not expected to contain social and economic policies that directly promote the more equitable distribution of urban environmental resources. Indeed, few local planning authorities address urban equity explicitly through local development planning, whether by making particular efforts to encourage those most disadvantaged in the market to participate in plan preparation, or by targeting specific plan policies towards their needs. Those that have attempted to promote equal access to urban services and facilities through statutory planning, such as Greenwich, have encountered an even greater challenge in connecting plan-making to implementation. The fragility of this link is therefore discussed in the next section.

Local planning and the implementation of development

According to Healey et al. (1988), the two most important rôles fulfilled by statutory local plans are land allocation, especially at the urban fringe, and open land conservation. Although in principle, such plans could help organize investment in new infrastructure, this relationship has often been problematic (Carter et al. 1990) Indeed, statutory local plans are usually too general to co-ordinate specific development. Moreover, though they may provide a useful background for the attraction of resources, they are not primarily bidding documents (Healey et al. 1988). Statutory local plans rarely attempt to organize all available resources into a phased implementation programme. Indeed, most plans contain a modest statement of two to three pages at the end of the document setting out the prospects for implementation.

The Surrey Heath Local Plan (Surrey Heath Borough Council 1985: 182) provided a typical example of such a statement. This suggested that: "In achieving development under the Local Plan, capital investment by all implementing agencies will be incurred. However, in view of the diversity of involvement, form of site development, infrastructure needs, phasing and as yet undefined detail, no predicted assessment of overall cost can be made. These costs, of course, will fall to be met and known by the respective agencies as projected schemes are planned in due time." In the consultation version of the subsequent local plan review (Surrey Heath Borough Council 1990), the section on implementation and monitoring accounted for only one per cent of a document of 200 pages. This section again acknowledged that the implementation would depend upon individual decisions taken by the public and private sectors and by the community as a whole.

Healey et al. (1982) initially investigated the implementation of planning policies in the South-East, and subsequently (1985) extended the work to Greater Manchester and the West Midlands. In the South-East, they found that planning policies that sought to restrict residential development to certain areas, zones and sites were successfully implemented. However, those that tried to limit the amount and rate of development to local needs, to phase development in a balanced way, or to organize it in relation to particular infrastructure investment, proved harder to implement. They concluded that planning policies were therefore most successful where they involved a limitation on land release in areas of high demand. The subsequent work in Greater Manchester and the West Midlands demonstrated that control over powers and resources, together with the level of agreement in a multi-agency context, were essential to successful implementation. In declining areas, implementation requires the ability to create or attract investment as well as to influence its location. If conflict over plan-making occurs between different public-sector agencies, or if policy runs counter to private sector trends, implementation is likely to be adversely affected.

Although power is concentrated in the hands of politicians and senior officials during plan-making, during implementation it is thus dispersed more widely (Blowers 1980). For in a multi-agency context, plan-making and implementation interact as plans are produced, applied, challenged and subsequently reviewed. Yet, statutory planning procedures still assume that the relationship between plan-making and implementation is hierarchical, and they insufficiently recognize the practical reality of the policy–action relationship identified by Barrett & Fudge (1981). As a result, statutory plan preparation is a prolonged and resource-intensive activity, eventually creating a product that may quickly become out of date, yet be unable to deliver the power, resources and agreement necessary for its smooth operation. The implementation of local development plans is thus twice undermined. Each of these weakness will now be examined.

Local planning and urban change

Statutory local plans remain fixed at a point in time, by-products of a continuous planning process that reflects the continuous nature of land management and development (Shaw 1989). Indeed, many statutory plans have already started to become out of date by the time they are adopted. Planning policy has begun to move on, and new proposals, not anticipated in the plan, will have been put forward by both the public and private sectors. Conflict may well arise between earlier policy expressed in a still-valid local plan and any policy subsequently revised outside the plan-making process (Bruton & Nicholson 1987). Statutory plans that are not kept up to date by frequent revision may therefore diminish in importance as material considerations in development control.

Furthermore, plans can fail to keep up with the speed of the development process, especially in a boom. This is well illustrated by the case of a rambling factory building near the centre of Greenwich, which was bought by a manufacturing company in 1983 for packaging operations. The People's Plan for Greenwich, which was started about this time, was subsequently published for consultation in 1985 and finally adopted in 1989. Throughout the planning process and in the adopted plan, the site was allocated for industrial use within an industrial improvement area. However, in 1988, when the statutory planning process was almost complete, the factory closed down. Subsequently, the manufacturing company recognized the potential for redevelopment and entered into partnership with the developer in 1988. Development proposals were drawn up for low-cost housing on most of the site, with some small industrial units on the remainder, to take part account of the local plan. Planning permission was subsequently given and development commenced in 1990. As this example reveals, statutory local plans can influence development proposals by providing a "baseline" for subsequent negotiations with the private sector (Healey 1983).

However, as the case also demonstrates, statutory local plans make assumptions about the continued future use of existing premises, which may well turn out to be incorrect. Indeed: "it would . . . be impossible for local planning authorities to anticipate all types of proposals that might come forward during the lifetime of the plan." (Department of the Environment 1992d: para 1.4). Development plans are therefore intended to be used flexibly. Nevertheless, the rapid pace of urban change restricts the extent to which such fixed documents can be effective in promoting regeneration or development. Statutory local plans that aim primarily to control development at the urban fringe are less likely to be affected in this way.

Powers, resources and agency support

Statutory local plans provide no effective basis for active intervention in the development process until the necessary powers, resources and agency support are mustered for implementation. Relevant statutory powers may be found not only in planning law but also related legislation such as that dealing, for example, with economic development or compulsory purchase. However, as Chapter 7 explained, the complexity of compulsory purchase legislation inhibits its use in the implementation of local plans.

Although the Nuffield Foundation (1986) argued that development plans should sit within a district or county strategy that would include a realistic assessment of the resources likely to be available for implementation, this view has never been accepted by central government. Indeed, as Carter et al. (1990) discovered, links between local plans and other public-sector expenditure plans are highly variable. Where resources for implementation are not available, local plans may raise hopes but never fulfil them. This is illustrated by the case in Greenwich of a listed building and its surrounding grounds, at one time owned by the Ministry of Defence. The site is located in an area of social stress, considered by the local planning authority to be deficient in open space. Although the authority allocated the site for public open space in the consultation plan in 1985, the Ministry of Defence objected. In 1986, the Ministry declared the property surplus to requirements, and sold it to private purchasers on the open market. This shows how landowners in the public sector, such as the Ministry of Defence, may not necessarily be any more committed to statutory local plans than those in the private sector. The new owners, who had no intention of making the grounds available to the public, began to restore the listed building for their own occupation. A commendable intention within a local plan thus proved impossible for a financially-constrained local authority to implement, because the cost of site acquisition was beyond its available resources.

No statutory local plan is guaranteed support from those agencies in the public or private sectors responsible for investment in new infrastructure and development. Although the privatization of many infrastructure agencies has not made the task of development co-ordination any easier, "institutional dispersal" in the public sector has always hampered the implementation of planning policies (Healey et al. 1988). For example, regional water authorities which took over responsibility for water services in England and Wales from local authorities in 1974, evolved corporatist investment strategies in direct liaison with key users, such as industrialists and developers, well before their eventual privatization in 1989 (Saunders 1985). Even now, the rôle of the state in the development process remains fragmented between a variety of separate agencies and three levels of government. The implementation of statutory local plans thus demands, but cannot always secure, commitment from elsewhere in government, as well as from landowners, developers, investors, infrastructure companies and other agencies.

Conclusion

Although statutory development plans were originally intended as the centrepiece of the planning system, they have since been marginalized as an **active** form of intervention in the development process. The status of statutory development plans as a form of **passive** intervention appears to have been enhanced by the requirement of the Planning and Compensation Act 1991 for specific planning decisions to be made in accordance with the development plan, unless material considerations indicate otherwise. Yet, as the private sector is responsible for the implementation of most development proposals, the agenda and content of such plans increasingly reflects the priorities of landowners, developers and other powerful interests, especially in areas needing to attract investment.

More innovative policy statements therefore grew in popularity in the late-1980s and early-1990s. As Chapter 7 explained, many local authorities sought to promote efficiency and equity by drawing up local economic development strategies. As global environmental concern was reflected in heightened political interest in the concept of sustainable development, environmental audits, again prepared outside the statutory planning process, were pioneered by authorities such as Lancashire County Council (Steeley 1990). These aimed to define local policy for environmental management in the context of available environmental data.

Although some commentators doubt the eventual significance of the legislative priority accorded to statutory development plans by the Planning and Compensation Act 1991 (Gatenby & Williams 1992), it does reflect a political determination to link development control more closely to development planning. Yet, as Chapter 8 indicated, the cost of such linkage is already apparent in the increasing length and complexity of local plan inquiries. Mynors (1991) considers that the record-breaking inquiry into the 1,200 objections to the South Cambridgeshire Local Plan, which cost the local planning authority over £200,000 and lasted for almost 10 months (Hussell 1991), may become commonplace in the future. Indeed, according to the Department of the Environment (1993), each local plan inquiry already costs the average local authority £170,000.

Furthermore, the Planning and Compensation Act 1991 is likely to ensure that such inquiries become even more dominated by professional expertise, thereby helping to sustain the workload of planning consultants, planning lawyers and other specialists. As a result, the direct cost of the planning service, which Willis (1988) calculated at £45 per household per annum in 1985, may substantially increase. Unless statutory local plans are reformed to provide an effective basis for the promotion and co-ordination of development as well as for its control, their costs, and the time and effort they consume, may increasingly be considered poor value for money. The final chapter therefore suggests a basis for such reform.

Notes

1. After the abolition of development land tax in 1985, capital gains tax became the main method by which, in certain circumstances, development value is part taxed.

PART 4
LOOKING TO THE FUTURE

CHAPTER TWELVE

An agenda for urban planning practice, education and research

If urban planning did not exist, but its pioneers were now gathering to promote the concept and establish the discipline, the occasion would be quite different from that which occurred nearly a hundred years ago. This chapter seeks to imagine what might be discussed today and what type of agenda would be set for planning practice, education and research. If such an agenda were to gain broad support, it could significantly change the working lives of both those already in professional practice, and those about to enter it on completion of their studies.

It is likely that the purpose of urban planning would now be defined as the promotion of equity, efficiency and sustainability in the built environment, rather than the mere pursuit of amenity, convenience, safety or public health. Indeed, any thought that urban planning could *control* or direct the process of urban change would quickly give way to the realization that, in a market economy, it should seek instead to *influence* such change. It is possible that urban planning would thus be hailed as a means to ensure that the social costs and benefits of development are identified and given equal weight to private costs and benefits, and perhaps even acclaimed as a method to balance the market's short-term valuation of environmental resources with a more profound longer-term perspective.

Moreover, today's planning pioneers would be unlikely to seek recourse to the simplistic and abstract notion of the public interest to justify their manifesto. Rather, they would recognize that institutional factors such as land ownership help produce winners and losers in both planning and development. They would therefore require the varying impact of urban planning on competing interests to be explicitly identified and fully acknowledged. Indeed, it is probable that they would place high priority on outcome evaluation in order to demonstrate how urban planning could successfully challenge and transform market failure.

If urban planning were to be remodelled in this way, and marketed afresh to a public unaware of past planning mistakes, it might well command widespread popular support. Unfortunately, urban planning does not have the advantage of such an untainted starting point. Despite recent changes, the statutory planning process remains rooted in a philosophy, long since discredited, which mistakenly believes that urban change can be controlled, and not merely influenced, by planning. This static view narrows the scope of statutory development plans, restricts their potential for dynamic intervention in the development process, and explains why plan-making is so poorly linked to implementation.

The contemporary agenda for planning practice, education and research, suggested in this chapter, is not intended to be comprehensive, since alternative recommendations to reform the planning system as a whole have already been proposed from a variety of sources (see, for example, Jones 1982, Adam Smith Institute 1983, British Property Federation 1986, Nuffield Foundation 1986, Healey 1989, Montgomery & Thornley 1990, Labour Party 1992). Instead, the agenda seeks to highlight what follows once it is accepted that urban planning is primarily a form of state intervention in the development process, rather than an exercise in civic design, a style of corporate management or a type of systems analysis. Readers are invited to imagine that they are present and perhaps even participating in the very meeting at which today's planning pioneers formulate their manifesto. The extravagant assumption is made that the meeting is fully aware of what would have happened over the decades (and in our minds, did happen), had urban planning been established as proposed about a hundred years earlier. Such unrealistic but imaginative thinking is essential to break the stranglehold of past misconceptions on current practice, statute and policy.

Today's planning pioneers are politically streetwise, acutely conscious that the planning system is merely a set of procedures to be filled "with whatever content politicians, officials and pressure groups consider important at a particular time" (Healey 1992b: 411). Although political confrontation has surrounded wider land policy, especially in land taxation (see Ch. 4), the need for urban planning is broadly supported across the political spectrum. Indeed, politicians on the Right appear to regard urban planning as a means to promote economic efficiency, while those on the Left believe it can promote social equity. As Healey (1992b: 430) therefore notes: ". . . the planning system has a high degree of adaptability. This allowed the substantial shift to a narrow agenda in the early-1980s, to a negotiated project-based practice dominated by development-market values in the later 1980s, and to strategic concerns for the integration of economic, environmental and social issues in the arena of managing land-use and environmental change in the early 1990s." Since politicians on both Left and Right are keen to add sustainability to the planning agenda alongside equity and efficiency, it is assumed that the nature or type of planned intervention in the development process will continue to vary more than its extent (Healey 1983).

Planning pioneers today may well admire the best that market processes can achieve, but would refuse to ignore the capacity of land & property markets to fail. They are well aware of market fragility in some locations, but robustness in others. This, they consider, needs to be reflected in a variety of policy responses, sensitive to the specific locational characteristics of different submarkets. Aware of the true rôle of urban planning as a form of state intervention in the development process, they sit down to formulate some recommendations for planning practice, education and research, which are brought together in the following statements.

An agenda for practice

Development plans will play a critical rôle in informing and guiding state intervention in the development process. By the vision they create and the direction they provide, development plans will capture the imagination of developers and investors, and articulate the hopes and aspirations of local people for an equitable, efficient and sustainable environment. Development planning will seek to balance strategic certainty with flexibility of response to subsequent site-specific events. Indeed, a strong strategic planning framework, in which socioeconomic policy is articulated at both national and regional levels, will allow local planning to respond imaginatively to the fast-moving pace of the development process. Local plans will therefore be more concerned to promote development of high quality than to restrict it. Regulatory planning, intended merely to control development, will be of limited importance, except in locations where severe restraint needs to be the keynote of policy. Indeed, local planning authorities will wish to avoid devoting too much professional planning time to the administration of small-scale regulations and too little to more significant matters (Simmie 1990).

Development plans at the local level will be prepared on an action basis, rather than on an area or topic basis. Implementation will certainly not be relegated to two or three pages at the end of the document. Individual sections will set out proposals to attract investment, enhance land quality, tackle dereliction and ensure a regular flow of sites to the market, etc., irrespective of whether particular sites are proposed for housing, employment or other uses. Each part of the plan will bring together the necessary powers, resources and agency support for effective implementation. Site-specific allocations of land will be made only in plans that are reviewed at least every four years.

When local planning authorities seek to implement urban plans in partnership with landowners, developers and investors, specific private-sector partners will be selected only after careful examination of their past experience and their present interests and strategies. Not all landowners, developers or investors behave in the same way. Some landowners adopt more active land management and development strategies than others (see

Ch. 5). Some developers and investors are more adventurous than others in the type and location of development undertaken (see Ch. 6). Local planning authorities will take particular care to ensure that the needs of property users are fully reflected in the strategies of developers and investors whom they partner.

Although development promotion is already undertaken by many local authorities outside a planning framework, the new planning system will provide strategic management and co-ordination for such vital activity, and furnish it with renewed purpose and direction. Urban planning will be able to ensure that land is ready for development when needed. Site constraints will be clearly identified in development plans and remedial action recommended. Grants and subsidies, for example, may help overcome physical constraints such as site dereliction, but the removal of ownership constraints may involve direct challenge to passive landowners. Simplified compulsory purchase will therefore be available, when required, for implementation of any proposal in an adopted development plan.

The state will seek to buy agricultural land in the market well in advance of development potential and to sell it only when eventually needed for development. Profits will be ploughed back into further purchases. Urban planners will partner surveyors and estate managers in the management and eventual development of such land. In some areas, local planning authorities may be best placed to create planning-orientated land banks, but in other locations regional land agencies could be established to achieve this. In the meantime, new powers and resources will facilitate the assembly of land required for the implementation of development plans.

In many areas, remarkably little information of any accuracy is published at the local level on property markets and development activity. This breeds market uncertainty and undermines confidence. Although few local authorities have previously sought to monitor local property markets, this is now changing. In 1990, for example, Bristol City Council decided to appoint a senior research assistant to undertake property research within the planning department. The advertisement sought "someone with skills in property research and a knowledge of the development industry to broaden the capacity of the city council in carrying out our research into economic development issues . . . The research section already carries out extensive monitoring of commercial development in the city It is planned to extend this work as part of its research into economic development and proceed to the development of a property market information system" (*Planning* 1990: 17).

Through close co-operation between local authorities, district valuers, regional and local property agents and others involved in property and development, existing knowledge on local markets and development activity will be brought together with methodological rigour and published at regular intervals. In some locations, local planning authorities may well be the most appropriate agency to publish such comprehensive information, but elsewhere it may be better undertaken by enterprise agencies, research institutes or other organizations.

Such information will make a vital contribution to the more efficient operation of market processes. It will help pinpoint property shortages at an early stage and provide the confidence for development to start without further delay. Subsequently, it might highlight the danger of excess supply and prevent a crisis of overbuilding. If better local market information reduces risk, financial institutions may be prepared to invest more in the inner city (McNamara 1993). This knowledge will also enable the outcome of planning policies, and particularly their impact on different interests, to be properly monitored and evaluated. Since more active intervention in the development process will require improved knowledge of local markets, property market monitoring and forecasting is considered as a much a task of urban planning as population or employment monitoring and forecasting.

Political consensus is more likely to be established by the gradual extension of planning gain (or development reimbursement, as it will now be called) than by any return to development land taxation. On the political Right, planning gain is already seen as a means to reduce public expenditure on infrastructure, while on the Left it is regarded as a way in which local communities can share in the profits from land development. Moreover, unlike development land taxation, planning gain is intended to benefit the local community rather than the national exchequer. Development plans will specify standard local impact fees to reduce the uncertainty of individual bargaining between developers and local authorities. The more certain such fees, the more likely they are to be borne by landowners, through lower residual site valuations, than by developers or users. A broad definition of development reimbursement will be adopted to enable it to meet the full social costs of development. For example, development of greenfield sites on the urban periphery will be expected to contribute to the restoration of brownfield sites at the urban core, since decentralization reinforces urban decay. Such restoration funds will be established on a regional rather than a district basis. They represent an extension of community amortization funds, originally proposed by Lichfield & Darin-Drabkin (1980).

Unless plan preparation is simple and speedy, development plans will be unable to provide the necessary dynamic basis for continuous intervention in the development process. Particular attention needs to be paid to ensure that no time is wasted between the publication of a draft consultation plan and its eventual adoption. It is therefore proposed that the period of public participation or consultation on local plans will culminate in a local plan inquiry. Matters for debate before the inquiry inspector will emerge during consultation. Those interests who can neither muster multiple representations nor afford professional expertise to make their views known will be offered independent advice or professional support. Local plan inquiries will be short and will concentrate on testing the merits of a plan as a whole through open debate.

Site-specific objections to local plans will be handled through written representations. This will prevent the domination of local plan inquiries by professional experts appearing on behalf of property and development interests. These interests will be invited and expected to register their proposals with the local planning authority at the start of plan preparation so that they can be fully examined throughout the process, rather than be first discussed at the inquiry. This will more than balance any disadvantage that such interests might otherwise suffer from the lack of opportunity for lengthy cross-examination during a local plan inquiry. However, failure to register site-specific interests when first invited, will mean that subsequent written representations at the time of the inquiry, will be considered only at the discretion of the inspector.

As commentators such as Hall et al. (1973), Simmie (1974 & 1981) and Reade (1987) have long pointed out, unless the social impact of urban planning is clearly evaluated, urban plans may merely promote the interests of those with most power in the market. Although some politicians may wish to use the planning system precisely for this purpose, such choices should be rendered quite explicit. Social or community impact analysis will therefore be required for all development plans and major development proposals. This would expose policies that nominally aim to benefit those most disadvantaged, but which in practice exacerbate their position. It is therefore essential that urban planners both acknowledge the conflicting claims that competing interests make on the planning system and identify the particular interests that each act of intervention is intended to promote.

An agenda for education

In recent years, planning education has been helpfully restructured around a core curriculum, which all students are expected to cover, and specialist material which varies from school to school. The balance between core and specialized studies is open to considerable interpretation, but each is expected to comprise no less than one third and no more than two thirds of the curriculum as a whole (Royal Town Planning Institute 1991). Some planning schools specialize in fields such as strategic planning, regional planning, rural planning, or environmental management. This section is not therefore intended to evaluate planning education as a whole, particularly as the relevant substantive matters have already been debated at length (see, for instance, Batty 1990, Healey 1991c). Rather, attention is concentrated on the specialized studies of a planning school which considers itself at the leading edge of urban planning practice.

Urban planning education will be concerned above all to sharpen the intellectual vitality and encourage the creative talent of men and women about to enter the profession. At the centre of the curriculum, critical analysis of planning practice will be set within the broader context of development and investment processes. As an example, the uneven and volatile nature of property development will be fully explored. Welfare economics will become a important component in explaining and justifying the work of the urban planner. Particular emphasis will be placed on research methods relevant to social and economic policy analysis, in order to facilitate future outcome evaluation.

Planning techniques that assume a dominant rôle for the planner in directing urban change will become redundant. In contrast, a knowledge of development appraisal and methods of valuation will be vital for future planners who wish to influence development activity. Indeed, as urban planning practice becomes more closely integrated with development, urban planning education will increasingly give attention to economic and financial skills. Similarly, no attempt will be made through practical work, to simulate the plan-making process in the rarefied atmosphere of a planning school, as this would tend to give students a false impression that they will be able to control the urban environment rather than merely influence it.

Instead, greater emphasis will be placed on rôle play and on the encouragement of negotiation and bargaining skills. Such exercises will be most valuable when undertaken in collaboration with related disciplines. Urban planning education will increasingly involve planning students in partnership with, for instance, students of architecture, estate management, law and other related disciplines at the same institution. This will strengthen team-working skills and facilitate such collaboration in later professional life. Moreover, no pretensions will be made that urban planning education offers comprehensive and detailed treatment of all relevant subjects such as architecture, economics, finance, politics, sociology, and surveying (Reade 1987). Attention will focus instead on the rôle of the planner in shaping market behaviour and influencing development processes.

The growing importance of continuous education and training (CET) or continuous professional development (CPD) as it is otherwise known, reflects the awareness that professional education does not finish on graduation. Many professions, including the Royal Town Planning Institute expect their members to take responsibility for keeping their professional expertise up to date. This may happen in a variety of ways, such as personal reading, in-house training, or attendance at seminars or conferences. Many of those in senior positions in the planning profession were originally trained at a time when planning education gave insufficient consideration to the development process. Through CET, the planning profession could throw open the debate about the real nature of its relationship to the development process and help clarify the implications for urban planning practice.

An agenda for research

Substantive new research in planning and development could make an essential contribution to understanding the context for urban planning practice and making it more effective as a form of intervention. The most important substantive research areas are the extent to which planning practice can alter development processes and change market outcomes, and the measures by which this can best be achieved. Healey & Barrett (1990) have already identified four themes around which research into land and property development processes could helpfully be organized. These themes can usefully be applied and extended to define critical areas of research interest that link urban planning to the development process.

The first theme aims to examine the relationship between the financial system as a whole and investment in land and property development. For example, this would seek to identify the importance of property development within the investment strategy of financial institutions. It would explore the way in which finance capital flows into and out of the built environment. This could enable planners to understand more fully how their own particular areas compete for funds with other locations and with other types of investment. Within this theme, the necessary methodological work could be promoted to enable local land markets and development activity to be monitored accurately.

The second theme aims to consider the changing composition and strategies of firms involved in the production of the built environment. Particular attention might be given, for example, to the land management and development strategies of different types of landowner and to the changing activities of various types of development companies and consultants. Such work could help planners to understand more clearly the aims and objectives of those with whom they negotiate on a daily basis.

The third theme explores the way in which the state sets a framework for land and property development. Comparative analysis of the respective merits of development plans, control and promotion as forms of intervention in the development process in various locations, would be beneficial under this theme. Attention could focus on the best way in which state resources can be deployed to influence development, comparing, for example, the return on development grants and subsidies with that on public investment. The relationship between planning and other types of legislation affecting development, such as land taxation, would be equally worthy of research consideration.

Healey & Barrett (1990) identify the fourth theme as outcome evaluation.

In this, they give particular emphasis to the impact of the land and property development process on local economic development, but they also suggest that it is important to consider the social and environmental consequences of particular types of development, and to evaluate distributive outcomes. They believe that this fourth theme presents researchers with the greatest challenge, conceptually and empirically, but offers the most significant potential to assess the contribution of land and property development to social and economic change.

By applying these four themes, planning research could be deflected from its earlier narrow preoccupation with procedural matters to the more substantive consideration of the relationship of urban planning to the development process. However, as Healey & Barrett (1990) acknowledge, such research raises challenging methodological problems and requires access to often-restricted data sources. Multi-causality is a particular problem, since outcomes cannot always be attributed to one source or event. Many local authorities have traditionally been willing to open their files to researchers, but the private sector is usually reluctant to do so for fear of disclosing commercial secrets. Although Healey & Barrett (1990) believe that the sensitive investigative researcher can penetrate development processes with considerable success, they emphasize that particular methodological awareness is necessary for an effective research contribution in the field.

Conclusion

This book has sought to contribute to the three related debates in urban planning identified by Yiftachel (1989) and introduced in the first chapter. In the context of the analytical debate, it has suggested that urban planning is a form of state intervention in the development process. In the context of the urban form debate, it has contended that a good urban plan is one that endeavours, through shaping market behaviour, to enhance equity, efficiency and sustainability in the built environment to an extent that improves – and is seen to improve – upon the outcomes that would otherwise be generated by the market alone. In the context of the procedural debate, it has indicated that a good planning process is one which is closely related to the development process, politically aware, and explicit about who will gain and lose from urban plans.

This final chapter has ventured into the past and into the future. Readers who were able to imagine participating in the meeting with today's planning pioneers may suggest that it reached different conclusions from those outlined above! Yet, urban planning in the 21st century may well contrast markedly with bureaucratic planning familiar in the 20th century. Who knows how practice, statute and policy will change, even in 10 years? If this chapter enlivens that wider debate, it will fulfil its purpose.

Bibliography

Adair, A. 1993. Financing of property development. In *Urban regeneration: property investment and development*, J. Berry, S. McGreal, B. Deddis (eds), 50–76. London: Spon.

Adam Smith Institute 1983. *Omega report: local government policy*. London: Adam Smith Institute.

Adams, C. D. 1987. Opportunities for landowner participation in local planning. *Planning Outlook* 30, 66–9.

— 1990. Meeting the needs of industry? The performance of industrial land and property markets in inner Manchester and Salford. In *Land and property development in a changing context*, P. Healey & R. Nabarro (eds), 113–27. Aldershot, England: Gower.

— A. E. Baum, B. D. MacGregor 1985. The influence of valuation practices upon the price of vacant inner city land. *Land Development Studies* 2, 157–73.

— — 1988. The availability of land for inner city development: a case study of inner Manchester. *Urban Studies* 25, 62–76.

— & R. F. W. Kent 1991. Landed interests and local planning in the UK. *Land Use Policy* 8, 36–49.

— & H. G. May 1990. *Local planning and the landowner*. Occasional Paper 25, Department of Planning and Landscape, University of Manchester.

— — May 1991. Active and passive behaviour in land ownership. *Urban Studies* 28, 687–705.

— — 1992. The role of landowners in the preparation of statutory local plans. *Town Planning Review* 63, 297–323.

— — T. J. Pope 1992. Changing strategies for the acquisition of residential development land. *Journal of Property Research* 9, 209–26.

— & G. P. Pawson 1991. *Representation and influence in local planning*. Occasional Paper 31, Department of Planning and Landscape, University of Manchester.

— L. Russell, C. S. Taylor-Russell 1994. *Land for industrial development*. London: Spon.

Allison, L. 1986. What is urban planning for? *Town Planning Review* 57, 5–16.

Alonso, W. 1964. *Location and land use*. Cambridge, Mass.: Harvard University Press.

Alty, R. & R. Darke 1991. A city centre for people, involving the community in planning for Sheffield's central area. In *Town planning responses to city change*, V. Nadin & J. Doak (eds), 119–31. Aldershot, England: Avebury.

Ambrose, P. 1986. *Whatever happened to planning?* London: Methuen.

— & B. Colenutt 1975. *The property machine*. London: Penguin.

Armstrong, M., T. Brown, P. Cook 1993. Intervention casts a shadow over bright new plans dawn, *Planning* 1002, 9.

Arnstein, S. R. 1969. A ladder of citizen participation. *American Institute of Planners, Journal* 35, 216–24.

— 1971. A ladder of citizen participation in the USA. *Royal Town Planning Institute, Journal* 57, 176–82.

Bailey, S. J. 1990. Charges for local infrastructure. *Town Planning Review* 61, 427–53.

Balchin, P. N., J. L. Kieve, G. H. Bull 1988. *Urban land economics and public policy*, 4th edn. London: Macmillan.

Ball, M. 1983. *Housing policy and economic power*. London: Methuen.

Barras, R. 1984. The office development cycle in London. *Land Development Studies* **1**, 35–50.

— 1985. Development of profit and development control: the case of office development in London. In *Land policy: problems and alternatives*, S. Barrett & P. Healey (eds), 93–105. Aldershot, England: Gower.

Barrett, S., M. Stewart, J. Underwood 1978. *The land market and the development process*. Occasional Paper 2, School for Advanced Urban Studies, University of Bristol.

— & C. Fudge 1981. Examining the policy–action relationship. In *Policy and action*, S. Barrett & C. Fudge (eds), 3–38. London: Methuen.

Batty, M. 1990. How planning education can survive the future: thoughts about new curricula. *Education for Planning Association Newsletter*, 57–73.

Baum, A. & N. Crosby 1988. *Property investment appraisal*. London: Routledge.

— & MacGregor B. D. 1992. The initial yield revealed: explicit valuations and the future of property investment. *Journal of Property Investment and Valuation* **10**, 709–26.

Begg, D., S. Fischer, R. Dornbusch 1994. *Economics*, 4th British edn. New York: McGraw-Hill.

Begg, H. M. 1991. Town and regional planning and the challenge of sustainable development. *The Planner* **77**(22), 7–8.

Bianchini, F., J. Dawson, R. Evans 1992. Flagship projects in urban regeneration. In *Rebuilding the city*, P. Healey, S. Davoudi, M. O'Toole, S. Tavsanoglu, D. Usher (eds), 245–55. London: Spon.

Bintley, M. 1993. Evaluation of urban development corporations. In *Urban regeneration: property investment and development*, J. Berry, S. McGreal, B. Deddis (eds), 254–72. London: Spon.

Blacksell, M., A. Blowers, T. Shaw 1987. Celebration or wake? 40 years of British town and country planning. *Planning Outlook* **30**, 1–3.

Blaney, T. 1993. Experience mounts on development plan lead. *Planning* **1031**, 26–7.

Blowers, A. 1980. *The limits of power*. Oxford: Pergamon.

— 1986. Town planning – paradoxes and prospects. *The Planner* **72**(4), 11–8.

Bourne, L. S. 1967. *Private redevelopment of the central city*. Research Paper 112, Department of Geography, University of Chicago.

Branson, C. 1989. In perfect union. *Chartered Surveyor Weekly* **29**(4), 88.

Breheny, M. 1993. Fragile regional planning. *The Planner* **79**(1), 10–12.

— & R. W. McQuaid 1985. *The M4 Corridor: patterns and causes of growth in high technology industries*. Geographical Paper 87, Department of Geography, University of Reading.

Brindley, T., Y. Rydin, G. Stoker 1989. *Remaking planning*. London: Unwin Hyman.

British Property Federation 1986. *The planning system – a fresh approach*. London: British Property Federation.

Brown, H. J., R. S. Phillips, N. Roberts 1982. Landownership and market dynamics at the urban periphery: implications for land policy design and implementation. In *World congress on land policy*, M. Cullen & S. Woolery (eds), 119–47. Lexington, Mass.: Lexington Books.

Brownhill, S. 1990. *Developing London's Docklands – another great planning disaster?* London: Paul Chapman.

Brundtland Commission (The World Commission on Environment and Development) 1987. *Our common future*. Oxford: Oxford University Press.

Bruton, M. J. 1983. *Legislation and the rôle of the town planner in society*. Papers in Planning Research 61, Department of Town Planning, University of Wales Institute of Science and Technology.
— & D. Nicholson 1987. *Local planning in practice*. London: Hutchinson.
— G. Crispin, P. M. Fidler 1982. Local plans: the rôle and status of the public local inquiry. *Journal of Planning and Environmental Law*, 276–86.
Burgess, E. W. 1925. The growth of the city: an introduction to a research project. In *The city*, R. E. Park, E. W. Burgess, R. A. McKenzie (eds), 47–62. Chicago: University of Chicago Press.
Butler, E. & P. Moore 1989. Sources of funding – public sector support. *Architects Journal* 190(7), 53–66.
Byland, T. 1989. Land Securities. *Financial Times Survey III* (30 June), vi.

Cadman, D. 1984. Property finance in the UK in the postwar period. *Land Development Studies* 1, 61–82.
— & L. Austin-Crowe 1983. *Property development*, 2nd edn. London: Spon.
— L. Austin-Crowe, R. Topping, M. Avis 1991. *Property development*, 3rd edn. London: Spon.
Cambridgeshire County Council 1985. *Cambridge Green Belt Local Plan: the inspector's report* (Report of Director of Planning and Research, 14 October). Cambridge: Cambridgeshire County Council.
— 1986. *Cambridge Green Belt Local Plan: considerations of representations on proposed modifications* (Report of Director of Planning and Research, 4 September). Cambridge: Cambridgeshire County Council.
Cameron, G. C., S. Monk, B. J. Pearce 1988. *Vacant urban land: a literature review*. London: Department of the Environment.
Carter, N., T. Brown, T. Abbott 1990. Policy planning: one step forward and two steps backward? *The Planner* 76(48), 9–12.
Chadwick, G. A. 1970. *A systems view of planning*. Oxford: Pergamon.
Chapin, F. S. & S. F. Weiss (eds), 1962. *Urban growth dynamics*. New York: John Wiley.
Charles Church Developments plc. 1987. *Report and accounts 1987*. Camberley: Charles Church.
— 1988. *Interim report for six months to 29th February 1988*. Camberley: Charles Church.
Chartered Surveyor Weekly 1987. Charles Church profits from house-building. *Chartered Surveyor Weekly* 21(9), 13.
Cheshire, P. C., S. Sheppard, A. Hooper 1985. *The economic consequences of the British planning system*. Discussion Paper in Urban and Regional Economics 29, Department of Economics, University of Reading.
— & S. Sheppard 1989. British planning policy and access to housing: some empirical estimates. *Urban Studies* 26, 469–85.
Chisholm, M. & P. Kivell, 1987. *Inner city waste land: an assessment of government and market failure in land development*. Hobart Paper 108, Institute of Economic Affairs, London.
Civic Trust 1988. *Urban wasteland now*. London: Civic Trust.
Clarke, L. 1992. *Building capitalism*. London: Routledge.
Crang, P. & R. L. Martin 1991. Mrs Thatcher's vision of the "new Britain" and the other sides of the "Cambridge phenomenon". *Environment and Planning D* 9, 91–116.
Community Development Project 1976. *Profits against houses*. London: CDP Information and Intelligence Unit.
Comptroller and Auditor General 1988. *Estate management in the National Health Service*. London: HMSO.

Coombes, T. 1991. Planning consultants. *Housing and Planning Review* **46**(3) 20–23.

Couch, C. & S. Fowler 1992. Vacancy and recent structural change in the demand for land in Liverpool. In *Rebuilding the city*, P. Healey, S. Davoudi, M. O'Toole, S. Tavsanoglu, D. Usher (eds), 100–13. London: Spon.

Cox, A. 1984. *Adversary politics and land*. Cambridge: Cambridge University Press.

Crispin, G., P. Fidler, V. Nadin 1985. *The process of local plan adoption*. Final report to the Department of the Environment. Department of Urban and Regional Planning, Coventry Polytechnic.

Cullingworth, J. B. & V. Nadin 1994. *Town and country planning in Britain*, 11th edn. London: Routledge.

Daniels, P. W. 1977. Office location in the British conurbations: trends and strategies. *Urban Studies* **14**, 261–74.

— & J. M. Bobe 1993. Extending the boundary of the City of London? The development of Canary Wharf. *Environment and Planning A* **25**, 539–52.

Darlow, C. 1987. Development finance: finding the funding. *Estates Gazette* **281**, 616–35.

— (ed.) 1988. *Valuation and development appraisal*, 2nd edn. London: Estates Gazette.

Davidoff, P. 1965. Advocacy and pluralism in planning. *Journal of the American Institute of Planners* **31**, 331–8.

Davies, H. W. E. 1988a. Development control in England. *Town Planning Review* **59**, 127–36.

— 1988b. The control of development in the Netherlands. *Town Planning Review* **59**, 207–25

— 1992a. *Address to Joint Planning Law Conference, New College Oxford, December 1992*. London: Sweet & Maxwell.

— 1992b. Britain 2000: the impact of Europe for planning and practice. *The Planner* **78**(21), 21–3.

Davies, J. G. 1972. *The evangelical bureaucrat*. London: Tavistock.

Dawson, J. & C. Walker 1990. Mitigating the social costs of private development. *Town Planning Review* **61**, 157–70.

Debenham Thorpe 1993. *Money into property*. London: Debenham Thorpe.

Delafons, J. 1991. Planning in the USA – paying for development. *The Planner* **77**(20), 8–9.

Denman, D. R. & S. Prodano 1972. *Land use: an introduction to proprietary land use analysis*. London: Allen & Unwin.

Dennison, C. E. 1988. *Planning by agreement: the need for new legislation*. MPhil thesis, Department of Planning and Landscape University of Manchester.

Department of the Environment 1984. *Circular 14/84: green belts*. London: HMSO.

— 1985. *Greenwich Borough Draft Local Plan (The People's Plan)*. Letter from Dennis Parker, Department of the Environment Greater London Professional Planning Service, to C. H. J. Pollard-Britten, Greenwich Borough Planning Officer, dated 8 October 1985. London: Department of the Environment.

— 1987. *Re-using redundant buildings – good practice in urban regeneration*. London: HMSO

— 1988. *Improving urban areas – good practice in urban regeneration*. London: HMSO.

— 1989. *Planning control in Western Europe*. London: HMSO.

— 1991a. *Circular 16/91: Planning and Compensation Act 1991: planning obligations*. London: HMSO.

— 1991b. *Circular 18/91: Planning and Compensation Act 1991: new development plans system: transitional arrangements (England and Wales)*. London: HMSO.

— 1992a. *The relationship between house prices and land supply*. London: HMSO.

— 1992b. *Planning Policy Guidance 1: General policy and principles*. London: HMSO.

— 1992c. *Planning Policy Guidance 12: Development plans and regional planning guidance*. London: HMSO.
— 1992d. *Development plans: a good practice guide*. London: HMSO.
— 1992e. *The use of planning agreements*. London: HMSO.
— 1993. *The efficiency and effectiveness of local plan inquiries: executive summary*. London: Department of the Environment.
Department of Transport 1992. *Developers' contributions to highway works*. London: Department of Transport
Dubben, N. & S. Sayce 1991. *Property portfolio management*. London: Routledge.

Edwards, D. 1988. The planning system and the control of development in Denmark. *Town Planning Review* **59**, 137–58.
Edwards, M. 1990. What is needed from public policy? In *Land and property development in a changing context*, P. Healey & R. Nabarro (eds), 175–85. Aldershot, England: Gower.
Etzioni, A. 1967. Mixed scanning: a third approach to decision making. *Public Administration Review* **27**, 385–92.
Evans, A. W. 1983. The determination of the price of land. *Urban Studies* **20**, 119–29.
— 1985. *Urban economics*. Oxford: Basil Blackwell.
— 1986a. The supply of land: a pedagogic comment. *Urban Studies* **23**, 527–30.
— 1986b. *House prices and land prices in the South East: a review*. London: House-Builders Federation.
— 1991a. Investment diversion and equity release: the macroeconomic consequences of increasing property values? *Urban Studies* **28**, 173–82.
— 1991b. "Rabbit hutches on postage stamps" planning, development and political economy. *Urban Studies* **28**, 853–70.
Eversley, D. E. C. 1973. *The planner in society: the changing rôle of a profession*. London: Faber & Faber.
— 1990. Inequality at the spatial level: tasks for planners. *The Planner* **76**(12), 13–8

Fainstein S. S. 1994. *The city builders*. Oxford: Basil Blackwell.
Fisher, M. 1986. The future of local enterprise boards. *The Planner* **72**(10), 18–20.
Falk, N. 1987. From vision to results – devising strategies to revive run-down areas. *The Planner* **73**(6), 39–43.
Fraser, W. D. 1993. *Principles of property investment and pricing*, 2nd edn. London: Macmillan.
Fordham, R. 1991. Planning gain: much obliged by better sense of balance. *Planning* **942**, 16–7.
— 1993. Why planning gain is not a tax on land betterment. *Planning* **1014**, 13.
Forsyth, J. 1985. *Local political party manifestos and local planning*. Paper given at Research into Local Land Use Planning seminar, Oxford Polytechnic.
Foster, M. 1986. Real progress from high-flying Mountleigh. *Estates Gazette* **279**, 913–4.
Fothergill, S., S. Monk, M. Perry 1987. *Property and industrial development*. London: Hutchinson.
Franzini, D. 1988. Ground rules for fair gain. *Planning* **790**, 2.
Friedman, M. 1962. *Capitalism and freedom*. Chicago: University of Chicago Press.

Gatenby, I. & C. Williams 1992. Section 54A: the legal and practical implications. *Journal of Planning and Environmental Law*, 110–20
Giddens, A. 1984. *The constitution of society*. London: Polity.
Gill, D. 1991. Planning gain: consequences for the developer and the land development

process. *Scottish Planning Law and Practice* **33**, 36–8.

Goobey, A. R. 1992. *Bricks and mortals*. London: Century.

Goodchild, B. 1990. Planning and the modern/postmodern debate. *Town Planning Review* **60**, 119–37.

Goodchild, R. & R. Munton 1985. *Development and the landowner: an analysis of the British experience*. London: Allen & Unwin.

Gore, A. & D. Nicholson 1985. The analysis of public sector land ownership and development. In *Land policy: problems and alternatives*, S. Barrett & P. Healey (eds), 179–202. Aldershot, England: Gower.

— & D. Nicholson 1991. Models of the land-development process: a critical review. *Environment and Planning A* **23**, 705–30.

Grant, M. 1982. *Urban planning law*. London: Sweet & Maxwell.

— 1986. Planning and land taxation: development land tax and beyond. *Journal of Planning and Environmental Law*, 4–19, 92–106.

— 1989. Directions for change in the British planning system: comment on the paper by Patsy Healey. *Town Planning Review* **60**, 322–3.

Green, R. 1990. Sustainable development of the built environment. *Town and Country Planning* **59**, 142–3.

Grigson, W. S. 1986. *House prices in perspective: a review of South East evidence*. London: SERPLAN.

Gyford, J. 1991. *Citizens, consumers and councils*. London: Macmillan.

Hall, D. 1989a. The case for new settlements. *Town and Country Planning* **58**, 111–4.

— 1989b. Community-based planning. *The Planner* **75**(2), 19–24.

Hall, P., H. Gracey, R. Drewitt, R. Thomas 1973. *The containment of urban England*. London: Allen & Unwin.

Harding, A. 1991. The rise of urban growth coalitions, UK-style? *Environment and Planning C* **9**, 295–317.

— 1992. Property interests and urban growth coalitions in the UK: a brief encounter. In *Rebuilding the city*, P. Healey, S. Davoudi, M. O'Toole, S. Tavsanoglu, D. Usher (eds), 223–32. London: Spon.

Harris, C. D. & Ullman, E. L. 1945. The nature of cities. *American Academy of Political and Social Science, Annals* **242**, 7–17.

Harvey, D. 1982. *The limits of capital*. Oxford: Basil Blackwell.

— 1985. *The urbanisation of capital*. Oxford: Basil Blackwell.

Harvey, J. 1987. *Urban land economics: the economics of real property*. London: Macmillan.

Harwood, M. 1975. *English land law*. London: Sweet & Maxwell.

Hayek, F. A. 1960. *The constitution of liberty*. London: Routledge & Kegan Paul.

Hayton, K. 1992. Scottish Enterprise: a challenge to local land use planning. *Town Planning Review* **63**, 265–78.

Healey, P. 1983. *Local plans in British land use planning*. Oxford: Pergamon.

— 1989. Directions for change in the British planning system. *Town Planning Review* **60**, 125–49.

— 1991a. Models of the development process: a review. *Journal of Property Research* **8**, 219–38.

— 1991b. Urban regeneration and the development industry. *Regional Studies* **25**, 97–110.

— 1991c. The content of planning education programmes: some comments from recent experience. *Environment and Planning B* **18**, 177–89.

— 1992a. An institutional model of the development process. *Journal of Property Research* **9**, 33–44.

— 1992b. The reorganisation of the state and the market in planning. *Urban Studies* 411-34.

— J. Davis, M. Wood, M. Elson 1982. *The implementation of development plans*. Report of an exploratory study for the Department of the Environment. Department of Town Planning, Oxford Polytechnic.

— A. Doak, P. McNamara, M. Elson 1985. *The implementation of planning policies and the role of development plans*, Final report to the Department of the Environment, Department of Town Planning, Oxford Polytechnic.

— P. McNamara, M. Elson, A. Doak 1988. *Land use planning and the mediation of urban change*. Cambridge: Cambridge University Press.

— & S. M. Barrett 1990. Structure and agency in land and property development processes: some ideas for research. *Urban Studies* **27**, 89-104.

— S. Davoudi, M. O'Toole, S. Tavsanoglu, D. Usher (eds) 1992a. *Rebuilding the city*. London: Spon.

— F. Ennis, Purdue M. 1992b. Planning gain and the "new" local plans. *Town and Country Planning* **61**, 39-43.

Herington, J. 1984. *The outer city*. London: Harper & Row.

Hewitt, W. E. 1988. *Report on objections to the South Westmorland Local Plan*. Bristol: Department of the Environment Planning Inspectorate.

Hindle, B. R. 1993. Salford Quays 2: development and planning procedures. In *Urban waterside regeneration: problems and prospects*, K. N. White, E. G. Bellinger, A. J. Saul, M. Symes, K. Hendry (eds), 82-93. Chichester, England: Ellis Horwood.

Hodge, I. & G. Cameron 1989. Raising infrastructure charges on land development: incidence and adjustments. *Land Development Studies* **6**, 171-82.

Hooper, A. J. 1988. Planning and the control of development in Federal Republic of Germany. *Town Planning Review* **59**, 183-205.

Hough, B. 1992. Standing in planning permission appeals. *Journal of Planning and Environmental Law*, 319-29.

House of Commons Committee of Public Accounts 1989. *Sixteenth Report: Control and management of the Defence Estate* (House of Commons Paper 88). London: HMSO.

Howell, M. 1983. Swansea: a case study of working together. *The Planner* **69**, 196.

Howes, C. 1989. Special report land assembly: private sector gets a boost. *Chartered Surveyor Weekly* **26**(3), 61-3.

Hoyt, H. 1939. *The structure and growth of residential neighbourhoods in American cities*. Washington DC: US Federal Housing Administration.

Hurd, R. M. 1903. *Principles of city land values*. New York: The Record and Guide.

Hussell, D. 1991. Get your timing right. *Planning* **914**, 23.

Investment Property Databank 1991. *Property investors digest*. London: IPD.

Jacobs, J. 1961. *The death and life of great American cities*. New York: Random House.

Jones, R. 1982. *Town and country chaos: a critical analysis of Britain's town and country planning system*. London: Adam Smith Institute.

Kaiser, E. J. & S. F. Weiss 1970. Public policy and the residential development process. *American Institute of Planners, Journal* **36**, 30-7.

Kane, F. 1992. Slow death for merchant developers. *The Guardian* (1 December), 13.

Ketelby, H. 1983. Planning comes of age? A comment on the liberal perspective. *The Planner* **69**(3), 83-4.

Keogh, G. 1985. The economics of planning gain. In *Land policy: problems and alternatives*,

237

S. Barrett & P. Healey (eds), 203–28. Aldershot, England: Gower.

Kitchen T. 1990. A client-based view of the planning service. *Planning Outlook* **33**, 65–76.

Kirk, G. 1980. *Urban planning in a capitalist society*. London: Croom Helm.

Kivell, P. T. & I. McKay 1988. Public ownership of urban land. *Institute of British Geographers, Transactions* **13**, 165–78.

— 1993. *Land and the city*. London: Routledge.

Klosterman, R. E. 1985. Arguments for and against planning. *Town Planning Review* **56**, 5–20.

KPMG 1990. *Planning gain*. London: KPMG Peat Marwick Management Consultants.

Kynoch, R. 1988. Rosehaugh profits from asset strength. *Chartered Surveyor Weekly* **25**(7), 11.

— 1992. UK clearing banks face big property writedowns. *Chartered Surveyor Weekly* **39**(5), 7.

Labour Party 1992. *Planning - a new agenda*. London: Labour Party.

Law, C. M. & E. K. Grime 1993. Salford Quays 1: the context. In *Urban waterside regeneration: problems and prospects*, K. N. White, E. G. Bellinger, A. J. Saul, M. Symes, K. Hendry (eds), 72–81. Chichester, England: Ellis Horwood.

Leung, H. L. 1979. *Redistribution of land values: a re-examination of the 1947 scheme*. Occasional Paper 11, Department of Land Economy, University of Cambridge.

Lichfield, N. & H. Darin-Drabkin 1980. *Land policy in planning*. London: Allen & Unwin.

Lindblom, C. E. The science of "muddling through". *Public Administration Review* **19**, 79–88.

Lloyd, G. 1992. Property-led partnership arrangements in Scotland: the private sector domain. In *Rebuilding the city*, P. Healey, S. Davoudi, M. O'Toole, S. Tavsanoglu, D. Usher (eds), 233–44. London: Spon.

Lock, D. 1988. Planning and opportunism. *The Planner* **74**(9), 26–8.

— 1989. New communities in Britain: the rôle of the private sector. *The Planner* **75**(2), 33–6.

— 1991. Bias against private sector. *Planning* **918**, 2.

— & L. Shostak 1985. New country towns in the South East. *The Planner* **71**(5), 19–22.

Low, N. 1991. *Planning, politics and the state*. London: Unwin Hyman.

Lowe, P. 1988. The politics of land. In *Who can afford to live in the countryside?* M. Winter & A. Rogers (eds), 36–49 Occasional Paper 2, Centre for Rural Studies, Royal Agricultural College, Cirencester.

Maitland R., P. Newman, M. Salter 1991. The use of consultants by local planning authorities. *The Planner* **77**(28), 9.

Marriot, O. 1967. *The property boom*, London: Pan.

Martin, D. 1992. Europe 2000: Community actions and intentions in spatial planning. *The Planner* **78**(21), 18–20

Marsden, T., J. Murdoch, P. Lowe, R. Munton, A. Flynn 1993. *Constructing the countryside*. London: UCL Press.

Massey, D. & A. Catalano 1978. *Capital and land: land ownership by capital in Great Britain*. London: Edward Arnold.

Matthews, P. (ed.) 1993. *The Guinness book of records 1994*. London: Guinness Publishing.

McAuslan, P. 1980. *The ideologies of planning law*. Oxford: Pergamon

McClenaghan, J. & C. Blatchford 1993. Development plan slippage. *The Planner* **79**(2), 29–30.

McConnell, S. 1981. *Theories for planning*. London: Heinemann.

McDonald, A. 1986. *The Weller way.* London: Faber & Faber.

McLoughlin, J. B. 1969. *Urban and regional planning: a systems approach.* London: Faber & Faber.

— 1985. *The systems approach to planning: a critique.* Working Paper 1, Centre of Urban Studies and Urban Planning, University of Hong Kong.

McNamara, P. F. 1983. Towards a classification of land developers. *Urban Law and Policy* 6, 87–94.

— 1986. The growth of multi-functional agents in the outer South East: a comment. *Land Development Studies* 5, 191–6.

— 1993. Parameters for institutional investment in inner-city commercial property markets. In *Urban regeneration: property investment and development,* J. Berry, S. McGreal, B. Deddis (eds), 5–16. London: Spon.

MEPC 1988. *Report and financial statements to year end 30 September 1988.* London: MEPC.

— 1992. *Report and financial statements to year end 30 September 1992.* London: MEPC.

Merrifield, A. 1993. The Canary Wharf debacle: from TINA – there is no alternative – to THEMBA – there must be an alternative. *Environment and Planning A* 25, 1247–65.

Millichap, D. 1993. Clear reasoning needed to avoid planning by appeal. *Planning* 1029, 14 5.

Ministry of Housing and Local Government 1955. *Circular 42/55: Green belts.* London: HMSO.

— 1969. *People and planning,* Report of the Skeffington Committee on public participation in planning. London: HMSO.

Montgomery, J. R. 1987. The significance of public landownership: local authority land trading in Oxford and Sheffield. *Land Use Policy* 4, 42–50.

— & A. Thornley 1990. *Radical planning initiatives: new directions for urban planning in the 1990s.* Aldershot, England: Gower.

Moore, V. 1992. *A practical approach to planning law,* 3rd edn. London: Blackstone.

Morrell, G. 1991. Property performance analysis and performance indices. *Journal of Property Research* 8, 29–57.

Moss, G. 1981. *Britain's wasting acres: land-use in a changing society.* London: Architectural Press.

Muth, R. 1969. *Cities and housing.* Chicago: University of Chicago Press.

Mynors, C. 1991. The Planning and Compensation Act 1991: (3) development plans, minerals and waste disposal. *The Planner* 77(31), 7–8.

Nabarro, R. 1990. The investment market in commercial and industrial development: some recent trends. In *Land and property development in a changing context,* P. Healey & R. Nabarro (eds), 47–59. Aldershot, England: Gower.

Nadin, V.
— & S. Jones 1990. A profile of the profession. *The Planner* 76(3), 13–24.

— & R. Daniels 1992. Consultants and development plans. *The Planner* 78(15), 10–12.

Nuffield Foundation 1986. *Town and country planning.* Report of a committee of inquiry appointed by the Nuffield Foundation. London: Nuffield Foundation

Oakeshott, M. 1985. Institutional attitudes to property investment in the UK – last waltz of the dinosaurs round the "prime property" totem pole? *Land Development Studies* 2, 147–56.

Oatley, N. 1989. Evaluating UDCs. *Planning Practice and Research* 4(3), 6–12.

Parker, H. R. 1985. From Uthwatt to DLT – the end of the road? *The Planner* 71(4), 21–8.

Pavitt, J. H. 1990. Urban renewal in Wales – the role of the Welsh Development Agency. *The Planner* **76**(49), 70–4.

Pearce, B. J., N. R. Curry, R. N. Goodchild 1978. *Land, planning and the market*. Occasional Paper 9, Department of Land Economy, University of Cambridge.

Planning 1990. Advertisement by Bristol City Council for senior research assistant (property research). *Planning* **863**, 17.

— 1992. Hampshire gives notice to quit on housing land. *Planning* **989**, 1.

Plender J. 1990. Property investment: the current conundrum. *Estates Gazette* **9047**, 14.

Pike, D. & G. Warren 1983. Planning for the 1880s. *The Planner* **69**(3), 81–2.

Price Waterhouse, Casco, Chesterton 1989. *Financing inner cities: a casebook*. London: Price Waterhouse.

Potter, S. 1990. Britain's development corporations. *Town and Country Planning* **59**, 294–8.

Punter, J. V. 1988. Planning control in France. *Town Planning Review* **59**, 159–81.

Reade, E. 1987. *British town and country planning*. Milton Keynes: Open University Press.

Rhind, D. & R. Hudson 1980. *Land-use*. London: Methuen.

Richardson, H. W. 1971. *Urban economics*. London: Penguin.

Rifkin, A. & L. Williams 1991. Greenwich partnership takes waterfront initiative. *Planning* **927**, 18–9.

Roberts, J. 1987. Mountleigh's Midas. *Chartered Surveyor Weekly* **19**(4), 31.

Robson, B. 1987. *Those inner cities*. Oxford: Oxford University Press.

Rowan-Robinson, J.
— & M. G. Lloyd 1988. The infrastructure lottery and the land development process. *Land Development Studies* **5**, 17–30.
— & R. Durman 1992. Conditions or agreements. *Journal of Planning and Environmental Law*, 1003–11.
    — 1993. Planning policy and planning agreements. *Land Use Policy* **10**, 197–204.

Ross, S. 1991. Planning and the public interest. *The Planner* **77**(40), 55–7.

Royal Town Planning Institute 1991. *The education of planners. Policy statement and general guidance for academic institutions offering initial professional education in planning*. London: Royal Town Planning Institute.

Rutterford J. 1993. *Introduction to stock exchange investment*, 2nd edn. London: Macmillan.

Rydin, Y. 1986. *Housing land policy*. Aldershot, England: Gower.

— 1993. *The British planning system*. Basingstoke: Macmillan.

Sainsbury, Lord 1989. New attitudes for better decisions: a business view of the planning system. *The Planner* **75**(29), 16–19.

Saunders, P. 1985. The forgotten dimension of central–local relations: theorising the regional state. *Environment and Planning C* **3**, 149–62.

Self, P. 1989. Planning's search for a political consensus. *The Planner* **75**(24), 20–1.

Sellgren, J. M. A. 1991. The changing nature of economic development activities: a longitudinal analysis of local authorities in Great Britain, 1981–1987. *Environment and Planning C* **9**, 341–62.

Shaw, M. 1989. Development plans and local discretion. *Planning and Development* **1**, 39–43.

Shoard, M. 1987. *This land is our land*. London: Paladin.

Short, J. R., S. Fleming, S. Witt 1986. *House-building, planning and community action*. London: Routledge & Kegan Paul.

Simmie, J. M. 1974. *Citizens in conflict*. London: Hutchinson.

— 1981. *Power, property and corporatism*. London: Macmillan.

— 1990. Planning theory objects of analysis: a response to Forester. *Planning Theory Newsletter* (winter), 105–7.

— S. Olsberg, C. Tunnell 1992. Urban containment and land use planning. *Land Use Policy* **9**, 36–46.

Simmons, M. 1992. Offices show strategic gap. *Planning* **963**, 2.

Smyth, H. 1984. *Land supply, house-builders and government policies*. Working Paper 43, School for Advanced Urban Studies, University of Bristol.

Sorauf, F. J. 1957. The public interest reconsidered. *Journal of Politics* **19**, 616–39.

Sorensen, A. D. 1982. Planning comes of age: a liberal perspective. *The Planner* **68**(6), 184–8.

— 1983. Towards a market theory of planning. *The Planner* **69**(3), 78–80.

Steeley, G. 1990. An agenda for a new mode of behaviour. *Town and Country Planning* **59**, 149.

Stoker, G. 1989. Urban development corporations: a review. *Regional Studies* **23**, 159–67.

— & S. Young 1993. *Cities in the 1990s*. Harlow, England: Longman.

Sunman, H. 1990. Market mechanisms and environmental planning. *Town and Country Planning* **59**, 146–7.

Surrey Heath Borough Council 1985. *Surrey Heath Local Plan*. Camberley, England: Surrey Heath Borough Council.

— 1990. *Surrey Heath Local Plan review: consultation draft*. Camberley, England: Surrey Heath Borough Council.

Sutherland, D. 1988. *The landowners*, (2nd edn). London: Muller.

Synnott, M. 1986. *Water privatisation and the local planning authorities*. Paper presented at Research in Development Planning Seminar, School for Advanced Urban Studies, University of Bristol.

Taner, O. & Tiesdell S. 1991. The London Docklands Development Corporation (LDDC) 1981–1991. *Town Planning Review* **62**, 311–30.

Thornley, A. 1992. *Urban planning under Thatcherism – the challenge of the market*. London: Routledge.

UK Government 1990. *This common inheritance: Britain's environmental strategy*. Cm 1200. London: HMSO.

Valuation Office 1988. *Property market report: Autumn 1988*. London: Inland Revenue.

— 1993. *Property market report: Autumn 1993*. London: Inland Revenue.

Walker, B. 1982. *Welfare economics and urban problems*. London: Hutchinson.

Wates, N. & C. Knevitt 1987. *Community architecture*. London: Penguin.

Webster, B. & A. Lavers 1991. The effectiveness of public local inquiries as a vehicle for public participation in the plan making process: a case study of the Barnet unitary development plan inquiry. *Journal of Planning and Environmental Law*, 803–13.

Weiss, S. F., J. E. Smith, E. J. Kaiser, K. B. Kenny 1966. *Residential developer decisions*. Center for Urban and Regional Studies, University of North Carolina.

Westwell J. & R. Johnston 1987. Fund profile: Guardian Royal Exchange. *Estates Gazette* **282**, 1197–8

Whitehand, J. W. R. & P. J. Larkham 1991. Suburban cramming and development control. *Journal of Property Research* **8**, 147–59.

Whitehouse, B. P. 1964. *Partners in property*. London: Brin Shaw.

Whitmore, J. 1992. MEPC may face £60m Alban Gate writedown. *Chartered Surveyor Weekly*

41(3), 9.

Whitney, D. & G. Haughton 1992. Structures for development partnerships in the 1990s: practice in West Yorkshire. In *Rebuilding the city*, P. Healey, S. Davoudi, M. O'Toole, S. Tavsanoglu, D. Usher (eds), 256–65. London: Spon.

Wilkinson, S. 1992. Towards a new city? A case study of image-improvement initiatives in Newcastle upon Tyne. In *Rebuilding the city*, P. Healey, S. Davoudi, M. O'Toole, S. Tavsanoglu, D. Usher (eds), 174–211. London: Spon.

Williams, C. 1989. Planning gain: guidance gaining ground. *Planning* **848**, 7.

Williams, R. H. 1993. *Blue bananas, grapes and golden triangles: spatial planning for an integrated Europe*. Working Paper 19, Department of Town and Country Planning, University of Newcastle upon Tyne.

Willis, K. G. 1988. Planning and the market: changing analytical contexts. *Planning Outlook* **31**, 2–4.

Wiltshaw, D. G. 1985. The supply of land. *Urban Studies* **22**, 49–56.

— 1988. Pedagogic comment and the supply of land for a particular use. *Urban Studies* **25**, 439–47.

Yiftachel, O. 1989. Towards a new typology of urban planning theories. *Environment and Planning B* **16**, 23–39.

Young, G. 1992. Government position: main school opening address. *The Planner* **78**(21), 3–6.

Young, S. C. 1993. *The politics of the environment*. Manchester: Baseline Books.

Index